MUSIC AND THE POLITICS OF NEGATION

MUSICAL MEANING & INTERPRETATION

Robert S. Hatten, editor

INDIANA UNIVERSITY PRESS

Bloomington & Indianapolis

MUSIC AND THE POLITICS OF NEGATION

JAMES R CURRIE

This book is a publication of

INDIANA UNIVERSITY PRESS
601 North Morton Street
Bloomington, IN 47404–3797 USA

iupress.indiana.edu

Telephone orders 800–842–6796
Fax orders 812–855–7931

♾ The paper used in this publication
meets the minimum requirements of
the American National Standard for
Information Sciences–Permanence of
Paper for Printed Library Materials,
ANSI Z39.48–1992.

Manufactured in the
United States of America

Library of Congress
Cataloging-in-Publication Data

Currie, James R., [date]
  Music and the politics of negation /
James R. Currie.
    pages. cm. – (Musical meaning and
interpretation)
  Includes bibliographical references and
index.
  ISBN 978-0-253-35703-8 (cloth : al-
kaline paper) – ISBN 978-0-253-00522-9
(ebook)
  1. Musicology. 2. Postmodernism. 3. Music – Political aspects. I. Title. II. Series:
Musical meaning and interpretation.
  ML3797.C87 2012
  780.72 – dc23
                                      2011051853

1 2 3 4 5   17 16 15 14 13 12

FOR THE WORLD OUTSIDE THIS BOOK.

TO MY BELOVED PARENTS

JENNY AND DAVID CURRIE

CONTENTS

· Preface: A No-Music *ix*

· Acknowledgments *xix*

1 VEILS (*Mozart, Piano Concerto K. 459, Finale*) *1*

2 DREAMS (*Fugal Counterpoint*) *34*

3 EXILE (*Haydn, String Quartet Op. 33, No. 5*) *65*

4 ENCHANTMENT (*Mozart, La clemenza di Tito*) *100*

5 FORGETTING (*Edward Said*) *139*

· Notes *179*

· Bibliography *203*

· Index *211*

PREFACE

A No-Music

Music says yes – to its historical and cultural participation in the worldliness of social life and its meanings. The past twenty years and more of politically oriented musicological thinking in the academy has been adamant on this point. It has claimed to bring music back from banishment within formalist abstractions; it has striven to make it autonomous of aesthetic autonomy. Music can now benefit *once more* from the warmth and wisdom of belonging to the already existent human worlds that have both engendered it and continued to offer it a place to stay when it finds itself abroad. As a result, music study in the academy today enjoys many intellectual liberties that would not have been possible had certain scholars not been prepared to fight for them for us, sometimes at considerable professional cost – a point this book neither forgets nor takes lightly.

However, the implications of "once more" in the penultimate sentence above should give us pause. On the one hand, what we might broadly label as this postmodern turn of contemporary academic music studies has often perceived itself historically as the manifestation of something particular to its own moment; and so, on one level, as something new. (Hence its most obvious symptom, the "New Musicology.") Yet, on the other hand, it has also validated itself by means of a sometimes transhistorical set of assumptions. For this new turn has simultaneously also been considered as a *re*-turn, in which musical discourse reasserts (once more) music's fundamentally located and determined status within and by culture and so wakes up (at last) from the nightmare of what postmodern musicologists often consider to have been the disastrous turn it took, particularly in Germanic lands, toward aesthetic autonomy at the end of the eighteenth century. Thus, with no apparent qualms, Susan McClary can effectively assert that we have always been postmodern musicians[1] – the problem was simply that a frequently privileged Western minority spent nearly two hundred years actively forgetting this point, often as a means of solidifying their own ideological ground. Or so the argument often runs.

But if postmodern musicology asserts that music must be understood in terms of the particularity of its relations to, broadly conceived, its various contexts, why is it that its own claims are sometimes allowed to exceed such bounds and become, as I say, transhistorical? In fact, as a particular discourse located in a specific context that nevertheless frequently rests on such transhistorical assumptions (acknowledged or not), postmodern musicology is formally speaking not unlike its own formulation of the discourse of aesthetic autonomy. Thus, it replicates the structural dynamics of the very object that it nearly always rejects in order to validate itself, as if, in psychoanalytic terms, it were suffering from some kind of projectional disavowal. Is it therefore possible that postmodern musicology itself, like aesthetic autonomy, is also ideological? After all, a key defining feature of an ideology is that, by means of a state of exception to an established law, a certain politics of exclusion can be kept afloat. Exception is created here by the fact that postmodern musicology insists on an interpretive law of contextual particularity for music but is relinquished from full submission to such restrictions itself. So what is being excluded?

This book gives two answers: music and politics. And stated in such a stark fashion, they must undoubtedly seem harsh. After all, as the 1990s progressed, musicology seemed increasingly to be enjoying the creation of an academic environment that could at last let music be music, and attendant on this was the assumption that musicology could now discuss politics. Today, at the beginning of the second decade of the new millennium, such assumptions in musicology are quite pro forma. But without any desire to play the Grinch, this book nevertheless does not align itself with the discipline's general sense of political well-being. And this, primarily, is because my arguments are haunted by a historical analogy whose broad implications as stated in this preface will appear somewhat crude, but whose basic provocation the following set of essays frequently returns to reinvestigate.

If postmodern musicology, particularly in the later 1990s, sometimes celebrated the historical particularity of its arrival as a moment when a certain transhistorical set of values in relationship to music could at last establish themselves, we should remember that during the course of that decade, the vast majority of Western discourses (political, economic, intellectual, journalistic, commercial, technological, lifestyle, and otherwise) were likewise wrapped up in similar forms of partying.[2] For with the demise of Eastern European communisms, the West in the 1990s took to celebrating its particular historical moment as one that would soon, in Francis Fukuyama's famous pseudo-Hegelian terms, usher in the end of history: the beginning of a world in which the transhistorical truths of social democracy would reign *in perpetuum* by means of the similarly transhistorical truths of the market. Over ten years on, with the political stability of the planet in a catastrophic state, the market unmasked in all its spectacularly raw and excessive indifference, and the prospects for democracy, even in democratic countries, worrying, the best one can say about the West's optimism in the late twentieth century is that it was preemptively narcissistic. More realistically, I think we should just see it as a purchase made with often quite willful myopia regarding who would have to foot the bill. It was a fantasy quite knowingly constructed by the increasingly indistinguishable realms of finance and government, and many opted for a completely uncritical relationship toward it.

In much public political discourse, the 1990s were taken up with a lot of talk about the claims of different identity groups. It was as if the question of what the basic political-economic structure of the increasingly global world should be had been answered by the fact that the power of Western capitalism had been able to dissipate the focus of Eastern European communism until it collapsed – as if capitalism's force here were the unalloyed sign of its value. The foundation stone of the new millennium seemingly in place, we set about making sure that there would be as many rooms available for difference in the mansion we were then to build. The obvious proviso was that accommodation could only be secured by signing an agreement to support the landlord; and for a relatively large percentage of westerners in the 1990s, lulled into a totally bogus sense of security by a fundamentally fantasmatic world resting on seductive credit and insane financial speculation, that seemed fair enough. The world of politics in its epic nineteenth- and twentieth-century form was deemed to be over, and citizens could now vote for politicians according to their ability to act as economic caretakers rather than formulators of ideas. Attendant on this was the practice of seeing the presence of ideas in politics as denoting the intellectual's betrayal of a commonsense empirical understanding of what is, for the supposedly anti-humanist idea of what should be, a sacrifice of pragmatics for utopia. A particularly telling symptom of this historical moment would be the triumph of so-called New Labour in the United Kingdom, whereby the British, believing that the market itself could create the conditions for a well-functioning democracy, ended up with a left-wing government that managed to expunge its politics of anything left-wing, and thereby, I would argue, opened up the way to the steady eradication of what remained of the welfare state, particularly the education system, which is now in a disastrous condition. Blair, we should remember, was one of Thatcher's favorite backbenchers.[3]

It is not so much that the discussion of questions concerning identity and difference are not necessarily important – although there are indeed instances where they are not as pressing as sometimes default assumptions might insist. Rather, it is that in the context of Western life in the 1990s it was possible to discuss such things without dialectically mediating the analyses in terms of global capitalism, since the privileged (and essentially fake) conditions in which many of us were then living meant that most of the time we could avoid much direct exposure to the price that has to be paid in order for such a set of economic relations to function. For example, true to its reliance on the concept of surplus value, capitalist manufacturing had been exported from the West to where it now ensues, according to most reports, in appalling conditions – conditions that are not an aberration within the economic coordinates of our world but constitutive. The problem here, then, is not that differences are not being made, but precisely that they are: there is one way of life for one group, where questions of identity and the like seem pressing, and another way of life for those who provide the material conditions for the former group. What the latter group needs is not to be distinguished from the others but to be treated on the *same* terms – which of course it is not possible to do without simultaneously and directly critiquing and changing the presently existing set of global economic relations. As a result, much of what tended to constitute political debate in musicology in the 1990s now appears somewhat like a red herring: a politically flavored distraction that potentially enabled politics in its proper transformative sense *not* to happen.

If I were to attempt a summary of the problematic of the 1990s, I would probably begin by noting that much of the rhetoric of political life in that decade was primarily oriented around the affirmation of things both particular and universal that were *already existent:* on the one hand, this was quite consciously performed, as was the case in relationship to various particular identity groups, often within mostly Western contexts; on the other hand, this was inadvertently achieved, since one of the resultant effects of affirming particulars was, as I state, precisely to allow for an affirmation of the increasingly universal economic forces. Since many prominent governments were kept in power by the popularity of the economic bubble that they were able to pass off as if it were the result of their own wise financial planning, they were also more than happy to follow suit. The 1990s was a decade that wanted to say yes to what was, rather than adopting a politics of negation and saying no so that something genuinely different, and actually necessary, might emerge. In many prominent instances, musicology tended to follow along and, with a certain insensitivity to context that is somewhat ironic considering that it usually claims that context is its business, it has often continued to do so. What constitutes political work in the discipline is still predominantly oriented toward the affirmation of the claims of particular groups – toward a music that says yes. Moreover, should one invoke the economy and its effects on music in any kind of fashion that would directly question the validity of capitalism in its present disastrous global form, one can still easily find oneself either being dismissed as lunatic or condemned by the violent sophistry of certain public intellectuals as being guilty of uncritical support of the totalitarian projects of the twentieth century. The fact that there have indeed been intellectuals who *have* been guilty as charged does not mean that one therefore *is* simply because you have raised the question of whether or not what constitutes

political debate in musicology is reliant on ignoring the staggering violence of the set of relations that perhaps have allowed for that academic
context to exist in the first place. The one small but not insignificant ray
of light that might come from the present dire straits in which many uni-
versities in the Western world now find themselves is that such a political
avoidance is increasingly untenable, since what was avoided now turns
its attention, with unambiguously sinister intent, toward the academy.
In a sense, we have fallen into the frame that we had ignored in order to
picture ourselves attractively.

If it is indeed the case that what we need is a politics of negation
rather than of affirmation, and if we continue to assert that music can
or even should be the bearer of the values that might inspire and edify
us, then maybe it would be strategically expedient now for musicology
to investigate once more how music says no – and so to formulate a no-
music. This is one of the things that this book sets out to achieve, and
in each chapter, with the exception of the last, which concerns Edward
Said and the West-Eastern Divan Orchestra, it does so by means of a set
of historical short-circuits between political and intellectual concerns
of the present and the historical moment that, as I have already noted,
many postmodernist musicologists locate as the point at which things
started to go wrong: the late eighteenth century. In part, then, this book
is a reaffirmation of the continuing import and relevance of the so-called
Viennese classical repertoire and of the founding arguments of mature
modernity that resonate through it. Each of the first four chapters lets
the pressure of contemporary political concerns be felt in the workings of
close readings (ranging across formal, stylistic, expressive, and historical
parameters) of examples drawn from pieces of late eighteenth-century
music: in chapter 1, the finale of Mozart's Piano Concerto in F Major,
K. 459; in chapter 2, a generalized consideration of fugal counterpoint
in Viennese classical instrumental music; chapter 3 turns to Haydn's
String Quartet, op. 33, no. 5 in G Major; and chapter 4 to an extensive set
of multiple readings of one aria from Mozart's late opera *La clemenza di
Tito*. Moreover, each of the chapters is organized around an idea that attempts to capture the different ways in which music negates what already
exists. So instead of mirroring the world, chapter 1 shows music veiled.
Instead of being awake to its surroundings, chapter 2 investigates how we

might conceive of music asleep and dreaming. Instead of being at home, chapter 3 shows music taking up residency in its own exile. In chapter 4, music is allowed to enchant us into believing that the aesthetic is more real than the world of human concerns that has produced it. Finally, in chapter 5, music's profound indifference even encourages us to forget who we are.

This is a dialectical book; the word "negation" in its title is there to make this allegiance unambiguous. But it is not a studied attempt to apply the details of dialectical philosophy to music, as for example Maire Jaanus Kurrik famously did for literature back in the late 1970s.[4] I neither claim to sustain engagement with a particular dialectical philosopher's line of argumentation consistently, nor do I argue against remarkable examples of such endeavors by which I have been inspired: amongst others, Berthold Hoeckner's work on the idea of the moment in nineteenth-century German music, Michael Spitzer's monograph on late Beethoven, Daniel Chua's critique of absolute music, particularly in relationship to Beethoven, Lydia Goehr's ongoing projects, much of Richard Leppert's more recent commentaries, many of Martin Scherzinger's publications, and Alastair Williams's study of the claims of the post–World War II avant-garde.[5] Since it was only at a relatively late stage in the progress of the various essays that are gathered here that I was fully aware that negation was my theme, I saw no reason to posture as if I'd been organized enough to have known so from the get-go.

Nevertheless, it transpired that the overall orientation was dialectically orthodox enough that my conclusion could not merely be a prescription for a large dosage of "no." After all, repeating "no," ad infinitum, merely creates a kind of endless deferral; something that a Hegel might have termed "bad infinity," or a Freud, hysteria. Of course, what is so politically laudable about "no" when employed dialectically is that it halts the fake immediacy of that which smugly presents itself as "just the way things are." This is what the discourse of the hysteric performs in Lacanian psychoanalysis, and considering that the violence of the economy has been increasingly scripted as a kind of fact of human nature – rather than the historical product of a consciously made set of mostly clear-headed, if deeply cynical, decisions – hysteria is not necessarily to be dismissed simply as poor behavior. When we witness angry

demonstrations on the streets of Athens or London, to take but two examples, it should make us feel optimistic: that there is still the possibility
of the antagonism which, following the position of Chantal Mouffe and
Ernesto Laclau, is defining of political culture proper.[6] But if we make
a law out of no-saying, then "no" becomes just as smug as an uncritical
indulgence in affirming one's privileged comforts as if they were simply
organic constituents of the natural way of the world. And the result of
such a convention of no is that the possibility of a political act devolves
into mere acting out – a dialectical paradox that I return to more analyti-
cally in chapter 3. One could argue, for example, that one of the many
problems with supporters of Democrats in the United States is that they
are so often wrapped up in endlessly quibbling and no-saying about what
their party should be doing that they are unable to affirm a political vision that could solidify their control of power.[7] "No" makes a space in
things, a potentially productive absence or lack; what the Republicans
can sometimes better understand strategically at this historical moment
is that you need to put something in that space in order to gain control
of government. In other words, without some kind of rectifying presence, the hollowing out achieved by negation verges toward politically
indulgent quietism. So at times I can admire the Republicans for their
present historical understanding of power, even though I consistently
consider their policies utterly contemptible.

   In the earlier stages of my thinking about the following studies, I
had still believed that intellectual investigation into music justified its
validity by making manifest political values that could either inspire
or repel. As such, this book began very much within the methodological orbit of musicology within the postmodern academy, even though I
was already concerned about what constituted politics there. To a not
inconsiderable degree this remained the case, and so since it was felt
that political negation required presence, then the question of where
presence could positively manifest itself within music without becoming mere bullish assertion became pressing. Thus, as the project ensued,
affirmation increasingly emerged from within the predominantly dialectical proceedings. In this regard, chapter 1 is the odd one out, since it
concludes with the most uncompromising negations of the whole book.
But in two of the later chapters, the work of negation is only able to

preserve its credentials and persevere authentically because something resists the restlessness of its movement and the resulting production of lack. In chapter 3, for example, the dialogic critique of the handed-down quality of musical conventions is preserved from becoming merely a litany of theatrical interruptions by a concluding acceptance of certain conventions. In chapter 4, the most densely argued and theoretically sprawling part of the book, the possibility of a political subject that can dissent and say "no" is only made possible when that subject is periodically able to emanate a certain presence; like the enchanted work of art, the political subject can only negate when it somehow affirms its own unique self-sufficiency.

All this affirming and negating bespeaks of music's fundamental engagement with the human world, and so if I had merely remained on this level of illustrating the complexities of music's acts of agreement and dissent, this study, dialectical as it may be, would still have been a work of postmodern musicology: it would have questioned how postmodern musicology tends to relate music to the human world without having disputed whether music had the relationship per se. What distinguishes this study, then, are the places where it articulates how music can also be quite indifferent to the human worlds from which it, and also its performers, have come – where instead of saying yes or no, music simply looks elsewhere, or closes its eyes completely. This thread begins most forcefully in the second chapter, where I try to articulate how the dynamics created by music's formal tendencies open up something other than the cultural intentions that had perhaps initially set them in motion. It then makes its pressure felt at certain moments in the arguments of chapters 3 and 4 until it becomes the presiding theme of the final chapter, where I argue that music's value can just as easily lie in its ability to make us forget cultural origins. On the one hand, I let the pressure of this line of thinking have its way with my thinking because I had come to feel that so much attention had been given to how music was cultural that it had become almost impossible, both logically and ethically, to say how music might be musical. Or to put it another way, there was such an insistence that music must say yes that we had ended up with no music.[8] Not only does this state of affairs strike me as symptomatic of an exceedingly Western, late twentieth-century version of the Protestant work ethic – where music, caught in a not infrequently politically self-righteous matrix, must always be doing cultural work – but also that the great benefits that can arise from situations where musical participants neither perceive nor want to perceive their musical activities as culturally located were being barred. On the other hand, I had come to hold the suspicion that the use of the cultural argument as a means of making music politically active was perhaps symptomatic of what in psychoanalysis is called fetishistic disavowal: the overdetermining of one object (in this case music) in order to mask a lack in another (here, politics). For in the Anglo-American academy, music started being most consciously scripted as capable of a political act precisely at the moment (the late 1980s) when the possibilities of such a thing in the West started to radically disappear. (My brief political sketch of the 1990s above was an attempt to given some sense of this.) So it is perhaps not ridiculous to pose the question whether in our present historical moment the freedom to allow for some instances of the musical in music might be the positive sign that we still believed that there was anything to be achieved by the political in politics. And since it is still too early historically to tell, this book answers neither yes nor no.

ACKNOWLEDGMENTS

Academic acknowledgments often give the impression that scholarly work takes place at parties, and that the resulting books are but the progeny of all the wonderful conversations that have been had there. The research experience for some is evidently a jolly and inspiringly collective one. But this book came into being in a colder climate: in the early years of the new millennium my then partner, Carlos Arévalo-Gómez, died a nasty death from AIDS, and, as if aping a pathetic fallacy, the hopes and delusions of 1990s political culture in the West were brought to a sharp halt through a series of sobering and traumatic events whose repercussions we are still thoroughly enmeshed within. It would be ridiculously narcissistic to conflate the two worlds – even though any death from AIDS is always en-route to being politically bruised. But the sad outrage that fueled my response to what I considered to be the shocking, if inadvertent, superimposition of the personal and the political, also fueled the quite pronouncedly solitary activities of this book's protracted beginnings. So although this book has its fair share of jokes and playful formulations, the marks made upon my outlook by the grim light in which I first tried to see the page I was writing upon have been allowed to remain. Perhaps the book would have been better if I'd applied some gentle cosmetics. But even now, years later, my petulance snaps back: the dead died! And something of that fury refuses to aestheticize for the sake of a smile. So, rightly or wrongly, I acknowledge it before others, even if it can hardly be thanked.

Considering how well formed my edges were for the inflicting of wounds, it is perhaps remarkable how much kindness I encountered as an author, especially in the final years of the book's messy adolescence. Richard Leppert, a marvelous mentor and comforting friend, took me seriously when it seemed that practically nobody else could be bothered. At a point when, as an unknown scholar, I had seriously started to wonder whether any of this was worth it, he inspired me to keep on board, and so I remain enormously in his debt. Similarly, Robert Hatten, gentlest and firmest of editors, was patient during the lunch in which I snarled at him that he wouldn't be interested in what I was working on, and by following through allowed me to think that maybe I wouldn't have to spend the rest of my professional life as a lunatic shouting at myself in private. Other editors who had read earlier versions of some the material in this book (Mark Burford, Simon Keefe, Elaine Sisman) were similarly generous. The one part of this book that did socialize properly, the final chapter, benefited from the kindness of invitations to give talks: from Olle Edström in the Department of Cultural Studies at the University of Gothenburg (Sweden), from my dear friend Tia Dinora at the Department of Sociology at the Univeristy of Exter (UK), and Nicholas Cook at the Department of Music, Cambridge University (UK). Various colleagues, in particular Michael Long, Peter Schmelz, and Stephanie Vanderwel, had the good grace to play the well-behaved audience when I wanted the stage for extended aria practice. And where other presses can make one feel that in approaching them with a project one is approaching the deity itself, the staff at Indiana University Press, by contrast, have been unfailingly human. Easy, proficient, pleasant, professional, and full of humor and grace, they made the whole process seem utterly normal, pragmatic, and never cause for undue concern. I raise my glass to you all – to Jane Behnken, Nancy Lightfoot, Sarah Wyatt Swanson, Eric Schramm, Mollie Ables. Thank you!

Although it is the case that I did not tend to discuss directly the material of this book with others, I have done a lot of talking over the years, and so acknowledgement is particularly due to those special ones who have been the rare combination of both dearest of friends and intellectual interlocutors. Most importantly here would be Jenny Marsh. As a poised adult professional, she listened to my nonsense when I was but a messy sixteen year-old lugging self-consciously on a cigarette in her living room. Although every conversation I have had with her since has offered me the strange kind of hope and happiness that only the pleasures of intelligent talk with those one loves can give, our first talk, sitting on the sofa, looking out into the magical world of her garden, is one of the few genuinely unsullied memories I hold: then I was truly happy. To Jo Malt, who has been so dear to me since that foggy day in Cambridge all those sad, sad years ago when first we spoke. You were heard, my love, and thank you for listening. To Andrea Spain, mighty mountain woman, desert companion, inspiration, and maker of space; I have been honored indeed. And finally to Martin Scherzinger, fellow foreigner and accompaniment in late-night walks through the empty streets of the cities of this world. You relinquished me from feeling ashamed when I did not have a home, and at times that has meant everything to me.

Then, of course, there are all of those who gave not a hoot about this book and what it was about, and in so doing gave me a life elsewhere. To Jessica Mckinnon, who, like truth, even when hidden, was there. To Beth Evans, amongst many other things, for an afternoon of sublime hysterics that nearly made me wet myself on a street corner in Lisbon. To Danny Chiarelli, the only ludic genius I know. (As only you will understand, you are the sister I've always wanted to be.) To the outrageously witty Scott Stevens, who I am lucky enough to have as my beloved boyfriend – for cutting off any attempt I might make to discuss this project with an immediate "Music?! Gross!!" which always made me laugh. And finally to my remarkable parents: hardy, funny, generous, life-loving, Jenny and David Currie; better humans than I could ever hope to be. With apologies if the poorly behaved vitriol of parts of this book disappoint. You are the sweetest thought I have. This pittance I dedicate to you.

1

Veils

(Mozart, Piano Concerto K. 459, Finale)

HAPPY BIRTHDAY!

Once a year we acknowledge our love for others by making them queen of a touchingly comic realm of pantomime fanfares from plastic trumpets, cakes aglow with candles, champagne overflowing from popping bottles. But what are we really doing at this birthday party? Only the morally Spartan would insist that the event is solely concerned with celebrating the particularity of a dear friend, for surely we are also celebrating the reciprocity of love: that I love my friend not only for who she is, in and of herself, but also for what she enables me to actualize surprisingly from out of myself; I celebrate her because she makes celebration overflow from out of me, like champagne from popping bottles at a birthday party. And so in 2006 we raised a glass to Mozart (250 years old!) and made a toast: to the "who he is" that allows this celebrating somebody else from out of us to emerge.

If Mozart can still activate a celebration within our being, then that is indeed remarkable. But it is also somewhat disturbing, a fact that encourages me to kick-start this book into motion with a hysteric line of attack: for we are all participants in a world that, even though it has had 250 years of opportunity to listen to Mozart's music, is nevertheless catastrophically broken. Just one quotation is needed here, from Derrida, over fifteen years ago, when many in the West might not have imagined how bad things were about to become:

> It must be cried out ... never have violence, inequality, exclusion, famine, and thus economic oppression affected as many human beings in the history of

1

the earth and of humanity. Instead of singing the advent of the ideal of liberal democracy and of the capitalist market in the euphoria of the end of history, instead of celebrating the 'end of ideologies' and the end of the great emancipatory discourses, let us never neglect this obvious macroscopic fact, made up of innumerable singular sites of suffering: no degree of progress allows one to ignore that never before, in absolute figures, never have so many men, women, and children been subjugated, starved, or exterminated on earth.[1]

So thank you Mozart! But for what exactly? For helping us to preserve the fundamental humanity that glows from out of the heart of our celebration of you? Or for helping us to forget the fundamental inhumanity of a world that, in our day-to-day lives, we are inextricably implicated in sustaining?

MIRROR MOZART

Mirror Mozart on the wall, who is the fairest of them all? It is a relative given of reception history that each age seems both to ask this question of Mozart and also to find the same answer: "You are the fairest." Maybe this narcissism that Mozart's music can inspire in us is not only a negative shadow cast by historical relativism. Maybe Mozart's music does, in fact, have the ability to reveal a certain best in us – not just our best, but a best that is indistinguishable from the best that other ages have had to offer. Maybe we are the fairest not because we are human at a particular time and place, but simply because we are human, per se. Maybe Mozart's music is the mirror that reflects not us, but the universal within us.

In the still pervasively postmodern climate of contemporary academia, such statements are unfashionable, if not deemed politically irresponsible. To talk about the universal is to avoid the matter at hand. At best, the universalist is inconsiderate, like someone lecturing about metaphysics to a mother trying to cook dinner for three screaming children. At worst, she is someone who puts Mozart on and turns up the volume while violence takes place outside her front door. Within the court of postmodernism, the notion of the universal has been found guilty of war crimes (both literally and metaphorically). However, as my essay will show, this should neither lead us to conclude that postmodernism has had an unfruitful relationship with mirrors, nor that it would reject the concept (in the style of Jeff Koons) of a mirror-coated

Mozart.[2] Although postmodern thinking in general would undoubtedly reject the notion that Mozart's music reflects the universal in man, a certain line of inquiry within musicology can in contrast validate a particular set of reflections between Mozart and the postmodern present. In this essay, I examine these reflections so as to negotiate my opening challenge regarding how Mozart's music is to be celebrated in the face of the political catastrophes of the present. Organizing my discussion around the metaphor of the mirror, I start by outlining the reflections between art and politics that postmodernism has set in place. This is followed by an improvisation on some suggestions from Wye Jamison Allanbrook concerning Mozart and postmodernism, in which I discuss the late eighteenth-century discourse regarding learned and *galant* styles via an extensive reading of the stylistic processes of the finale of Mozart's Piano Concerto in F Major, K. 459. To conclude, I suggest why certain political situations demand that mirrors should be smashed or veiled and what that might mean in terms of the relationship between Mozart's music and the possibility of a better world, should we even consider it still appropriate to talk about such things in the same breath.

POLITICAL REFLECTIONS

At the end of the eighteenth century, after nearly two uninterrupted centuries of confidently reflecting how the West wished to understand itself and its art, the metaphor of the mirror started to tarnish. Instead of grounding the understanding of reality, reflections (particularly of the self) acquired the potential to cause great anxiety, exiling the human subject from out of the validating home she had once found in the recognition of her own appearance and the appearance of her world, and into a realm of the uncanny, the *Unheimlich*, where the comforts of home became the horrors of alienation. Like ghosts, reflections of the already existent were things to be avoided at all costs – a warning that the Romantics were to communicate particularly through *Doppelgänger*, that cast of terrifying reflections that Romantics allowed periodically to haunt and sometimes penetrate the secure limits of narrative and discourse. However, contrary to a common understanding of Romanticism, one might provocatively argue that the problem was not so much a fear of what unexpected horror might suddenly stare back at one from the mirror's surface. It was not that we might suddenly come face-to-face with the Other looking over our shoulder; Glenn Close in the famous bathroom scene finale to *Fatal Attraction*, dribblingly mad, wielding a kitchen cleaver. Rather it was that there might not be anything more than what one already saw. Looking into the mirror we see ourselves looking back at ourselves looking at ourselves in the mirror, ad infinitum; an unending ricochet between reality and reflection stretching without variation into a future of the infinite same. Horrified, we smash the mirror, but are then confronted by an even greater trauma: that our terrifying anxiety is but a trick played by the light on a flat surface. For the Romantics there had to be depth, for in the depths lay the possibility that there might be something more to life than the merely apparent. The exploration of depth did, of course, run the risk of confronting unforeseen, even annihilating, terrors, but it was a risk that had to be taken in the name of a certain political hope.[3] As is now well documented, Romantic music became a prime medium by which such depths could be fathomed. Romantic hermeneutics, remaining consistent to this discourse, argued that what was most important about this music was not its immediately heard surface but the secrets that it kept hidden down below. And so Keats was famously to write in "Ode on a Grecian Urn": "Heard melodies are sweet, but those unheard / Are sweeter."

Thus, at the very moment that music assumed her position at the top of the hierarchy of the arts, her acceptance song became inaudible, a state of affairs that causes eyebrows to be raised among certain critics. But as Allanbrook asks rhetorically: "Should one really be disturbed to think that music could concern surfaces?"[4] Indeed, why shouldn't the tangibility of music's surface, its inextricable embodiment in audible sound, constitute the alpha and omega for celebrating it in the first place? Surely we should work with the already existing plenitude of music as it is, rather than, to appropriate E. T. A. Hoffmann, the "infinite longing" created by the question of what it might be hiding.[5] As Susan Sontag famously once put it: "In place of a hermeneutics we need an erotics of art."[6]

Such statements have the quality of calls for hedonistic luxuriation in the merely sensuous, for an aestheticization of all existence including thought. Undoubtedly, there is an element of this in certain postmodern writings, most notably the later work of Roland Barthes. Critics of postmodernism, such as Eagleton, are then perhaps right to question the political validity of such positions.[7] But across the disciplines, postmodern suspicions regarding the hermeneutic impulse toward depth and the art that encourages it have also been motivated by perfectly justifiable political anxieties.[8] On the one hand, postmodernists often suggest that the tendency to talk first and foremost of what lies beneath the surface of art may be analogous to the means by which, time and again in the sphere of our political consciousness, our gaze has been directed away from the self-evident political and economic inadequacies of reality and redirected toward claims either of an underlying political order or of a more broken (but strangely invisible) part of reality that has greater moral and ethical claims on our attention. Thus, in part, postmodernism seriously entertains the notion that analysis of depth may be isomorphic with the disavowals of consciously constructed projects of political oppression. In doing so, it is strangely in accordance with the Enlightenment critique of authority that tends to work on the assumption that arcane mysteries are merely functional, acting as smokescreens for the machinery that supports the elite and inequality. (As I soon articulate in more detail, postmodernism, irrespective of its suspicions regarding metaphysics, is somewhat like the Enlightenment in this regard; it seeks to shine a certain light onto all existence, thus banishing the smoky theatrical shadows that are so much a part of depth's dramatic success.)

On the other hand, postmodernism has been concerned not only with how depth obfuscates the problems of our political reality, but also how it disempowers us by training us in a second nature, whereby we then assume that the first move to be made in negotiating the difficulties of our world (whether personal or political) is to look for an underlying cause or origin that must be known or confronted before further progress can be made. In the collaborative work of Gilles Deleuze and Félix Guattari, for example, such depths, whether they occur in the scene of psychoanalysis or broader social dialogues, are considered chimerical; they are dangled in front of us as unattainable goals that merely make us forget that we could, to use their terminology, "become" the skills of which we are already in possession (on our surface, as it were) but whose revolutionary potential we have as yet failed to activate.[9] In following this line of thought, postmodernism has shared similarities with the methods of critique that led Marx to assert, for example, that religion was the opium of the people.

So postmodernism's famous celebration of surface is not just to be taken as an avoidance of seriousness (although, taking its cue from Dada and surrealism, it has at times made a form of political commitment out of its rejection of what normatively constitutes seriousness in art). In fact, its call for depths to be collapsed into completely self-present surfaces issues from the radically democratic project that it claims lies at the heart of most of its discourses. In the context of postmodernism, we should aim at hiding nothing, and also at making everything as available as possible. On a musical level this can lead, as in Alfred Schnittke's discussion of the "polystylistic method," to talk of a kind of "documentary objectivity of musical reality, presented not just as something reflected individually but as an actual quotation"; the third part of Luciano Berio's *Sinfonia* has thus been explained not just as a collage of quotations, but also as "musical 'documents' from various ages – reminding one of the cinema in the 1970s."[10] On the other hand, this discourse of availability helps to explain postmodernism's reassertion (purportedly in contradistinction to modernism) of the virtues of pleasure, quotation, citation, representation, communication, convention, functionality, sociability, dialogue, style, self-evidence, mass culture, consumer-oriented values, and populism. To take but one musicological example, Robert Fink writes that Schenker "had no interest in analyses that appeal to the general experience of listeners untrained in structural hearing." By comparison, "our more democratic, materialist era may demand a stricter accountability to listener response – and thus to musical surface."[11] Hence the value of a supposedly postmodern musical style such as minimalism: "Minimalism is so obviously *flat* that even the most flexible depth theorist must quail before it: what is there on this surface that needs generating or explaining through a theory of structural levels?"[12] By maximizing visibility we move toward maximizing availability, and the more of the world that is made available, the more likely it will be that we will move toward an equality of representation and a respect for difference, which, by implication, should eventually result in an equality of human rights and economic distribution. Postmodernism seeks to transform the entirety of social existence into one massive surface by relocating the economically and representationally dispossessed from the invisible depths, where they act as a foundation, and on to the visible surface; by comparison, to date the economically and ideologically dispossessed have provided a supportive foundation enabling the minuscule minority of the world's privileged to have something on which comfortably to rest. If this re-location could be achieved, then a certain conceptual gravity would take over, since putting a foundation on the place that the foundation is meant to support would cause the entire structure to fall down to the same flat surface of equality, thus creating – to invoke a phrase of Mc-Clary's again – a pile of rubble in which to revel.[13]

Whereas Romanticism banishes mirrors since they threaten to erad-icate the possibility of a redemptive something else offered by depth, postmodernism seeks to better the world precisely through making all of its surfaces as reflective as possible. In so doing it strives to guaran-tee that there will be no place where the world cannot be confronted by itself, no gated mirror-free community where the agents of oppres-sion, domination, and inequality can hide from the reflection either of their own agency or from the reflected images of their victims. Total "mirrorization" of the world will in essence erase censorship, leaving oppression standing naked. It is in the context of this discourse of reflec-tive surfaces that we can most fruitfully understand the deeply political implications of postmodern art's most characteristic feature: its plural-istic, collage-like surface, constituted from a kind of euphoric babble of samples, fragmentary representations, quotations, vignettes of ironic mimicry, straight-faced pastiche, (mal)appropriations, snap-shorts, *ob-jets trouvés,* and stylistic clashes between trash and transcendence. Like an enormous (global?) disco ball, the polyglot surface of postmodern art is, in a sense, coated with a collage of mirror-coated fragments, end-lessly reflecting anything and everything that comes within the enor-mous orbit of its voraciously mimetic appetite. As Schnittke puts it with regard to the "polystylistic method": "It widens the range of expressive possibilities, it allows for the integration of 'low' and 'high' styles, of the 'banal' and the 'recherché' – that is, it creates a wider musical world and a general democratization of style."[14] Since everything gets reflected, yet no reflection gets to dominate (since all are fragmentary), the mirror-coated surface of postmodern art thus provides us with a powerful analogy for the characteristic dynamic of any democratic politics of difference: that our fundamental right to be represented must always resist the hegemonic tendency that encourages us to turn our representations into rolls of wall paper with which we then set about covering every surface of discursive space. Unlike paintings, which do not change, and encourage us through static images to entertain narcissistic delusions of permanence and universality, images caught in mirrors are images that can never be caught. The people reflected there are either constantly twitching and moving about as they try (always unsuccessfully) to get a complete picture of themselves, or someone walks between them and their reflections, thus momentarily projecting them into that supposedly primary ethical realm, where someone else must be acknowledged. Mirrors do not humiliate but create humility. Reflections should make us reflect.

POSTMODERN MOZART

Let us now invite Allanbrook to do the honors and ask the question: "Is Mozart himself post-modern?" In balancing an awareness of historical relativism with a pragmatist's preference for the functional rather than truth-value of assertions, Allanbrook's answer reveals her postmodern inclinations: "Frankly I like this seemingly absurd idea, or at least I have learned something about Mozart and his contemporaries by entertaining it."[15] Mozart's music, like postmodern art, is mirror coated, and endlessly draws on the "universe of topoi," in V. Kofi Agawu's phrase, that "thesaurus of *characteristic figures*," in Leonard Ratner's terms, that music in the early eighteenth century developed "from its contacts with worship, poetry, drama, entertainment, dance, ceremony, the military, the hunt, and the life of the lower classes."[16] It is drenched in reflections.

Allanbrook's stylistically exquisite work combines sophisticated interpretations of Mozart's stylistic discourse that are contextualized within eighteenth-century thought with an approval of the values that she finds therein (an approval that is laudable for its complete unambiguousness). By co-opting this work in my construction of a Postmodern Mozart, I open up two hitherto unexplored lines of inquiry. First, in insisting on the importance of stylistic play and surface in Mozart's music, Allanbrook allows for Mozart to reflect postmodernism's documentary tendency, in which, as already mentioned, the realities of the world's existing surface appearances are recorded in political repudiation of the disavowals of depth. Thus, *Le nozze di Figaro* "is not a revolutionary's manual. . . . Mozart had no desire to obliterate class distinctions, because for him the way to the most important truths lay through the surface of things as they are. The attempt to shrug off one's skin," rather like feigning blindness in the face of one's reflection in the mirror, "is a vain and ultimately circumscribing act of violence; one struggles impotently, caught in the coils of the unwilling self." And so "true freedom begins with carefully articulated orders, true knowledge with the patience of the receptive eye," that mirror reflecting the truth of the world's appearances.[17] Second, for Allanbrook, the polystylistic, mixed surfaces of postmodern art are "mongrel, democratic; they cannot pretend to be elite."[18] And so Mozart's music, in reflecting the postmodern, is therefore democratic. As Allanbrook writes of the first movement of the Piano Sonata in F Major, K. 332: "The movement's stylistic multiplicity neutralizes any suggestion of a thematic hierarchy: the aria gives way to learned counterpoint, which in turn moves to closure by way of a hunting minuet."[19] If we raise the question as to which of these styles is most important, we are missing the sonic image of a certain political freedom that this music offers: "With comic flux – the mixture of stylistic modes – comes a democracy of thematic material not possible in the monoaffective style of the Baroque."[20] As in life, so too in music; a true politics of difference knows no colonization of one particularity by another. Thus, "one such moment is not reducible to another: an aria is not the same as a minuet";[21] and in a similar vein: "Simply by co-existing, these various *topoi* frame and undermine one another, in the course of a single movement ceding stylistic authority playfully one to the next."[22] In short: "*Topoi* articulate each other's differences in the same way as modern linguistics understand phonic units as delimiting each other: by juxtaposition and opposition, by rubbing shoulders, 'jostling each other about.'"[23]

STYLISTIC INTERPLAY IN THE
AGE OF ENLIGHTENMENT

We can elaborate further on our reflections by turning to the discourse on learned and *galant* styles that arises in response to the stylistically mixed language of Mozart and his contemporaries. This discourse propounds the musical values of popularity, clarity, comprehensibility, approachability, pleasure, and familiarity, which it attempts to validate via an implicit co-opting of late eighteenth-century Enlightenment philosophy of history. This philosophy, manifest in numerous texts – from Charles Burney's *A General History of Music from the Earliest Age to the Present Period* (1776–1789) and Edward Gibbon's *History of the Decline and Fall of the Roman Empire* (1776–1788) to Immanuel Kant's essay "Idea for a Universal History with a Cosmopolitan Purpose" (1784) and the Marquis de Condorcet's *Sketch for an Historical Picture of the Progress of the Human Mind* (1795) – views history as a rational, optimistic, and progress-oriented process toward the *telos* of its own already enlightened age, or the one that was, it was believed, soon to come. As such, it was critical historiography, antithetical to historical relativism, and completely comfortable with taking the past to task for failing to live up to the ideals of the present.[24] The past was either to be rejected for failing to be the enlightened present, or appropriated as something that could be educated (or coerced), as it were, into being adapted to the needs and ideals of Enlightenment.

Within musical discourse, this philosophy of history was used to script the Baroque past, as manifest in the strict contrapuntal artifices of learned styles, as an authoritarian Other: difficult, stiff, inflexible, arcane, lacking in a clear expressive immediacy, and thus dissonant in relationship to the democratic accessibility of the contemporary musical language.[25] This was a reading that was supported, in part, by the continuing association of fugal counterpoint with the church. Johann Georg Albrechtsberger, for example, bluntly stated that "fugue is the kind of music most necessary for the church."[26] Such a critical view of learned styles was, of course, hardly new to discourse on music in the second half of the eighteenth century; both Jean-Jacques Rousseau and Johann Adolf Scheibe – to cite two obvious examples – had railed against counterpoint and the musical culture of the baroque for failing to live up to the aesthetic benchmark of clarity.[27] However, in calling for a rejection of learned styles from composition, one might argue that writers such as Rousseau and Scheibe simultaneously turned the notion of composition into ideology, that is, a discursive space organized around a politics of exclusion. By contrast, in the later eighteenth century, it was argued not only that this authoritarian Other could, in fact, occur in the context of the accessible *galant* style (rubbing shoulders with it, to follow Allanbrook), but also that it could take on attributes of the *galant*. Learned style was now capable of acting in a less rigidly authoritarian manner and of being more flexible and open to stylistic interplay than supposedly had been the case during the Baroque.

For example, in *Der angehende praktische Organist* (Erfurt, 1801–1808), J. C. Kittel states that "the strict [Baroque] style of fugal writing is troublesome in that it favors fiery enthusiasm but not clarity. The course of modulations, at least for anyone who is not exactly a connoisseur, is not sufficiently intelligible, lacking in points of repose, in light and shade, in illustrative episodes. In recent times, therefore, composers have begun to merge stricter and freer styles, thereby creating a third genre in which solemn seriousness can be united with charm."[28] In particular, the difficulty arising from the musically demanding experience of contrapuntal artifices was perceived as being lessened by the adaptation of those artifices to the clear harmonic and melodic syntax of the normative *galant* instrumental style of late eighteenth-century music. In his *Historisch-biographisches Lexicon der Tonkünstler* (Leipzig, 1790–1792), Ernst Ludwig Gerber writes the following about Haydn: "Every harmonic device is at his command, even those of the gothic age of grey contrapuntalists. But instead of their former stiffness, they assume a pleasing manner as soon as he prepares them for our ears. He has a great gift for making a piece sound familiar. In this way, despite all their contrapuntal artifices, he achieves a popular style and is agreeable to every amateur."[29] And in an anonymous review of 1809, one reads that "Haydn's fugues, almost without exception, are distinguished by the popularity of their invention and organization, by simplicity and excellent flow of each part, by the general clarity which results from this, and by many erudite devices, though these are employed only incidentally."[30]

The fact that commentators were prepared to believe that fugal counterpoint had become more enlightened was mirrored by the fact that late eighteenth-century descriptions of different contrapuntal styles were frequently more fluid than might have been expected from an age still so seemingly devoted to taxonomy. Johann Friedrich Daube in *Der musikalische Dilettant* (1773) rather bizarrely designates symphonies, arias, and concertos as "ungebundene oder uneigentliche Fugen" (unbound [free] or pseudo fugues).[31] Elaine Sisman has pointed out similarities between Heinrich Christoph Koch's 1802 definitions of *thematisch* and *kontrapuntisch* and comes to the conclusion that "what we think of as 'thematic working-out' or motivic development may have had eighteenth-century applications comparable to the 'strict' techniques of double counterpoint."[32] Even as late as the 1820s, Anton Reicha in his *Traité de haute composition musicale* (1824–1826), groups together interpolated fugal expositions both with other contrapuntal techniques and, similar to Koch's definitions, with thematic development. Moreover, Reicha does this without feeling the need to make any strong distinction between the different functions that these styles could perform: "In the course of a movement of a quartet, quintet, overture, symphony, etc. (above all in the second part of a movement) one may employ with great success a fugal exposition, imitations, strettos, more or less canonic, the inversion of a double counterpoint, the partial development of one or several motives."[33] And Kirkendale, in a discussion of an exchange in 1798 between Privy Councillor Karl Spazier and Johann Anton André, notes that "vagueness about the concepts 'fugue' and 'fugato' was widespread at that time."[34]

In scripting learned styles as more flexible than they had been during the Baroque period, this later eighteenth-century discourse was able to explain stylistically mixed music of the late eighteenth century as evidence of historical progress. At a broader level, in revealing learned style to be capable, as it were, of negotiating aspects of its identity with other styles for the good of the musical whole, the discourse created a set of potential reflections between the behavior of musical styles and the social responsibilities that autonomous individuals were meant to honor in order to qualify as enlightened: that without a moderating, social counterbalance, unrestrained individuals might be drawn into rampant and essentially socially destructive and dominating forms of behavior.[35] For political and moral purposes, the desires of the solitary individual or groups had to come to some kind of compromise with those of other individuals or groups, creating the compromise called society.[36] This society would neither be rigid nor repressive, but fluid and diverse while retaining stability.

In the following section I investigate what seems at first to be a credible musical reflection of such a society, the remarkable finale of Mozart's Piano Concerto in F Major, K. 459, which Charles Rosen asserts to be the "greatest of all Mozart's concerto finales."[37] In general, the movement is important for my argument in that it highlights the two features that are vital for an enlightened stylistic discourse in music to function: negotiation and resolution. The need for negotiation is forefronted in this music by the sheer variety of different influences and associations with which the movement juggles. As Rosen writes, the "movement is a complex synthesis of fugue, sonata-rondo-finale, and *opera buffa* style. The weightiest and the lightest forms of music are fused here in a work of unimaginable brilliance and gaiety.... [It is] the synthesis of Mozart's experience and his ideals of form. Everything plays a role here – operatic style, pianistic virtuosity, Mozart's increasing knowledge of Baroque counterpoint and of Bach in particular, and the symmetrical balance and dramatic tensions of sonata style."[38] And resolution is highlighted, not only because this is a finale, but also because Mozart has framed it in such a way that, in the words of Cuthbert Girdlestone, it acts as the "center of gravity of the concerto,"[39] a point supported by Rosen's observation that the "first two movements of this work are already heavy with Baroque sequences and contrapuntal imitation, as if to prepare for the final Allegro assai."[40] Similarly, Simon Keefe, in an impressive systematic examination of dialogue in Mozart's piano concertos, has shown how in K. 459 the piano and orchestra "demonstrate a teleological relational development, carefully establishing and reinforcing dialogic cooperation in the first and second movements and reaping the rewards of their toil in the finale's uninhibited affirmation of cooperation" – although he is careful to point out that this process is counterbalanced by a sophisticated set of references in the finale back to earlier procedures from the first two movements.[41]

THE FINALE OF MOZART'S K. 459

The movement begins with a solidly homophonic, rondo-like theme, whose undemanding, relaxed comic grace is created by the playful and slightly cheeky dialogue between the solo piano and wind instruments, the solid four-bar antecedent and consequent of the theme, and a highly repetitive rhythmic structure based on a motive of two eighth notes followed by a quarter note. We are immediately dropped into the "here and now" world of *opera buffa,* and the particular images the music evokes are therefore those of rapid interactions between people in complex social situations. Admittedly, we should be wary of making such an association too easily, since, as Allanbrook remarks, "*opera buffa* is not responsible for every witty, quicksilver passage of instrumental writing we may encounter, in the concertos or anywhere else." For Allanbrook, "*Buffa* contributed to concerto writing not so much its materials as its procedures. . . . In short, the ability to embed references to many musical styles in the continuous context of a piece."[42] Indeed, such stylistic pluralism is one of the defining features of this movement. However, we can locate specific *buffa* gestures in the concertos in the endings, cadences, and finales, where "in both low- and high-level structure [they] serve as signs of termination and areas of arrival."[43] And so at the end of the movement the underlying *buffa* qualities of the opening theme are made unambiguous when that opening material appears in the context of a mixture of patter-song style and rapid interchanges between the solo piano and orchestra from m. 486 to the end, which anticipates the comic antiphonal interplay between Papageno and Papagena in the act 2 finale of *Die Zauberflöte* (1791).[44]

The fugato starting in m. 32, though, immediately transports us into the different and more authoritarian world of learned style. In fact, Mozart emphasizes the sense of authority here by invoking the idea of quotation, since the fugal subject is made up of a learned *alla breve* vocal head motive, recalling the motet style and the imitative ricercar of the Renaissance, followed by a specifically instrumental-style continuation (**x** and **y**, respectively, in Example 1.1a).[45] The intensity of this passage of fugal counterpoint is also emphasized by the fact that it begins with entries of the subject already in stretto, and when the second set of entries begins in m. 43 the stretto overlap is made even shorter. Although the sharp divide between these two styles at the opening of the movement nicely illustrates Allanbrook's notion of the different styles "jostling each other about" (perhaps like people at a busy corner in a large city), it doesn't capture the full democratic potential of fugal counterpoint that emerges in late eighteenth-century discourse of stylistic interplay. Later in the movement, however, such potential is momentarily realized.

The movement that follows is essentially a sophisticated sonata rondo form in six sections: **A (1)**-**B (1)**-**A (2)**-**C**-**B (2)**-**A (3)**. The first section, **A (1)** (mm. 1–202), is all in the tonic and can be divided into two main sections, the first (mm. 1–119) being for the orchestra alone and the second (mm. 120–202) for orchestra and piano; **B** (mm. 203–54) introduces new thematic material and is all in the dominant; **A** and **B** combined hold a certain similarity to the double exposition of the first movement of a concerto. **A (2)** (mm. 254–87) immediately begins back on the tonic but quickly deflects onto D minor for the beginning of **C**, which begins with an intensified reworking of the fugal material starting in m. 32 of **A (1)**, passing in mm. 322–53 through developmental-style material and then concluding (mm. 354–90) with a transposed reworking of mm. 166–202 from **A (1)**. **B (2)** (mm. 399–433) presents **B (1)** in the tonic, and then the movement is rounded off with **A (3)** (mm. 453–506), which functions as a coda. After the opening (starting in m. 32 of **A (1)**), elements of the learned style passage subsequently appear on five prominent occasions: as a closing theme at the end of both **B (1)** (mm. 228–44) and **B (2)** (mm. 415–29); in section **C** at mm. 288–322 and in the passage that follows in mm. 332–45; and in Mozart's extant cadenza for this movement (m. 453).

In the closing-theme passages of **B (1)** and **B (2)**, the musical style is a mixture of *opera buffa* and concerto style. From the language of the *opera buffa* finale there are short two-bar phrase groups that reiterate perfect cadences, and from the world of instrumental virtuosity there are running scalar passages in the piano, the kind of brilliant-style bravura entirely to be expected in an Allegro concerto movement. This is a very different stylistic world from the passage of learned style (mm. 32ff.) that I have been discussing and, obviously, any material that is transported from the learned-style passage into this new one is going to have to be altered in order to be comfortably recontextualized. Thus, when the fugal

1.1a. Mozart, Piano Concerto in F, K. 459, 3rd movement, measures 32–43

subject is transplanted into this musical environment, it relinquishes its status as one line in a contrapuntal texture and adopts the garb of a theme in a homophonic texture. In order for this to happen, Mozart forefronts an extension of the length of the instrumental continuation of the subject, which had only been presented in passing in the flute and first violin in mm. 42–45 (compare -**y**- in Example 1.1a with Example 1.1b from the end of **B (1)**). Onto that he then appends a cadential cliché (-**z**-, Example 1.1b). Later on in the cadenza the descent of -**y**- is extended further (Example 1.1c).

Not only might one hear a pleasing mixture of the learned and the *galant* in these passages, one could also say that the two styles come to some kind of democratic compromise. And this interpretation does give the movement a satisfying form: as the movement progresses, the "difficulty" created by the mildly intrusive entrance of learned style in m. 32 is eased out when learned style allows its fugal subject to be transformed by its interaction with the less demanding and more pervasive *buffa* style. Learned style is, thus, made softer and more flexible without it having to relinquish its identity. In fact, one might perceive that the slightly problematic and socially embarrassing gap between learned style and less elevated styles already begins to be bridged from m. 44 onward.

1.1b. Mozart, Piano Concerto in F, K. 459, 3rd movement, measures 225–44

1.1c. Mozart, Piano Concerto in F, K. 459, 3rd movement, cadenza (extract)

Here the contrapuntal texture of the fugato begins smoothly, and almost imperceptibly, to transform itself into the passage of brilliant style homophony that eventually leads to the cadence in m. 65. Thus, although learned style enters as a mildly disruptive character that creates a stylistic disjunction, it exits graciously and considerately, leading the music back toward a more popular style and then modestly stepping aside in order to let that style speak. In the next chapter, I offer a more dissonant reading of what happens here.

Up to this point, Mozart's finale seems nicely to reflect the ideals of enlightened social interaction that I have articulated. Yet in the midst of the movement's *bonhomie* there is a passage (mm. 288–322 in **C**) whose expressive severity calls attention to itself: an intense passage of learned style, a double fugato, whose two subjects are derived from the opening passages of *buffa* and learned styles, respectively. Stylistically, one could interpret this as another moment of stylistic synthesis: as *buffa* appropriates learned-style material at the end of **B (1)**, so learned style appropriates *buffa* in **C**. Interpreted thus, these two passages pleasantly balance each other out. However, this interpretation is a little fragile.

The first problem of interpreting this passage as a counterbalance to the moment of stylistic appropriation at the end of **B** (1) concerns its formal location in the movement. The moment of stylistic compromise at the end of **B** (1) occurs as part of the kind of closing theme material that one might expect at the end of a sonata-form exposition. By definition, such material tends to express at a local level that the musical process has come to some kind of resolution; it is a brief moment of formal repose, particularly at a local harmonic level. This stable formal context provides a musical environment conducive to the seemingly happy democratic interaction of learned style and *buffa* style; formal and stylistic stability reflect each other in mutually supportive fashion. In contrast, the stylistic intermingling at the beginning of **C** occurs in a highly tense and unstable passage, fulfilling a number of different formal requirements: it acts as a radically altered restatement of the initial fugato from the opening of **A**; it is part of a complex mosaic of fragments of previously heard themes (mm. 288–389) that functions as a retransition to **B** (2) (now in the tonic, at m. 390); and it might also be heard as a means of creating a development-like tension within the otherwise carefree fun and games of the rest of this finale.[46] Such a musical environment is hardly as hospitable as the codetta-like ending of the first **B** section. As a result, instead of being brought together expressively by the fugal texture in which they are both placed, the learned style fugal subject and the fugal subject derived from the opening *buffa* material of the movement are involved in a rather disturbing game of attraction and repulsion. At the beginning of each new entry, the two subjects seem to be in opposition, particularly in terms of rhythm and articulation; they then move into a closer relationship (Example 1.2). But repeatedly, this new proximity and cohesion is quickly undermined by each new entry of both subjects, where the initial tension between the two subjects is, of course, reasserted by other voices. The whole process is made more fractious by the roving modulations of this passage, which starts in D minor (m. 288) and then passes through A minor (m. 293), G minor (m. 301), C minor (m. 308), finally cadencing on B-flat major (m. 316).

The impression that learned style and *buffa* style are in opposition here is accentuated by the uncomfortable proximity of the *buffa* fugal subject to its immediate origins, the *buffa* theme from **A** (2). In m. 288,

1.2. Mozart, Piano Concerto in F, K. 459, 3rd movement, measures 288–89

without any significant preparatory motivic development, and with only three taut measures of modulation preceding it, the main motive of the *buffa* material suddenly changes from a sprightly major-mode figure into a stiff and terse minor-mode version of a pathetic-style fugal subject – in other words, into one of the most venerable and learned of the Baroque fugal subject types to have survived into the late eighteenth century. The fact that each subject in the double-fugato passage can be distinctly heard as an identifiable subject type (mixed instrumental and pathetic, respectively) only adds to the impression of a lack of stylistic integration and of conflict between the two subjects. The sudden shift in the stylistic associations of the basic eighth note–eighth note–quarter note *buffa* motive makes it seem that the *buffa* style is not willingly taking part in an enlightened stylistic compromise. In fact, it sounds as if it has been caught off-guard, wrenched into this new environment, and quickly corseted into an uncomfortably tight new outfit before it has had time to put up a fight.

By comparison, when material associated with the learned style recurs at the end of **B (1)**, there is no immediate context for perceiving to what degree it has been transformed, for learned-style material has not been heard for 178 measures. Further, comparing the opening passage of learned style in the movement with its reincarnation at the end of the **B (1)** (Example 1.1b), one sees that they are stylistically and expressively relatively congruent. They are both in the major mode, and the instrumental continuation of the fugal subject feels as if it has been easily adapted to the *buffa* environment. The forefronting of the extension of the continuation -**y**- that happens at the end of **B (1)** adds, by means of its mild exaggeration, a subtly comic element of caricature to the fugal subject, which helps to soften the solemnity of the motet-style headmotive -x-. (This element of caricature is then highlighted in Mozart's extant cadenza, where -y- [Example 1.1c] is extended to ludicrous proportions – a point to which I return in the next chapter.) Finally, the strangely bare texture of violas and cellos and piano answered by violins and piano sounds like a less dense, unpacked version of the relationship between subject and answer in the opening fugato (see Example 1.1b). (This kind of relationship between instruments is possibly what Daube had in mind when talking of "ungebundene oder uneigentliche Fugen.")

Another problem with interpreting the double fugato at the beginning of the **C** as balancing the stylistic appropriation at the end of **B (1)** concerns its size. Up to this point, learned style has had a walk-on part in the stylistic interplay of the movement. The first passage of learned style was short; learned style material then disappeared, only returning to make a quick appearance appropriated into a *buffa* context at the end of **B (1)**. If the fugato at the beginning of **C** is a stylistic counterbalance, one would expect it to be similarly brief. Instead we get twenty-seven measures of intense, stylistically overbearing counterpoint, creating the impression that the passage is not particularly well integrated into the movement. The fact that this entire section up until m. 314 is the only place in the movement where the minor mode is firmly established adds to the fact that, in the seeming playfulness of the rest of the movement's stylistic negotiations, this passage of learned style cuts a conspicuous and rather uncomfortably stony-faced figure.

The sense created by this fugato in the recapitulation that integration is lacking is accentuated from m. 316 onward. There is a cadence on B-flat major in m. 316 when all the voices come to rest, and then the contrapuntal texture restarts with pairs of voices entering in sequential order. If for a moment we imagine that this movement is a full-fledged fugue, this break in the texture followed by a resumption of contrapuntal activity could be interpreted as a secondary exposition, or at least the beginning of a new section. In the context of this movement, though, it is confusing. In classical instrumental works whose primary textural orientation is homophony, fugal counterpoint generally occurs only as small, homogenous, and syntactically uninterrupted blocks. The reason for this is that within the homophonically and cadence-oriented world of classical instrumental music, an uninterrupted passage of strict contrapuntal writing can often act as a means of creating a unified block of tension between two points of repose. The interruption in m. 316 of the finale of this Mozart piano concerto therefore makes reference to an unconventional formal gesture. It creates a conflict between what ought to be a fleeting *stylistic reference* to learned style, and the expectations that are engendered by a self-contained *musical form* of the learned style.

Since unadulterated learned style has only presented itself as a fleeting stylistic reference so far in the movement's stylistic dialogue, the intimation of a full-fledged contrapuntal form raises a number of questions. Why all of a sudden does learned style seem to be trying to assert itself as a self-contained form, driving toward stylistic autonomy? If learned style is, as it were, growing arms and legs, is there not a threat that it might become dangerously autonomous, detach itself from the body of the movement in which it seemingly has been nurtured, turn around and seize control from the *buffa* style? The following interpretation is only one among many, and, in keeping with both postmodern and Enlightenment suggestions regarding the reflective relationship between mixed stylistic surfaces and the structure of social relations, it is unabashedly anthropomorphic.

Learned style holds the potential to be highly resistant to the stylistic cross-fertilization and compromise with which, in this movement, it constantly finds itself having to deal, because it has very little to gain from interaction with other styles. Since learned style's identity is founded on its authority, stylistic interaction will often produce a lessening of its characteristic effect, which, as Elaine Sisman has suggested, can be related to Quintillian's second kind of rhetorical figure, the *schema*, or "that which is poetically or rhetorically altered from the simple and obvious method of expression."[47] By comparison, not only does the *buffa* style in this movement imply fluidity, mobility, and a desire to interact, it also has very little to lose by interaction with *any* kind of style; *buffa* style can only profit from social engagement. In this context, the rather violent outburst of learned style at the opening of **C** makes sense. In the opening of the movement, learned style was able to uphold its authoritarian identity while appearing to take part in an enlightened dialogue with other musical styles. As already discussed, in m. 32 it presents itself in such a way that we are in no doubt as to its stylistic identity, and in m. 50 it graciously steps aside so that another style can be given space. Like an Enlightenment despot, learned style appears to recognize the existence of other stylistic identities and even gives them room to speak. But it does not actually dirty itself in getting fully involved with their business. In the codetta section of **B** (**1**), though, learned style finds its own clothes being worn by another style. One might argue that *buffa* style confuses the initially benevolent behavior of the learned style in m. 50 for a *laissez-faire* attitude. And so *buffa* style grabs the learned style's fugal subject, puts it on like an item of clothing, and trips off onto the floor of the small codetta party where it dances to its own *buffa* beat. Well-meaning as the *buffa*'s gesture may be, from the perspective of an elevated figure such as learned style this reinterpretation of sartorial code could be quite infuriating. Although it could be argued that *buffa* style endeavors to show how a learned style outfit can be made to function in a foreign environment, learned style would not be unwarranted in entertaining the sneaking suspicion that it is being ridiculed. After all, there is just a thin line between the impression that the forefronted expansion of learned style's **-y-** motive in the **B** (**1**) codetta is the *buffa* style's charmingly naive way of wearing a learned gown off the shoulder, and the possibility that *buffa* style is covertly undermining learned style's authority by showing how easily an item of learned clothing can be made to seem buffoonish and tasteless (see Example 1.1b). Similarly, there is an ambiguity as to whether the passing of the altered fugal theme from violas and cellos to violins is an approximation of a fugal texture, or a surreptitiously crude aping of a fugal subject and answer. Once one hears the musical events through the ears of the potentially wary learned style, one can start to imagine that around every corner *buffa* style is to be found trying to stifle a giggle.

When figures of authority feel they have been humiliated, one of their potential reactions is to relinquish decorum and angrily seek revenge. And this is exactly what learned style does at the beginning of **C**, by violently abducting the *buffa* figure. In particular, this act of sabotage by learned style is expressed by the way the music enters into this fugato at the beginning of **C**. In m. 32 at the opening of the movement, the start of the fugato was hitched onto the final chord of the *buffa* theme so that both styles were kept under the swathe of F major. Even though learned style was perceived as stylistically distinct, the unity of key helped to give us the impression that learned style was a cohabitant in a musical environment with other musical styles. By comparison, in **C**, the fugal counterpoint is separated from the *buffa* theme by a short modulation starting in m. 286, which though technically is not untoward is, nevertheless, both expressively and formally striking. Its affective power comes from the fact that it is literally tagged onto the end of the recapitulation of the *buffa* theme. Instead of having the quality of a natural and necessary link between two different keys, the passage sounds as if the harmonic foundations have been knocked out from underneath and the floor is collapsing. Moreover, it literally marks a formal divide between *buffa* and learned styles that had not existed at the beginning of the movement, when both materials had cohabited within **A (1)**. It is as if an insurmountable wall has suddenly been built through a once unified city.

In short, in m. 288 learned style hijacks control of the movement's stylistic processes from *buffa* style. As we have seen from the fraught dialectic of repulsion and attraction between the two subjects in this passage, *buffa* style does briefly attempt to struggle free from the straitjacket of its learned pathetic-style fugal subject. But by m. 316, the *buffa* figure seems to be taking part happily in the contrapuntal texture. (Either it has relinquished itself to the seemingly inevitable passing of its reign within the movement, or finally it becomes brainwashed by the seemingly indefatigable contrapuntal momentum that learned style exhibits here when it begins what sounds like a secondary fugal exposition.) In particular, the effect of *buffa*'s defeat is created by the change of mode from minor to major. On the one hand, this shift in the harmonic environment makes the *buffa* figure seem as if it were smiling inanely. On the other hand, it can express learned style's realization that it has successfully seized hegemony over the stylistic politics of the movement and that it can now sink back into its "comfy" major mode throne and enjoy the restoration of its authority without fear of a *buffa* counter-revolt. However, in m. 322 learned style's hegemony in this finale is cut short by the solo piano playing virtuoso figuration, which powerfully confronts the authority of learned style's distant historical aura with the immediacy of the musical

realities at hand: that is, that we are listening to a piano concerto. However, the effects of the learned style's attempted coup do not disappear
immediately, and learned style continues to cast an ominous influence
over the movement's stylistic processes.

From m. 322 onward, answering the piano figuration antiphonally,
the strings play a version of the *buffa* motive. Because *buffa* material and
virtuoso figuration have happily coexisted in the movement so far, one
might expect that the *buffa* material here would be expressively congruent with the piano. But the *buffa* material sounds as if it is working
against the piano's attempt to stamp out the unruly learned style, even
though *buffa* and solo piano material are related at this point. The *buffa*
material appears here to still be under the sway of learned style's su-
premacy within the dialogue; it has forgotten that it once had a role as an
autonomous stylistic character within the movement's stylistic processes
before it had been incarcerated within a contrapuntal texture in m. 288.
The continuing learned allegiances of the *buffa* material in this passage
(mm. 322–30) are underlined by the shift back to the minor mode. The
only other place in the movement when the *buffa* motive is played in the
minor mode is in mm. 288–315 – in other words, during the period of the
learned style's triumph. It seems appropriate that the link between the
buffa motive in these two passages should be modally highlighted.

Throughout the passage under discussion, the solo piano, with un-
flinching determination, has sustained its refutations of learned style
and continued to play figuration. Its efforts are repaid starting in m. 332
where there is a return of the *buffa* version of learned style's fugal subject
that had been heard in the codetta to **B (1)**. Finally brought to its senses
by the insistent message of the piano's figuration, *buffa* style regains its
powers and is once more able to appropriate learned material. Admittedly, in mm. 340–44 the learned style's fugal subject occurs in stretto,
as was the case in the very first passage of fugal counterpoint beginning
in m. 32, and we might interpret this brief moment of contrapuntal inten-
sification as the final blush of learned style's negative influence passing
across the movement's stylistic politics. This minor learned deflection,
though, is quickly corrected, the stretto entries being rapidly soaked up
by the textural modulation from counterpoint to homophony starting in
m. 345, leaving the focus on the piano, which then triumphs unaccom-

panied with ease in mm. 352–54, ending with an exalted trill on a high C that opens the door for a return of the *buffa* motive in its form from m. 166 in the second part of **A (1)**.

MOZART WRAPPED

It is still possible when wandering around the increasingly dilapidated amusements of seaside piers in England to come across a gallery housing deliberately deformed mirrors that reflect us back as caricatures, squashed into a vile homunculus, or variously stretched into the splat of a human pancake or the pencil-thin elongation of some wraith. The experience can be varied – side-splittingly funny, a depressing reflection of a hidden anxiety regarding how we think we appear, narcissistically flattering. At best, however, we leave with a quiet chuckle passing through the hint of a smirk on our faces: how prone we are as beings to distorting reality; how good it feels to see things as they truly are, reflected from the flat surface of a mirror without warps or buckling. This is the politics of the mirror, whose policy of reflecting the babble of plurality is wonderfully caught by the reflective surface of the finale of Mozart's K. 459, where we witness learned and *galant* styles not only at play, in dance, laughing and talking and sharing, but also in dispute, angry and greedy, and attempting to silence the democratic music of socially polyphonic dialogue with the terrifying monophony of the same. All mess and all magnificence is here, and if we are acting in a responsible postmodern fashion we do not attempt to organize this reflection by means of the priorities or hierarchies of some kind of overarching formal or political "meta-narrative." Not only, as Jean-François Lyotard was famously to assert early in theoretical debates about postmodernism, are such narratives now supposedly defunct,[48] but, as I have already suggested, the imposition of such schema can incarcerate the already dispossessed at the margins of the field, thus working to sustain an inequality of representation. To appropriate Allanbrook, if we treat the field of contrasting musical styles "as veils to be lifted to reveal deeper structural truths [we are] ignoring the kaleidoscopic expressive mutations that are a crucial element of this style. The variousness in this music is not contingent, not the merely necessary appearance of an inner reality, but a thing-in-itself, a being of the phenomenal world of temporal succession."[49] As it is in our world in general, "political" life in the finale of Mozart's K. 459 is a series of localized tensions and agreements, a reveling in the contingent mess of the day to day, and to pretend that there is any larger totality that controls such negotiations, both in our musical and political life, is, as many postmodernists have insisted, to put the cart before the horse. If the world is as broken as Derrida asserts in the quotation at the beginning of this essay, then for postmodernists that is because we have yet to learn to live within this human realm of negotiations. We are fatally attracted to the theoretical Leviathan, which, when brought to life, remains indifferent to the sounds of crackle and crunch that human life makes as it disappears under its vast feet. The first step en route to the mending of our world may simply involve you putting down this essay and smiling at whomever might be next to you – smiling like the ending of Mozart's concerto, with the full humor that comes from accepting oneself as just one moment in the endlessly transforming music of the here and now.

But before we return to the birthday party that I so rudely interrupted at this essay's start, we need to emphasize an important point. The postmodern notion that the world works according to localized disputes and resolutions is a vision of the world as it *could* and (*perhaps*) should be. However, the reality of our present condition is that it is more totalized than it perhaps has ever been. So postmodern euphoria over the notion of surface may well be a covert form of despair regarding the enormous totality, the depths, on which such surfaces slide. Turning back to Mozart, why should the authoritarian backlash of learned style that occurred in the middle of the finale of K. 459 not have consumed more of the stylistic negotiations of the entire movement? Does the mirrored surface reflect all we need to know? Or is there something more sinister at stake? For example, in his justly famous analysis of the postmodern cultural logic of John Portman's Westin Bonaventure Hotel in downtown Los Angeles, Fredric Jameson notes that the mirrored glass skin of the building repels the city outside. Moreover, it is

> a repulsion for which we have analogies in those reflector sunglasses which make it impossible for your interlocutor to see your own eyes and thereby achieve a certain aggressivity toward and power over the Other. In a similar way, the glass

skin achieves a peculiar and placeless dissociation of the Bonaventure from its neighborhood: it is not even an exterior, inasmuch as when you seek to look at the hotel's outer walls you cannot see the hotel itself but only the distorted images of everything that surrounds it.[50]

So is Mozart's music in the K. 459 finale – a music that in its bustling, Babelic plurality is thoroughly urban in orientation – merely a distorted reflection of its world? Moreover, is it a distortion that functions to repel both the world it claims to represent and us – to repel from both its potentially hidden depth and, to follow through on the analogy with Jameson, its surface too?

A writer such as Allanbrook might argue that the movement ends with a sense of resolution because this is a comic work, and the "happy ending of comedy celebrates the restoration of the proper orders, no matter what the difficulties in reaffirming them. Hence its job is to persuade us of this, and its ingratiating cadences are honed to this task, whereas in tragedy the pathos and ambiguity of the whole provide no patent point of view to which to persuade us."[51] Keefe has pointed out that in the piano concertos the "eventual outcome of Mozart's relational drama is not really in doubt," and so "the listener can turn his or her attention exclusively to interactive processes."[52] Again, there is the assumption (basically correct historically) that for late eighteenth-century audiences and theorists, resolution was simply expected to be achieved by works of art, thus making the question moot as to why it might not have been.

But to use a historical argument regarding convention to neutralize a perfectly valid political concern is to pervert history into a set of injunctions against critique. In terms of the understanding of Mozart himself, there is nothing particularly problematic if the status of resolution here is the product of convention rather than reflection, an imposed simulated order rather than the replication of one that actually was in existence. As I mention in this book's fourth essay, in Mozart there is often a slippery dialectic in play between what we might, tentatively, refer to as a proto-realist impulse and a kind of mid-eighteenth-century French neoclassical one, between a notion of art as real as life and art as but a fully constituted artifact. Perhaps for Mozart our postmodern musicological concerns would have been moot. However, in terms of the postmodern scholar everything depends on this point. For if we are dealing with musical convention here, then Mozart's music does not connect us with the world by means of its surface; rather, it has a constructed image of the world projected onto it by whatever power source it is that controls the circulation of the convention. Conventions, after all, are merely the set of practices by which a community decides, or has been coerced, to organize its behavior; the resultant forms of decorum that they engender may well represent how communities would like to appear to themselves, but they do not by definition therefore speak the communities' truths, a point to which I return in the third chapter. So if the postmodern musicologist were here to embrace convention as an acceptable solution to a somewhat unresolved surface antagonism, they would, in essence, be using a surface to hide a surface, thus employing an unacknowledged depth structure to clinch a deal against depth. Perhaps like the postmodern politics of the mirror, then, Mozart's music does not offer us a reflective surface, but rather a painting of a mirror reflecting a world that (still) has not yet existed. Although it is true that attention to the stylistic surface of Mozart's composition helped to articulate that there is, indeed, a problem, it provided next to no information as to why that problem should have disappeared. My argument (and it was a thin one) was simply that learned style was confronted by virtuoso piano figuration, creating a contradiction that somehow derailed it. But what really convinces us that we can pass beyond the threat of hegemony posed by the learned outburst on the surface is the underlying formal convention (the large-scale harmonic movements of the sonata style) that helps us to rescript this tense moment as merely necessary for the balance of the form as a whole, a dissonance that works to highlight the consonance of the ultimate resolution. We make a palliative from the formal resolution; its underlying normative gesture distracts us from the unresolved surface stylistic question. The mirrored surface of this movement has a concave representational warp in it that we fail, or perhaps choose not, to notice.

To smash a mirror may well be to behave in an adolescent fashion, substituting hysterical acting out for the sometimes unbearable confrontation with who we are, or even who we are not. And yet it can also be politically justified, since power warps mirrors in such a way as to comfort us into not seeing things that are already there, things which, in other circumstances, we might notice more clearly. We imagine that we would know when we are before the funny distorted mirrors in the amusements arcade, but frequently our perceptions prove themselves unreliable in this regard. So in these troubled times a rejection, *tout court*, of the depth hermeneutic should give us pause; likewise, we should be wary of the assumption that our desire to preserve depth is merely founded on an elitist attempt to neutralize the liberational force that, it is sometimes uncritically assumed, surface possesses. The notion of depth has, of course, proven itself to be vulnerable for conscription by suspicious forms of metaphysics, essentialism, colonialism, and much else. However, in its politically productive form it is driven by a basic insistence, that that which innocently and without complication appears as just what it is must nevertheless undergo critical scrutiny. Depth is, therefore, also a powerful tool of negation and thus an important means of checking that surfaces really are surfaces, as opposed to flatteringly bent reflections of power. After all, we should remember that postmodern critics of depth had to perform in the first place exactly this depth maneuver on depth-oriented scholarship in order to put their own ideas regarding surface into circulation.

As a move toward concluding this essay, we might therefore perform a little depth analysis on a pro forma move made by critics of depth, whereby depth-oriented models employed in music theory are criticized for oppressively denying the living, breathing exuberance of music and the joys it can bring (I merely sample here from the stock of phrases that are commonly plundered when making this point). Depth criticism, it is argued, eradicates pleasure. Now, I would of course be lying if I claimed that there was no such stingy element to be found in certain instances. However, what is problematic about this kind of critique is its frequent and somewhat morally righteous assumption that what constitutes and validates pleasure is self-evident, as if the mere fact that pleasure makes one feel good means that, in and of itself, it must therefore be a force of good. But from what ground does this confidence in pleasure speak? For Freud, we should remember, the pleasure principle was originally referred to as the unpleasure principle;[53] its function was to curtail excessive excitation of the organism, reducing pleasure to a minimum no longer threatening to the boundaries that constitute the subject. For Lacan, likewise, the pleasure principle is a regulatory force, a law; its allegiances are, thus, toward the Symbolic. Pleasure then, we might say, functions precisely in order that pleasure will not become too pleasurable and transform into enjoyment (*jouissance*). After all, enjoyment is on the side of what Lacan would call the Real, the constitutive impossibility at the heart of any signification system. It is under the sway of the death drive, and it therefore aims to overshoot all constitutive symbolic structures. (In effect, enjoyment heralds the death of such symbolic structures, and this explains why *jouissance* in Lacanian theory is conceived of both as excessive pleasure and also as pain.) In a strict dialectical sense, then, enjoyment negates the subject, for by confronting the subject with that something in it that seeks to transcend the very boundaries by which the subject recognizes it own seeming consistency, enjoyment also forces upon the subject a realization of the limitations of such consistency. Enjoyment confronts us with the trauma of our inconsistency; it brings the subject into an uncomfortable proximity with the realization that its identity only constitutes itself as whole through an act of censorship. It is perhaps for this reason that we can cry or feel unnerved after heavy drinking or sexual intercourse: we have had a confrontation with the limit within us (our extimacy, to cite Lacan's excellent term),[54] and so the return to whom we are normally feels like an uncanny homecoming. For we now know that within us there is something other than just ourselves in residence.

Enjoyment, we might say, is an affect of the sublime. By contrast, pleasure is an affect of the beautiful, which Lyotard, for one, equates with ideology.[55] Beauty emphasizes "unity of experience";[56] it creates pleasure since it allows us a means of not seeing what has had to be airbrushed out of the picture in order to create the aesthetically satisfying sense of our coherent worldview where parts, seemingly without coercion, equate with wholes. So when scholars talk about depth analysis regulating and denying them the plenitude of their pleasure, we should at least wonder whether the postmodern scholar's pleasure is not already the result of a submission to a law that enforces the practice of her/his own self-regulation and denial. Pleasure, in other words, is thus not necessarily full but lacking. In a certain sense, pleasure can be merely the surplus product of the structure of delusion. Since pleasure is therefore less, not more, and since pleasure is an affect often invoked by postmodern musicologists with regard to surface, we should perhaps entertain the possibility that surface is simply less too – not less than depth, just less than all. This does not mean that we must give up on pleasure and surface. Even if, as I have here argued, pleasure and surface can rely on the ideological gesture of excluding information and experiences, only a sadist would insist that we must be constantly exposed to the totality of the world's malfunction or the potentially destructive forces of *jouissance*. However (and it is a big "however"), to be at rest and yet claim that one is vitally involved politically with the world (because the world, it is claimed, is a surface that can be reflected by, for example, the mirrored surface of the piece of music that presently pleases us) seems distasteful. If musicology is in the business of circulating this notion as a model of political behavior worthy of emulation, then it is perhaps necessary to start circulating something that could say no to it.

So maybe we should reconsider the modernist values, sometimes maligned these days, regarding difficulty. For if we are to reside with the phenomenon of difficulty, we often have first to endure beyond the surface appearance of our own initial reactions, particularly if they arise from discomfort. Those reactions have to be unveiled of our certainty that since we are not being offered what we in our immediacy want, we are justified in our dismissals. If we find that hard to do, because we are distracted by what Lacan would see as the Imaginary – the beautiful, flattering, fantasmatic reflections of ourselves that we keep glimpsing in flight across the surface of that which pleases us – then maybe, to balance out the equation, we might then experiment with veiling. Maybe, after all, what we need is not a mirror-coated Mozart, à la Jeff Koons, but a wrapped one, à la Christo and Jeanne-Claude. For in their art – where epic geographical features (a portion of the Australian coastline) or iconic landmarks (the Pont Neuf in Paris) are wrapped in what appear to be enormous sheets – Christo and Jeanne-Claude employ veiling precisely to draw attention to objects that we usually consider to have fully comprehended. On the one hand, this results in a sort of euphoric process of defamiliarization, which encourages us to reengage with the world. Yet there are shades, too, of dead bodies under shrouds, protected from the obscenity of our greedy narcissistic gaze, a reminder of the persistence and presence of loss. So perhaps, as in certain death rituals, we should veil our mirrors until we are responsible and respectful enough to look in them once again. The role that Mozart's music might play in that process is up to us, for, like a mirror, it is only as good as we are.

2

Dreams

(Fugal Counterpoint)

THE MATERIAL UNCONSCIOUS

Shrouded objects are ambiguous. Too easily they can imply the sadness of things not in use, as in the somewhat period-piece image of furniture under dustsheets in summer retreats offseason. But things aren't so devoid of life as such initial impressions might imply, and death, as grief can sometimes make us understand, is not always dead enough. When characters in films find themselves in the unused house trailing their fingers along the shrouded top of the chair, it is frequently a cue for things forgotten to be drawn back close to life. And so the departed beloved stands at the window once more, the warmth of his laughter muted by the coldness of the passed time through which he has traveled to reach us. Already we might tentatively suggest the beginnings of a theory here, that veiling and its attendant practices are less singular actions than exchanges in which an initial gesture, seemingly of subtraction and withdrawal, makes a space available for an emergence: of a gift, since presents after all should be wrapped; or a shock, for a ghost, at least at Halloween, is usually a wailing mystery covered by a sheet.

A particularly familiar act of covering that most of us perform each night is to pull up the blankets as an overture to sleep. It is of course pragmatic, a protection from the cold. But the fact that it can still be felt to be necessary in some vestigial form even when, as in the heat of high summer, it is no longer required suggests that it is as much a signal to some Other part of our being. Wildly, we might wonder if it reactivates distantly some redundant archaic memory of a time when the descent into sleep simultaneously meant increased exposure to the dangers of the natural environment and so the necessity of guaranteeing that one was suitably protected and had covered one's ground. And one can easily improvise further, invoking for example the fact that a tried and tested way of avoiding harm is precisely to play dead, and that one way of doing so is to camouflage oneself as a corpse by lying still, perhaps shrouded as if by a mortuary sheet. If we are lucky, adopting covering allows the world's threat to pass us by, and so if there is a value in what I am teasing out here it is exceedingly close to ideas of escape, if not escapism, even though it is not such things per se. But if for sleep to be safe we need a little death, then that cessation also makes room for something else to come to life. So if I concluded the previous chapter by throwing a covering over music in part so as to veil it from the potential political distortions of reflection, it is not only so that it could die a little and sleep, but also open itself up to what then can follow, the life of dreams.

The association of music with dreams is a rich and venerable one that it is not my intention here to attempt to capture historically. What interests me is how what appears in dreams relates to its seeming origin in waking life and how such a form of appearance might in some instances offer us a better metaphor for the relationship between music and world than that offered by the mirror. In the somewhat popular understanding of the dream/reality relationship, aspects of objective reality appear in dreams usually in some form of distortion, and it is perceived that the job of dream interpretation is to tease out what latent dream thoughts (underlying desires, traumas, and so on) this manifest content of the dream text supposedly hides. Indeed, the kind of interpretation that I had started to propose at the end of the previous chapter was already en route to such a hermeneutic, for I had scripted the initial proposition – that the mirrored surface of Mozart's K. 459 finale reflects the world as it is – as a kind of dream text hiding a potentially more traumatic social reality. This interpretation can now be given further credence if we turn to Mozart's own written-out cadenza, which in part I had to avoid in order to make my initially mirrored interpretation.

The cadenza is divided in two and allows for a final presentation in one musical scene of the movement's two leading stylistic protagonists, the first half being centered on the learned fugal subject (example 1.1c, chapter 1), the second on the *buffa* material. Striking is the degree of the transformation that has overtaken the fugal subject. As we will recall, at numerous points throughout the finale's course this theme had undergone various processes of adaptation in order that an enlightened stylistic compromise could be achieved between it and other materials. Primarily these had tended to involve brief extensions of the subject's scalar continuation as a means of creating successful cadences. In the cadenza, however, extension no longer appears to take place within the ethical frame that had previously functionally scripted it as benefiting the stylistic and formal good of the movement as a whole. Rather than fulfilling the terms of some musical social contract, it occurs more for its own sake, as if it were simply enjoying itself in the excesses of its *jouissance*. As a result, the originally learned material now appears as if it were a somewhat saucy caricature.

An outrageous tumescence, the eighth-note continuation reveals itself over the course of six measures of the cadenza's opening as possessing nearly three octaves in length before kinking back on itself so as to land on an F. At an increasingly excruciating slower tempo it then descends again down to B-natural, which it suspends for seven measures of flagrant expectation-heightening before finally dropping to B-flat and then A. The rhetoric of this obscene revelation has all the lack of temporal subtlety, and thus all the fantastic effectiveness, of a knowingly crafted tawdry striptease. In this vein, we can admire the lewd mastery by which a rapid preemptive summary of the eight-note continuation is interpolated into the final moments of the descent at the point when the left hand hits the low B-natural, rather like the relinquishment of a feather boa; the right hand's final glitter-splattered arpeggiations articulate two cackling high kicks of sufficient abandonment to emancipate each shoe like a hand grenade into the audience. If we had forgotten our doubts regarding the somewhat glib manner in which difficulties arising from the learned outburst in the middle of the movement had been superseded, this cadenza easily resuscitates them. Certainly, the somewhat embarrassed chromatic hedging that initially characterizes the following *buffa* motive (before it, too, is overtaken by its own excesses) bespeaks the shock following an exposure to more than one had reckoned on. Either we have just witnessed learned style with devil-may-care abandon casting off its Enlightenment education and so refusing to know its place, or an act of ridicule of learned style that is so carnivalesque – the Rabelaisian association, via Bakhtin, with lower bodily functions is not inappropriate here – that one has to wonder if its overdetermination is not merely the reverse side of an acknowledgment that the forces it seeks to belittle can never ultimately be placed.[1] Of course, one might reject such hermeneutic excesses by pointing out that cadenzas are conventionally understood locations for the placement of improvisation and performative bravura. But as I continue to assert, we should be wary of assuming that because a community has decided to agree on a normative meaning for some conventional aspect of its cultural behavior that the meaning is therefore transparent in relationship to the community's purported claims. Indeed, this is the value of viewing things in music as if in dreams, for repeatedly dreams illustrate that the seemingly irrelevant thing at the corner of the frame of reference can transpire as the uncanny blot through which undermining forces will, during the course of the analysis, emerge. If the devil is in the details, then a cadenza can unmask the lie of the movement to which it has been conventionally scripted as merely supplemental.

But in going deeper, such a musical dream interpretation perhaps goes too far and so paradoxically ends up closer to, rather than further from, the mirror metaphor. In the terms of Carolyn Abbate's widely circulating argument, the kind of symptomatic interpretation that I have performed on Mozart's cadenza is just as oriented toward a "clandestine mysticism" whereby music becomes the cipher to some other nonmusical truth as the object of critique it tries to escape – if not more. It verges toward what Abbate, in a lovely formulation, calls the "cryptographic sublime," whereby the "more impenetrable or complex the mechanism by which it is assumed something important has been encoded by a medium, the deeper the fascination commanded by that medium becomes and the stronger the emotional and erotic charges it exerts."[2] And as Abbate rather naughtily points out, one of the side effects of this somewhat fetishistic scene (my formulation, not hers) is that relatively obvious points all of a sudden become imbued with a significance they would not possess if they merely presented themselves to us directly, rather than being made to loom up to the surface from out of the hidden depths of the musical work. This is the negative side of my theory that things covered nevertheless allow for something else to emerge, for by being placed within a wrapping of musical material, unremarkable things are made "less banal than they are by themselves. The ordinary becomes a revelation."[3] Even at the end of the eighteenth century, when optimism was perhaps in better health than now, one did not have to look that far to find acknowledgment that social life was not necessarily perceived as the well-functioning plurality that at times musical art and its attendant discourses might have wished it to be. It was hardly unconscious, and one did not therefore have to take the circuitous route through the cadenza of a piano concerto in order to arrive at the realization.

Such arguments, however, only invalidate the dream metaphor if dream interpretation continues to adhere to desires for the spectacle of an Arcanum to be magically made to speak its secret. But as Žižek, like other Lacanians, has argued regarding Freud's theory, "*There is nothing 'unconscious' in the 'latent dream-thought,'*" no devastatingly illuminating fact about the self waiting to be revealed. Rather, "this thought is an entirely 'normal' thought which can be articulated in the syntax of everyday, common language; topologically, it belongs to the system of 'consciousness/preconsciousness'; the subject is usually aware of it, even excessively so; it harasses him all the time."[4] Freud and Abbate are perhaps not dissimilar. What is truly unconscious is by definition constitutively repressed, cannot be translated into everyday language, and so has in effect no content. We come to know it not through some kind of hermeneutic unearthing of it itself, but through its effects. Like the wind in the trees, it is observed in the manner in which its force (repetition and desire) rattles the dream materials in the form of the so-called "dream-work" – the essentially formal, even stylistic, processes, such as condensation and displacement, which are enacted upon and through the content endowing it with its particular dream appearance. What is important is therefore "decidedly more 'on the surface,' consisting entirely of the signifier's mechanisms, of the treatment to which the latent thought is submitted."[5] My argument thus transpires as somewhat paradoxical, for surface has been veiled in order to rectify the fact that it was not surface enough; it has been encouraged to dream so that we might forget its content and concentrate on its form. So rather than exegesis, we should perhaps do something more musical, as one of Lacan's maxims for analysts attests: "The less you understand, the better you *listen*."[6]

Without doubt the distortions to which the learned fugal material is subjected in the cadenza of Mozart's piano concerto are available – almost alarmingly so – to cultural discourse as forms of signification. Even without the distortions, the various basic musical features that constitute the learned theme and the kinds of contrapuntal textures that one would usually expect to encounter it within can all with relative ease be shown to arise inextricably from out of the polyphonic web of histories in which they were formed and functioned as part of the work of culture. As we are used to hearing, there is no innocent outside to cultural mediation and so no need for guilt – and this being the case, then perhaps no need for psychoanalysis either. However, if learned style is like a piece of equipment that can be used to get a job done, then we should note that a piece of equipment can also nearly always be used for another purpose, even one completely unintended by the forces and agents that initially brought the equipment into being. The large hammer I had been using to hang a picture can suddenly be at hand as a suitably graspable weight for the purposes of bicep development or for smashing someone's skull; learned style can be part of a church service and then available to Mozart in a piano concerto as a means of pleasing an audience and guaranteeing the economic success of a series of subscription concerts. One might attempt to halt the beginnings of this equipment-based counterargument by simply invoking the notion of the dialogic work of cultural appropriation. But if we assert that the functional displacements of hammers and musical styles *only* result from the agency of culture, then the cultural position is en route to a kind of self-essentializing, absolute idealism in which everything takes place in its own head. And so one is tempted by the rather simplistic gesture of Dr. Johnson's in response to Berkeley's idealism: to refute the point by kicking a rock, and so asserting a certain materiality into the frame of debate.

Regarding the cultural position's potential self-essentialization, we can easily note a return of the repressed, and so, ironically, the continuing need for psychoanalysis, for the cultural position frequently validates itself ethically through the assumption of its own modesty: that rather than adopting some phallic observation point on the illusory metaphysical mountain of the absolute, it understands truth more respectfully from the ground level, where it can only ever be partial, contingent, fragmentary, relative, and so on and so forth. But the threat here, obviously, is that if there are no more mountains that might simply be because ground life has totalized itself into being the new mountain-top existence. The paradoxical result we could term absolute relativism, its common behavioral symptom being where pride is taken in the ability to be humble. The cultural position, content-oriented as it is, nevertheless has a formal moment, a point to which Martin Scherzinger's work has repeatedly drawn attention.[7] And as a whole panoply of philosophers have argued (amongst them, Hegel, Derrida, Lacan, Deleuze, and Žižek), that formal moment, rather than simply clamping content down or reinforcing its claims, creates a structure of excess whereby rigid consistency to a position's purported demand – for example, "Do not live on mountains!" – produces its own negation, so that humility can become pride, cultural materiality can reveal its moment of absolute idealism, and so on. So the cultural position requires psychoanalysis, or at least a homology of its gesture, because otherwise it cannot understand that there is by definition an Other scene created by the very structure that allows in the first place for the possibility of its conscious activities to function. In effect, it has an unconscious.

Returning to the example of a piece of equipment, I would make a similar kind of argument. The fact that it can be used for purposes other than those intended by the cultural forces that originally brought it into being is as much the product of what I am tempted to call its material unconscious as it is the result of culture's own agency. On the one hand, the decisions that culture can make regarding a culturally formed object reach a certain limit when they run up against the resistance resulting from the formed materiality of the object itself; there are certain desires to which a piece of equipment will simply not respond. On the other hand, when the object is able to respond to an attempted appropriation, that is perhaps less some displaced form of Enlightenment domination (the triumph of culture over its formed materials) than the act of grace arising from culture having chanced upon the excess potential available in the materiality of the thing itself. Through an act that is more play than work, culture thus productively experiences its own limit. Again: the forming of material into a piece of equipment is not only the harnessing of that material, the process of making it, as it were, consciously focus its energies toward one aim; it is also the means of creating a kind of unconscious excess of potentials in materiality itself. This is the fundamental paradox of form – like Schlegel's hedgehog, by closing in on itself through its structural set of relations, form thereby enables something else to stick out. So to enter the world of dreams, either literally or metaphorically, simply means that we now have increased awareness of the pressure exerted on us by this form-produced excess of potentiality. One of the privileged means we have of becoming awake to that pressure is the act of falling asleep offered by musical art. The rest of this chapter is concerned with making inroads into hearing this.

Taking my cue from the excess exhibited by learned style in the K. 459 finale cadenza, I center my attentions once more onto learned style and specifically to fugal counterpoint. My primary aim is to illuminate the potential limits of those later eighteenth-century cultural discourses that I discussed in the previous chapter and which asserted, somewhat moralistically, that fugal counterpoint could find its place within the stylistically varied world of late eighteenth-century instrumental forms. First, I suggest how fugal counterpoint in and of itself produces a certain dynamic excess, which I term *textural dissonance*. I then seek to show how this textural dissonance produced by the musico-cultural forming of the fugal material gets exacerbated when appropriated into the context of certain late eighteenth-century formal procedures. In effect, my aim will be to suggest how fugal counterpoint in late eighteenth-century instrumental forms exerts a kind of materially unconscious pressure on the more culturally "conscious" intentions of the music's form. The aim is not so much to assert the untruth of the conscious procedures against the verities of the unconscious. After all, the only way effectively to live wholeheartedly in the unconscious is through psychosis, and I have no intention of spinning that potential horror into a virtue. Moreover, it is absolutely not the intention once more to undermine the forms of late eighteenth-century music as some kind of pseudo-rational false consciousness. Rather, it is to extol the importance of this body of music: in this instance, for the way in which it allows the presence of the Other produced by its own forming processes to pulse through the dynamic of its unfoldings; for enabling us to hear, as it were, holographically, both what is conscious and unconscious; for the paradox of the sophistication with which it sometimes relinquishes responsibility, and so makes room for the advantages that arise from that which was not intended.

THE RIGHTS OF ROUSSEAU'S WRONG

Like some of the mid-eighteenth-century "galant" critics, such as Scheibe, Rousseau's view of fugal counterpoint was decidedly negative in orientation: "Fugues, in general, render the music more noisy than agreeable. ... In every fugue, the confusion of melody and modulation is what . . . is most to be feared and the most difficult to be avoided; and since the pleasure which this kind of music produces is always middling, we can say that a beautiful fugue is the unyielding masterpiece of a good harmonist"[8] – in short, a misguided waste of compositional effort. Rousseau preferred music whose expression was clear and natural, and this led him to a preference for homophonic textures; his understanding of counterpoint's difficulty is, by comparison, somewhat unappealing, since it provided him with the means of dismissing counterpoint as a compositional device. But however we might recoil from the image of what music might have looked like had Rousseau's suggestions become widely accepted – no finale of Mozart's *Jupiter* Symphony, no first movement of Beethoven's op. 131, for example – his disgruntlements nevertheless touched upon a potential musical truth regarding fugal counterpoint that other later writers were perhaps less comfortable with admitting. And so we can profit from elaborating for a moment on his position.

However the affective relationship between melody and accompaniment in a homophonic texture is to be understood, it is nevertheless the case that the accompaniment can work to fix what we will refer to as the listener's *aural gaze* onto the main melodic material, whose progression through the piece can then be followed with relative ease. It helps to create a highly effective form of musical perspective in which foreground and background can be clearly distinguished, thus enabling "*Unité de Mélodie*" to occur: "a successive unity connected to the subject, and by which, all the parts, well integrated with each other, compose a single whole, whose general effect and interconnections can be easily perceived."[9] By comparison, in fugal counterpoint the musical perspective fluctuates and is unstable because the melodic material keeps appearing in different voices. In chasing entries of the fugal subject around the texture, listeners repeatedly have to refocus their aural gaze onto different bearings within the thicket of the counterpoint in order to keep track of what is primary, a situation that is evidently compounded when more than one subject is present. This can create an almost constant state of mild distraction, at best a tenuous balancing act between the present moment of the musical experience and hypotheses regarding the location of the next entry; when strettos occur, refocusing of the aural gaze and second-guessing of the next entry may even occur at the same time. Expectancy, which is always present in the temporally incarcerated experience of music, is heightened when fugal counterpoint is present, thus increasing the sense of the music's dynamism and forward momentum. Fugal counterpoint can easily make one feel as if the music is running ahead of itself – a phenomenon familiar to anyone who has played keyboard fugues and noticed how often one seems to accelerate as the piece progresses.

Such characteristics can make the fugal experience both demanding and (paradoxically) tedious. For Rousseau, even "psalms sung in four parts" proved to be too wearing: "But having heard it for only a few minutes, my attention wanes, by degrees the noise makes my head swim, soon it fatigues me, and in the end I am bored by hearing only chords."[10] Thus, the longer fugal textures continue, the more likely it is that listeners might start looking forward – beyond expectations as to the hypothetical location of next entries – to where cognitive efforts, and perhaps disappointments also, might finally come to rest. Anxiety develops for the release that will be felt at the fugal passage's cessation, as if fugal counterpoint drives listeners into desiring resolution in the same way that a harmonic dissonance requires movement toward a consonance. Fugal counterpoint might therefore be characterized as *texturally dissonant*.

If for Rousseau fugal counterpoint disrupted one's piece of mind, because it shattered the ear's ability to impose a unifying point of perspective onto the sonic environment, other writers often emphasized its ability to placate, affirm, and homogenize. Heinrich Koch, for example, stated that, as part of learned style, fugue "is distinguished from the free style [and, thus, homophony] principally through the fact that the main subject is never lost sight of, as it is heard in one voice or another; this ensures that each voice partakes in the character of a principal part and shares directly in the expression of the sentiment of the piece."[11] A similar idea, expressed more dramatically, appears in the writings of Johann Nikolaus Forkel:

> Let us imagine a people made emotional by the account of a great event, envisaging initially a single member of this group, perhaps through the intensity of his feelings, being driven to make a short powerful statement as the expression of his feelings. Will not this emotional outpouring gradually grip the collective members of this people and will he not be followed by first one, then several, then the majority, each singing the same song with him, modifying it according to his own way of feeling to be sure, but on the whole concording with him as the basic feeling?[12]

Georg Joseph Vogler wrote that "the fugue is a conversation among a multitude of singers. . . . The fugue is thus a musical artwork where no one accompanies, no one submits, where nobody plays a secondary role, but each a principal part."[13] In these passages, the writers focus on the idea of voices united in a common cause, on an emotionally stabilizing experience as opposed to anxiety-inducing boredom.[14]

In Baroque music, fully fledged fugues can on occasion be well suited for the creation of the kinds of effects that Koch, Forkel, and Vogler outline, and indeed these writers seem to be referring to such an older musical style. Koch states that the fugal style is "best suited for church music," which in the late eighteenth century was colored by a decidedly retrospective streak.[15] The inspiration for Forkel's poetic effusions is J. S. Bach, whose works he considered as marking the zenith of musical achievement.[16] A connection between fugal writing, church music, and Baroque musical styles is also to be noted in Vogler's writings.[17] We should of course be wary of accepting the historical accuracy of these later eighteenth-century conceptualizations of earlier fugal compositions. As Adorno and more recently David Yearsley remind us, Baroque fugues, particularly Bach's, cannot be solely relegated to some kind of premodern worldview, as musical embodiments of a belief system founded on unchanging universal and cosmological truths; this music can sometimes be much more twitchy, modern, even subjective.[18]

Nevertheless, some Baroque fugues do indeed exhibit the ability of creating emotionally stabilizing experiences, and when that is the case, it is usually because they have tended to minimize musical salience. The weaving of different melodic lines and the recurrence of fugal subjects throughout can create a consistent, if not to say seamless, musical style. There is, to cite Koch again, a "serious conduct of the melody, using few elaborations. The melody retains its serious character partly through frequent closely-bound progressions which do not allow ornamentation and breaking up of the melody into small fragments . . . partly through the strict adherence to the main subject and figures derived from it."[19] In contrast, with homophony there is the potential for "many elaborations of the melody, and divisions of the principal melodic tones, through more obvious breaks and pauses in the melody, and through more changes in the rhythmic elements, and especially in the lining up of melodic figures that do not have a close relationship with each other."[20] Moreover, the stability in fugue that is created by means of the contrapuntal texture and the generally monothematic orientation is complemented by what Ratner has referred to as the "circular or solar harmonic schemes" of fugues.[21] Finally, the potentially stabilizing effect that Baroque fugues create, in and of themselves, is frequently emphasized by where they are placed. It is common in Baroque music to find a fugue at the end of a sequence of movements, such as in the fantasia and fugue, the toccata and fugue, the prelude and fugue, sometimes at the end of concertos or trio sonatas, particularly those in the church style, and in fugal gigues at the end of suites. In the context of these movement sequences, the fugue is the place where listeners are able to luxuriate in the conclusion of the musical events. The coordination of the different parts into a rigidly controlled rhythmic whole provides the composer with an impressive means of creating a musical peroration. Rather than the passing of the subject around the contrapuntal texture engendering unwieldy textural dissonance, the subject can be heard as echoing throughout the texture like a series of affirmations or a peal of bells, each statement grounding the *Affekt* into our perceptions and stabilizing the expression.

There are various places in classical music where fully fledged fugues of such a Baroque orientation are to be found. In church music, for example, certain texts (for example, the "Et vitam venture" and "Cum sancto spiritu" sections of the mass as well as passages from the *Te Deum*) continued to be set with fugal textures according to well-established traditions. Specific instances could include the "In Gloria" of both Haydn's *St. Cecilia* (1766) and *Lord Nelson* (1798) masses; the "Cum sancto spiritu" and "Et vitam venture" sections of Mozart's early masses in C Major, K. 66 (1769); C Minor, K. 139 (1768); C Major, K. 167 (1773); and C Major, K. 262 (1776); and the "Kyrie" in the *Requiem, K.* 626 (1791). As Kirkendale has shown, in instrumental music up until the 1780s composers were also still regularly employing essentially self-contained fugal movements with the stable rhythmic pacing, seamless consistency, and circular tonal schemes that were to be found as the concluding fugues of certain Baroque instrumental sequences.[22] Moreover, James Webster has written in the context of a discussion of the continuing influence of the Austrian church-sonata tradition on the instrumental music of the period that "the possibility that fugal finales were heard as culminations [in these works] cannot be dismissed."[23] Such fully fugal finales in Haydn's music are to be found in the Symphony no. 40 in F Major (1763) and the finales of his String Quartets op. 20, no. 2 in C Major, no. 5 in F Minor, and no. 6 in A Major (1772). Mozart used fully fledged fugues for the finales of his String Quartets K. 168 in F Major and K. 173 in D Minor (1773).

However, from the 1780s onward, fugal writing, particularly in instrumental music, increasingly holds the possibility of creating tension rather than stabilizing expression. This is particularly the case in self-contained instrumental movements geared toward the rhetorically emphatic punctuation and syntax of the so-called "sonata style," where points of repose and passages of flux can often be sharply distinguished from each other. Since the kinds of fugues that I have been discussing frequently rely on a steady rhythmic pulse and the sustaining of a seamless musical continuity and texture, the attempt to bring them together can easily produce a tense dialectic between the desire to stop and start (the syntactical rhetoric of the sonata style) and the attempt to move through to conclusion in a seamless fashion (the syntactical rhetoric of fugue). To return to the propositions of my introduction, the potential for textural dissonance that is produced from the initial cultural forming of musical material into fugal counterpoint is exacerbated by the attempt to then culturally appropriate that form into aspects of the cultural forms of a certain aspect of later eighteenth-century musical language. The resultant effect is therefore not just another cultural form whose content we can than seek to understand – a putting into musical effect of a set of discursive decisions – but an accident produced from out of the inadvertent activation of the potentiality in existence within the material form. It is, in effect, a symptom of the material unconscious, a complicating force, whose pressure composers must then seek to negotiate.

The pressure created by the attempt to sustain simultaneously fugal and sonata-style syntax can be witnessed as early as 1772 in the finale of Haydn's String Quartet op. 20, no. 2 in C Major. As this movement proceeds, pressure builds up, like water behind a dam, and a suppressed nervous strain enters the expression because the desire for a suitable musical resting point is constantly thwarted. The tension in the movement is then heightened by the fact that the first 129 measures are marked *piano*. As Kirkendale has pointed out, eighteenth-century fugues generally tended to be marked *forte* throughout.[24] When the counterpoint was not so strict, a *piano* dynamic might be used, creating what Johann Georg Albrechtsberger referred to as a "galanterie fugue."[25] Although there are passages in thirds and sixths in the last movement of op. 20, no. 2 (for example, mm. 49–55), overall the counterpoint is far from leisurely and *galant*. As a result, the seemingly relaxed *piano* dynamic marking is contradictory, a misplaced cultural signifier that ultimately adds to rather than detracts from the syntactical dialectic in place. One might think of it as a mask, at first glance appearing merely serene. But the mask does not stretch far enough and so, inadvertently, it periodically allows the movement's underlying twisted syntactical physiognomy to be espied; increasingly anxiety blushes across the *piano* composure.[26] The movement seems rather distant from Vogler's latter-day Enlightenment vision of fugue as an artwork where "no one accompanies, no one submits, [and] where nobody plays a secondary role."[27] Nor does it easily communicate the unified expression of one sentiment that Koch claims for fugue, nor the latter-day Enlightenment dream of Forkel's vision of fugue as a kind of universal song. Texturally, this is a threateningly dissonant movement, a fact strongly suggested in Keller's warning to players about the words ('*Sic fuget amicus amicum*') that Haydn wrote at the end of the movement: "If the players don't remember the *sempre sotto voce* right up to the *piano* that introduces the eventual *forte* 34 measures from the end, *amicus* will rather sound like a hefty full-back chasing a fleet-footed winger and employing a late tackle or two while the referee is looking the other way."[28]

Eventually, the pressure created by the attempt to sustain the deadlock between fugal and sonata-style syntaxes proves too much, and, after 129 measures of *piano,* the dynamic suddenly changes to *forte* and the underlying syntactical animosity manifests itself. First, in mm. 129–45, sonata-style syntax prevails: the cello part changes from a contrapuntal line into a harmonic bass and there is an uninhibited, clear harmonic progression leading us toward the strong dominant pedal starting in m. 146. Faced with this surge of strongly directed, classical-oriented harmonic activity, the fugal counterpoint has no choice but to abandon its densely woven texture and, as a result, the counterpoint from m. 129 becomes looser. But in m. 146, counterpoint suddenly reasserts itself, and the opening of the first fugal subject returns in a series of implied stretto entries including inversions that strain in a tortuous fashion against the dominant pedal. The dominant pedal attempts to strap this contrapuntal outburst back into the sonata-style syntax, but it is unsuccessful, and beginning in m. 151 there is a statement of all four subjects (Example 2.1). The movement is then brought to conclusion by all four instruments playing in unison an expanded variation of the first subject in inversion, which leads to the final cadence. One could say of these final seven measures that the conflict between fugal and sonata-style syntax is resolved by the adaptation of a fugal subject to a strong cadence. Perhaps fugal elements come to a happy dialogic compromise with the sonata style, in a manner redolent with the cultural discourses discussed in the previous chapter. Carl Dahlhaus has written of this movement – and, in fact, of the quartet as a whole – that "inner contradiction is not a deficiency deserving an aesthetic verdict but rather a stylistic principle." In his interpretation, the quartet cleverly explores the contrast between different musical procedures "without aiming at a reconciling 'synthesis.'"[29] But to return to the maxim of Lacan's cited earlier, it is just as feasible to listen rather than understand, and so hear the way in which the four instruments hammer out this final passage as akin to grinding teeth that only stop at the final two chords.

2.1. Haydn, String Quartet in C, op. 20, no. 2, 4th movement, measures 146–end (162)

The above reading does not suggest that the finale of op. 20, no. 2 fails.[30] On the contrary, the movement enjoys its symptom and so cashes in on the problematic relationship between fugal and sonata-style syntax. The exaggeration of the latent textural dissonance in fugal counterpoint, exacerbated by its collision with sonata-style syntax, creates an unmanageable forward momentum and dynamic that threatens the stability of the movement, and thus creates a thrilling drive toward the final cadence. Rather than being brought to rest, the quartet reverberates loudly into the silence that follows, like a set of railings in the wake of the car that has just smashed into it. Webster asserts that the final *forte* passage starting in m. 129 "is a true coda, the only one in [the op. 20] fugues [and] perhaps for this reason, it seems to provide closure not just for the finale, but for the entire quartet."[31] After op. 20, no. 2, though, the only time Haydn attempted to sustain a fugal texture for the entire course of an instrumental movement was in the finale of the String Quartet op. 50, no. 4 in F-sharp Minor (1787), a work that Keller tellingly refers to as "Haydn's only supremely difficult quartet."[32] Keller is primarily referring to the problems posed to players by this quartet. Nevertheless, in Keller's commentaries on Haydn's string quartets there is always the assumption that the technical demands Haydn places on his performers are meant to enhance important aspects of a work's particular expressive and formal character. The considerable difficulties of playing in F-sharp minor on string instruments helps to create the tense and nervy world of the quartet; the problematic relationship in the finale between fugal and sonata-style syntaxes is but one expression of this nervousness.

As Webster rightly warns us, we should be wary of assuming that Haydn does not repeat himself because a formal experiment has been unsuccessful, and thus we could assume that the finale of op. 20, no. 2 is "precisely radical enough."[33] However, apart from the finale of Haydn's op. 50, no. 4, it is not until Beethoven's late works – for example, the finale of the Cello Sonata op. 102, no. 2 (1815); the *Grosse Fuge,* op. 133 (1825); and the finale of the *Hammerklavier* Sonata, op. 106 (1817) – that we see again an attempt to combine a *continuously* sustained fugal texture *simultaneously* with classical syntax across the span of an entire instrumental movement of a multimovement work.[34] Even then, the results, though dramatically thrilling, are still, as with the finale of Haydn's op. 20, no. 2, exceedingly problematic. It is true that a composer such as Albrechtsberger, who died in 1809, continued to write fully fugal movements throughout his career, especially in the over 120 *Sonate* that he composed for various instrumental combinations after 1780. These two-movement works developed out of the Baroque church sonata and took the form of a slow homophonic movement followed by a fast fugue. However, even though Albrechtsberger "helped to create the atmosphere in which

Baroque polyphony and mid-century homophony fused to form mature Classicism ... unfortunately, his own music remained largely unaffected by this stylistic synthesis."[35] Albrechtsberger's own fugal writing remains fundamentally conservative throughout his career. Beethoven's contemporary Anton Reicha (1770–1836) also wrote a large number of fugues, in particular the thirty-six piano fugues, which were published in Vienna in 1803, dedicated to Haydn, and accompanied by an essay, *Über das neue Fugensystem*. In these radical if not to say downright quirky pieces, it is definitely possible to find examples of strong, classical-style cadences. Yet in order to incorporate such a syntax, Reicha had to loosen the rigid defining musical characteristics of fugue to such a degree that the music frequently bears no audible relationship to fugal counterpoint: expositions no longer follow the strict model whereby answers are at the fifth; any kind of melodic material is deemed suitable as a fugal subject, with peculiar results; and modulations are allowed to run riot, to the point that some of these so-called fugues do not even begin and end in the same key. The potential tension created by the interaction of fugal and classical syntax is dispelled by an extremely broad, and perhaps overly flexible, conception of what constitutes a fugue. As Beethoven succinctly put it, with Reicha "the fugue is no longer a fugue."[36]

In general, from the beginning of the 1780s, the standard form in which fugal counterpoint occurs in instrumental music is as fugatos: in other words, as relatively small passages interpolated *into* movements whose textural orientation is predominantly homophonic. I suggest that the increasing predominance of fugato can be interpreted as a tacit attempt to remove the problematic symptoms caused within sonata-style syntax by the presence of extensive passages of fugal counterpoint. Fugal counterpoint was relegated to the level of fugato so that the dialectical tension between its counterpoint and sonata style-syntax could be minimized and the resulting textural dissonance controlled.

At the most fundamental level, such control and accommodation is created by means of a process that I refer to as *textural modulation*, which is set into action when fugatos occur in mature classical instrumental music. Take, for example, the fugato beginning in m. 32 of the finale of Mozart's Piano Concerto K. 459 that I discussed in the previous chapter. Like a harmonic dissonance, the textural dissonance created by this fugato has to be resolved so that its disruptive force no longer holds sway. Resolution is achieved by gradually loosening the connections that bind the contrapuntal texture together, starting (as is most common in textural modulations in classical music) with the bass, and then reworking the relationship between the voices to form a homophonic texture. Thus, in m. 46 the eighth-note movement of the fourth measure of the fugal subject of the bass entry is altered from a descending scale figure into an arpeggiation (Example 2.2). As a result, a connection with the original subject is retained at the same time as the function of this part changes from a voice in a contrapuntal texture to a supporting bass part. This connection continues in mm. 47–48 with a reminiscence of the scale descent of the fourth measure of the subject. The brief move to a functional bass in m. 46 is significant enough a reorientation of texture to act as a catalyst for textural modulation amongst the other voices. Echoing the bass activity of m. 46, the viola part in m. 47 relinquishes the descending scale figure in its presentation of the subject, and then imitates the return of the scale figure from the subject in the bass in m. 47, creating parallel tenths with the bass in m. 48. The second violin entry in m. 46 retains its connection with the fugal subject for only two measures, changing in m. 48 from a contrapuntal voice into a part that fills in the harmony. The final subject entry in the first violin in m. 47 fares a little better. Nevertheless, by the time it reaches its third measure in m. 49, the other voices have relinquished their relationship to the original subject and, as a result, the first violin is transformed into a melody that is being accompanied. Bowing to the superior pressure exerted by the other voices in the texture, it alters the pitch height of the sixteenth-note triplet at the end of its third measure so as to create a pleasant melodic link with the passage of brilliant style starting in m. 50.

But even in the resolution of this relatively pro forma textural procedure, there are indications that something of the momentum produced by the fugal texture is not so easily quelled. The change of the cello part into a functional bass in m. 46 is confused by the fact that the arpeggiation that is created is then imitated by the violas in the following measure. As a result, the functional bass figure of m. 46 is retrospectively transformed into a motive in an imitative contrapuntal texture that

2.2. Mozart, Piano Concerto in F, K. 459, 3rd movement, measures 42–49

briefly continues until it is cut short in m. 49. Moreover, after the initial fugal exposition in mm. 32–42, a set of stretto entries begins in the bass in m. 43. Thus, before the workings of the textural modulation have asserted themselves, the opening fugal counterpoint has begun to *reassert* itself *and* intensify. Textural modulation does kick in quickly thereafter and homophony is then reestablished. But the impression of a series of stretto entries in mm. 43–49 remains strong, working dialectically against the increasing momentum of the textural modulation spreading up through the texture from underneath.

The image is of somebody desperately running up a hill while the hill collapses underneath, and this might lead us to caution that if a fugal cutting is placed in the soil of a predominantly nonfugal movement, it may attempt to suffocate the rest of the foliage by trying to grow back into a fully fledged fugue. The material unconscious, we might say, can be acknowledged and perhaps negotiated, but it cannot be expunged; the act of hubris in which pieces of music purport that they can collect their entire being fully into conscious presence might well result in momentary returns of the repressed like the strange contrapuntal backlash just discussed. And so, once more, we see the inadvertent right in Rousseau's wrong. For as Jacqueline Waeber has shown, Rousseau's problems with polyphony arose not only from the fact that it made listening more complex and so hindered a certain ideal of transparency. It was also a fear "motivated by a refusal of the sonic polysemy produced by an excess of melodic parts and its resultant – and frightening – excess of signs."[37] For Rousseau, fugue threatened to unleash a proliferation that could not then be suitably reined in. In this light, the shift in the discourse on fugal counterpoint in the 1790s toward the sublime could perhaps be understood in part as an attempt to make a virtue out of Rousseau's concern.

Although there are notable moments of sublime counterpoint in classical instrumental works, in formal terms fugal counterpoint tended to be associated with passages of flux such as transitions and developments where its tendency to create the impression of an incessant forward momentum could be exploited to complement harmonic instability and thus ultimately enforce rather than destabilize syntax. Thus, it is not usually used for the exposition of important thematic material. On the whole, homophonic textures are employed because they lend themselves more naturally to the periodic constructions that are necessary for a self-contained, clear, and stable thematic presentation. It is not uncommon for a theme that has been presented homophonically to be destabilized later on in the movement by being reworked contrapuntally, as with the opening thematic material of the last movements of Mozart's String Quintet in E-flat Major, K. 614 (1791) and Beethoven's Piano Concerto no. 3 in C Minor, op. 37 (1803). Similarly, one often finds fragments of thematic material recurring later in a fugal context as a means of creating some kind of thematic development. Hence, in the **B** section of the ternary-form finale of the String Quartet op. 64, no. 5 in D Major, *Lark* (1790), Haydn reworks thematic material from the **A** section into a series of fugal entries, which create the impression of a development-like section in this otherwise non sonata-form movement. These processes, though, are generally used as a means of emphasizing the sense of resolution that is created when the theme, or the motivic constituents of the theme, comes home to the original homophonic environment. Finally, on the rare occasions when important thematic material is first presented as the subject of a passage of fugal counterpoint, it is usually reworked into a periodic theme and placed in a homophonic texture later in the movement. This happens in the finales of both Mozart's String Quartet in G Major, K. 387, and his Piano Concerto in F Major, K. 459. In such instances, the use of fugal counterpoint for thematic exposition creates a problem that the ensuing movement has to attempt to resolve. We might say that the thematic exposition is unstable, just as if it began in the wrong key, as in the first movement of Haydn's String Quartet op. 33, no. 1 in B Minor, or if it included a particularly salient dissonant pitch, such as the famous C-sharp in the opening theme of Beethoven's *Eroica* Symphony.

But again, the fact that the formal effects of the material unconscious in music can sometimes be encouraged in order to stabilize the conscious structure does not mean that they have now been annulled. Take, for example, the last movement of Haydn's Symphony no. 95 in C Minor (1791). At the opening of the movement, a clearly periodic theme is presented as the melody of a solidly homophonic texture. Starting in m. 32, this theme appears as the subject of a fugato that acts as the beginning of the transition to the dominant, where we might expect a homophonic texture and the presentation of either a new theme, or (this being Haydn) a variant of the opening theme. The arrival of the dominant in m. 78, though, is marked by a fugal texture based, like the transition, on the opening theme. In a seemingly self-defeating fashion, the transition has, in effect, led us back to a passage that sounds like the beginning of the transition. The formal expectation and momentum of further harmonic transition that is engendered by the fugato starting at the arrival of the dominant is then confirmed by the fact that the music carries on modulating straight through to the submediant. Finally, the opening theme returns in m. 106 in its original homophonic form in the tonic. On one hand, the confusing of the conventional textural expectations could be interpreted as a means of illustrating the fact that this movement starts in the tonic, modulates straight through to the submediant, and then jumps back to the tonic. The tonal confusion of the first part of the movement is then cleared up when the opening theme returns in the tonic *and* in its original homophonic form. On the other hand, the recurrence of fugal counterpoint where the second subject should have been can be viewed, like the example from Mozart's K. 459, as a symptom born out of the difficulty of resolving the fugal textural dissonance into sonata-style syntax. Having already established its roots in the transition, fugal counterpoint sprouts up in the second subject group of the finale of Symphony no. 95, thus creating a strange counter-dynamic not unlike that created by the unnerving contrapuntal undercutting noted earlier in the K. 459 example. As a result of its textural dissonance, a dangerously inexorable forward momentum is created that makes it difficult for the dominant to be satisfactorily rested upon and which, in turn, drags the music through to the submediant. In effect, texture destabilizes the harmonic structure of the movement.

STRATEGIC PLACEMENTS

If fugal counterpoint is potentially so unmanageable, we must consider why in classical instrumental music it occurs most frequently in finales, where the tying up of loose ends and the neutralizing, expunging, and resolving of difficulties would seem to be most pressing. In part, the prevalence of strict fugal counterpoint in final movements can be explained in terms of the changing role of the finale. In earlier classical music, finales were where the music leveled out, "even if it was a spirited windup";[38] relatively few early classical finales ended in the "difficult" and less satisfying minor mode, and musical forms tended to be of a simpler ilk, less argumentative. Further, except when the finale was a fugue, the expressive level would, in general, migrate to a low-to-middling stylistic ground. However, starting with Haydn's "Sturm und Drang" works of the 1770s, finales became increasingly emphatic and difficult.[39] They either became "capable of balancing a serious opening movement, but without abandoning its traditionally lighter character,"[40] or they might actually outweigh the first movement and, thus, function as the culmination of a multimovement cycle, as in Mozart's *Jupiter* Symphony. One way in which this extra weight was produced was by introducing some kind of difficult musical problem into the formal and rhetorical drama. The ability of the music to overcome this problem helped both to emphasize the irrefutability of the ending when it arrived and to create an impression of musical argument that could match a first movement sonata-allegro. The difficulty of fugal counterpoint provided an excellent means of achieving such goals.[41] However, I propose that passages of fugal counterpoint in finales also retain strong connections to the already mentioned Baroque practice of concluding movement sequences with a "stable" fugue. And so the reason why such tense and overbearing textures occur at the point where conclusiveness is most important is not only that finales had become better equipped to deal with textural difficulties; it is also that the stability *associated* with the Baroque fugal practice tempers the textural dissonance that is *created* by the interaction between fugal counterpoint and sonata-style syntax. Therefore, in an ideal last-movement situation, the opposing forces of stability and instability created by the associations with both the old and modern uses of fugal counterpoint, respectively, could conceivably balance each other out, creating a kind of cross-historical Enlightenment compromise, not unlike that discussed in the previous chapter.

These claims are strengthened by observing that classical composers tended to use extended passages of fugal counterpoint less in earlier movements, particularly sonata-allegros. Perhaps if a fugal exposition could not be tempered by its association to the stabilizing Baroque concluding fugue, then it was potentially too intense and disruptive to be freely used. In fact, it is not until the first movement of Beethoven's String Quartet op. 59, no. 1 in F Major (1806) that we find a first movement sonata-allegro that is expansive enough, in and of itself, to be able to soak up the shock waves of an extended passage of fugal counterpoint.[42] As Joseph Kerman writes of this movement, "Contrapuntal episodes had haunted the development section of the Op. 18 Quartets, but Beethoven had never before worked in a scale that allowed or demanded the massive formality achieved by counterpoint here."[43] And even here the balancing act was hardly without problems.[44] Indeed, in general, when extended passages of fugal counterpoint occur in earlier movements, their potential for disruptiveness is either employed in order to resolve a musical problem or to create one; they are marked in a different way than in a finale.

For example, Haydn uses fugal counterpoint in the development section of the second movement sonata-allegro of his *Razor* Quartet,

op. 55, no. 2 in F Minor (1788) to resolve problems created by the fact
that the cycle starts with a relatively slow set of alternating variations
(*Andante più tosto Allegretto*).[45] Beginning a multimovement work with
a slow set of variations is hardly a rare procedure in Haydn's works, and
therefore not so odd.[46] However, in the sonata-allegro second movement, the decidedly marked quality of the uneasy silence in m. 16 that
concludes the opening antecedent and consequent can set in motion a
set of queries that retroactively cast a critical light back on the formal
suitability of the first movement for this particular multimovement work
(Example 2.3). In the context of a sonata-allegro, the opening silence is
incongruous because it rhetorically overhighlights tonic tonal closure.
Obviously, it is not that tonal closure in itself is unusual here, but that
too much attention is being drawn toward it too early, before any of the
essential large-scale tonal movement of the form has occurred. And
so it works to cast a self-conscious light forward onto the future possibility and necessity of modulation to new keys – there being little to
cramp one's style more effectively than preemptively giving away one's
punchline. It is as if the formal characteristics of the first movement's
variations have infected the sonata-form processes of the second movement; variation form, after all, requires strong tonic closure at regular
intervals and repeated returns to both the beginning of a regularly constructed periodic theme or its variations and the tonic.[47] The sturdy
sixteen-measure theme (mm. 1–8: I-V, mm. 9–16: I-I) of the opening of
the second movement, and the perfect cadence in mm. 15–16, which is
made rhetorically emphatic by the silence that follows, would seem to be
more at home in such a formal context than in the opening of a sonata
form. And the fact that this cadence is "controlled" by or related to the
processes of the first movement is stressed by the connection between
the first violin's pitches (D♭-C-E-F) and pitch height, and those of the
first violin in each of the cadences that end the minor theme sections of
the first movement (mm. 24–26, 83–84, and 140–142, Example 2.4). As
a result, the initially confident tone of the silence in mm. 16–18 quickly
turns into an uncomfortable question mark hanging in the air: Will
sonata or variation procedures prevail?

In m. 19, the threat of tonal stagnation posed by the silence of mm.
16–18 is dispelled by a presentation of the opening theme on G-flat ma-

2.3. Haydn, String Quartet in F Minor, op. 55, no. 2 (*Razor*), 2nd movement, measures 1–21

jor, instigating the transition to the relative major and another variation of the opening theme. The second movement seems to extricate itself from its lapse into the first movement's formal behavior. But in m. 84 in the development section, after another variation of the opening theme, this time in D-flat major, the uncomfortable silence of mm. 16–18 recurs again. As in the exposition, this silence is followed initially by a rather sheepish presentation of the opening theme in a remote key (A major). This statement, though, develops into an extensive passage of fugal counterpoint starting in m. 98 that eventually leads back to the somewhat unorthodox recapitulation starting in m. 145. The textural dissonance created by the fugal counterpoint emphasizes the tonal fluidity that is

2.4. Haydn, String Quartet in F Minor, op. 55, no. 2 (*Razor*),
1st movement, violin 1, measures 24–27, 83–85, 140–42

vital for a development section to be able to fulfill its assigned structural function. It intensifies the second movement's tonal dynamic by working against tonal closure and, in so doing, acts against the stagnation of the general pauses that result from the influence of the first movement. Its success is marked by the fact that the next time the general pause occurs is at the very end of the movement, where it is no longer disruptive and puzzling, but authentically expressive of where we find ourselves syntactically.

In contrast to Haydn's quartet op. 55, no. 2, the fugal counterpoint in the allegro of the first movement of Beethoven's Piano Sonata in C Minor, op. 111 (1823), creates rather than resolves a compositional problem. The theme of the first subject group, with its rhythmically stiff head motive and efficiently mechanical continuation, is strongly reminiscent of the conventional bi-partite structure of many Baroque fugal subjects, and thus raises an expectation that the music acknowledges, with the result that fugal textures keep asserting themselves throughout the course of the movement. On the one hand, the fugal tendencies of the allegro work with the double-dotted rhythms of the slow introduction to create a distant association with the French overture that we might argue works to ground the work by means of historical association. However, the resulting fugal tendencies come into a dialectical conflict with the also present sonata-form principles at work creating a rather unmanageable dynamic, which in turn spawns a set of counter-reactions in the form of a number of sudden *ritardandos* and reflective *adagio* passages, which in turn act like brakes throughout the course of the movement.[48] That these gestures do not go far enough is attested by the fact that Beethoven follows the first movement with the enormously expansive set of *adagio* variations that conclude the work. The stability created by the repetition of the tonal and phrase structure of the opening theme in each of the variations, added to the *adagio molto* tempo marking, acts as a huge sponge that soaks up the unresolved dynamic energy from the first movement until all that is left is the impression of a delicate and gently throbbing sheet of sound. In comparison with Haydn's *Razor* Quartet, where fugue occurs in order to rectify a problem created by variation form, variation form here resolves a fugally created imbalance.

Another example of a problematic occurrence of counterpoint, though not strictly fugal, is the second movement of Beethoven's String Quartet op. 18, no. 4 in C Minor (1798).[49] Throughout the movement each new section begins with an imitative texture, thus inverting classical instrumental music's usual mode of employment in which counterpoint is for transitions and developments, and homophony is for thematic statement. Kirkendale has written of this movement that it is "a final expression of the courtly rococo, and has not hitherto been sufficiently appreciated in that capacity."[50] Kerman interprets the use of counterpoint as evidence that "Beethoven was working for droll simplicity of procedure ... in the *scherzoso* humor. Such was surely the case when the fugue subject returns in the coda, now throwing in its lot with the *Teutsche* of the Viennese ballrooms, and rattling itself away to nothing."[51] But one can also hear the prevalence of contrapuntal textures as a nervously comic reaction to the slightly gauche and melodramatic angst of the first movement, as if the emotional gusts from the previous movement had blown the textures of the second movement into a sniggering and embarrassed contrapuntal disarray that keeps breaking out after failed attempts to adopt more straight-faced homophonic behavior. The movement has the mixture of messiness and overdetermination that characterizes the drunken behavior of the aristocracy. Moreover, the fact that the predominant textures never satisfactorily settle into themselves acts as a means of creating through-composition, for the movement's textural problems encourage the projection of our expectations into the remainder of the quartet, where one hopes for more self-assured textures that will ground our experiences and bring the work as a whole to rest. In a similar vein, Haydn uses counterpoint to create through-compositional relationships between movements in his String Quartet op. 76, no. 2 in D Minor, *Quinten* (1796). The famous third-movement minuet is in strict canon at the octave throughout and, as a result, the final cadence is sparse and feels unsatisfactory because the instruments do not all come to rest on one final, affirming sonority. Thus, we expect (or rather hope) that we will be given a pleasantly spaced, full-string-quartet texture at the very beginning of the next movement so that the uncomfortable feelings engendered by the end of the minuet will be dispelled.[52]

MARSYAS

The associations that words hold for us can hinder our ability to see what might be otherwise. Form is such a word. All too easily it invokes the idea of an ecologically benign order where everything can find its place without disruption to the social environment at large. In many ways such a form, even if it is of comic orientation, is attendant on the mirrored Mozart of postmodern discourse that I discussed in the previous chapter. And there is a certain irony to this, since the project to mirror Mozart that began in the late 1980s was performed under the aegis of content (a celebration of images of the world reflected) and precisely as a means of liberating this remarkable music from incarceration in the formal tomb of Apollonian classicism, to which it undoubtedly has been periodically condemned. With but little pressure, form in contemporary musicology seems to invoke a corseted Victorian world of behavioral rectitude accompanied by wraps on the knuckles should that not be attained; form for form's sake, tight, constricted, and lacking in the space for life. But our own images of life may in fact be just as formally punitive, even when we are laughing and happy and nice, a point to which I return in chapter 4 ("Enchantment"). So it can easily transpire that we are inadvertently just Apollo in Dionysian garb.

If it is the case that we cannot escape Apollo, then, as Nietzsche reminds us in *The Birth of Tragedy,* nor can Apollo so easily distinguish himself from Dionysus and his various understudies. Take for example the tale of the music competition between Apollo and Marsyas. For

Vladimir Jankélévitch, when Marsyas fails, the right order of being is restored, "for the odes of Marsyas 'bewitch' us."[53] Marsyas plays upon Dionysian technology, "the orgiastic flute of disgraceful intoxication,"[54] and it is Apollo's job, like his son Orpheus (at least according to Janké-lévitch), to reinstate a music that makes us gentler, "pacifies the monsters of instinct in all of us and tames passion's wild animals."[55] But Janké-lévitch achieves his moral victory through a grotesque indifference to the incomprehensibly excessive penalty that Marsyas must pay for his cheeky dare: to be flayed alive, a point Jankélévitch never once mentions. Ovid, by comparison, writes this history in terms of the looser:

> Apollo stripped his skin; the whole of him
> Was one huge wound, blood streaming everywhere,
> Sinews laid bare, veins naked, quivering
> And pulsing. You could count his twitching guts,
> And the tissues as the light shone through his ribs.[56]

In this telling, no one thanks Apollo:

> The countryfolk, the sylvan deities,
> The fauns and brother satyrs and the nymphs,
> All were in tears, Olympus too, still loved,
> And every swain who fed his fleecy flocks
> And long-horned cattle on those mountainsides.[57]

If dismemberment is the potentially problematic *telos* of the Dionysian ritual, for Apollo, chillingly, it is just business as usual. And this is also the case in the dream, which for Nietzsche, at least, is under Apollonian jurisdiction.

Perhaps, then, content-oriented concerns regarding form are right but for the wrong reason. The problem is not that form prohibits, but that it is already too excessive; it is *jouissance* rather than pleasure, a point that any fetishist will recognize. Form's first move is to violently distinguish some particular victim from out of the undifferentiated world. Marsyas screams, "Why tear me from myself?"[58] But as a result of being wrenched from the ground, the newly distinguished part, rather than withering away, begins to foliate excessively. Marsyas, tersely identified at first (simply "the satyr"), becomes a horrific litany of excessive descriptions, a proliferation of dismembered parts, and then through metamorphosis, this being Ovid, a river that "hurries to the sea, / Through falling banks, the river Marsyas, / The freshest, clearest stream of Phrygia."[59] Form makes the whole less, but the newly made part swell. And so Marsyas overflows himself – like fugal counterpoint in classical instrumental music. Cultures make music through a violent assault on the sonic universe. The resultant music then makes more.

3

Exile

(Haydn, String Quartet Op. 33, No. 5)

We are in high spirits and decide to pay a visit on someone. Upon her opening the door we immediately realize that she is in high spirits, too, and we take comfort in what we assume to be the accurate reflection of each other's smiles. We are friends and so our coming together is an end in itself, a closed system in which roughly hewn questions of means leading to ends – purpose, profit, necessity – cannot flourish. Nevertheless, like an act of grace, the warmth of friendship offers us what seems to be an authentic point of rest and stable ground amidst what can frequently strike us as the twitchy, fractured landscape of our world. It calms our nerves, and in doing so intimates that maybe some kind of consolation might be found for us within the larger "nervous system" of the world, into which darkness, as our friend closes the door behind us, we return once more.[1] Friendship offers us hope that with the help of our comrades we will be able to survive intact the situation in which we now find ourselves.

But on another day when we make our call once more, our friend's opening of the door confronts us with despair. We recognize her still. Strangely, we may even feel closer to her since there is a certain physical tangibility to those in distress, the particularity of the turn of her head as she attempts to hide an overflowing of tears, the anxious scratching of one hand by another. But we no longer understand her. Surely the friend who looks out from this prison is a broken friend, difficult to discern in the midst of her metamorphosis back into the very fractured landscape of the world from which she had once provided us with respite. She may well be physically nearer, but as a result we now feel her differently, more literally, materially, for she has crumpled into roughness and sharp edges that cut us in our witnessing. Hijacked by melancholy, she is now too close and so is Other to the friend whom we had once found in her place. As a result, something of the world we had hoped to keep at bay encroaches upon us, perhaps to do us wrong.

This underworld of friendship where our friend appears lost as a shadow can make us deeply uncomfortable. "What is to be done?" she seems to ask. And her sad-eyed look as she waits for us to answer challenges us to confront a lack in our sense of happy self-possession. The heaviness of her melancholy (in Dürer's famous etching, melancholy has wings but cannot fly) suggests to us that when our spirits are high in flight, they are potentially just "high" on a cruelly pragmatic perspective that exiles certain other truths to the margins of our frame of reference. She understands us – that we are not one – rather than the other way around. To tell her to pull herself together can be tantamount to insisting that she perform being a static whole so that we might avoid confronting the restlessness underlying our own smiling sense of self-completion. And so in ethical terms, the truth of our friendship is marked by when our friend no longer strikes us as herself and yet we remain in attendance upon her. We assume the responsibility of accompanying her in her exile.

In a striking remark, upon which I have just been improvising, Adorno views our relationship to music in similarly loaded terms: "We do not understand music – it understands us. This is as true for the musician as for the layman. When we think ourselves closest to it, it speaks to us and waits sad-eyed for us to answer."[2] Adorno is not just poeticizing a common frustration that can plague academics when they find themselves unable to finalize a classification, to contextually or historically pin things down, or generally to bring an intellectual mission regarding a certain piece of music to rest. Rather, music is sad like the beloved. She worries as to what will happen once her prince realizes that there is a disjunction between herself and his idea of her, for she is often as confused and wrapped up in the process of trying to work out who she is as he is secretly about himself. If her lover is a musicologist, her anxiety most likely concerns the revelation of the gap that exists between herself and her determinants. And so it is not that music doesn't love musicology. It is rather that she waits sad-eyed to find out whether it might acknowledge its own homelessness and so accompany her in her exile, where love must survive amidst restlessness, wandering, and waiting.

This chapter is an attempt to respond to such an expectation. The following section is primarily theoretical. In it, I aim first of all to show what being at home and being in exile might mean for music, and to articulate some of the political reasons for why exile can be justified as a value. This then leads me to argue for the continuing necessity of the sometimes-maligned notion of autonomy for debates concerning music's political value. I argue for a kind of dialectical form of autonomy, one produced at the changing points of intersection between home and exile and their various analogies. In the remainder of the chapter, I return once more to the music of the late eighteenth century, specifically to a long reading of Haydn's String Quartet op. 33, no. 5. On the one hand, I do this is in order to show how such an autonomy might manifest itself historically; on the other hand, I seek to show how such a historical argument can itself enable this music to be autonomous of its historical inscriptions.

MUSIC IN EXILE

From what perspective can we view music as being at home? I would argue that music has been conceived as such when it and the human subjects that have produced it seem to be experiencing a high degree of integration and productive interaction and collaboration between themselves and the contexts of their social world.[3] At home, music is embedded in what I would call human belongings: the specific realms of human activity and meaning-making that enable us to belong to a certain social locality and which, in turn, therefore belong to us. Lawrence Kramer writes that "classical music can become a source of pleasure, discovery, and reflection tuned not only to the world of the music, rich though that is, but also to *the even richer world beyond the music.*"[4] Here music is at home because it participates in a broadly conceived politics of relationship formation. In collaborating with and so saying "yes" to what already exists in human life ("indispensable human concerns, the stuff of real life"),[5] music encourages us to do likewise: "Classical music enlarges the capacity of all music to attach itself, and us, more closely to whatever we care about."[6] And so although Kramer offers a number of different reasons for why classical music still matters, one of its primary values for him is its socializing capacity: "Music of all kinds invokes bonding; classical music dramatizes and reflects on it in the act of invocation."[7] This is particularly brought out in Kramer's discussion of an essentially therapeutic role performed by music in the United States in the immediate period following 9/11. At that time, music for Kramer helped reestablish the connections to the social that the traumatic event had seemingly destroyed, starting the process of rebuilding home in a time of the uncanny.

The notion of home – and then with suspicious rapidity the word homeland, as in Homeland Security – acquired formidable currency at that time. And this was achieved primarily through the circulation of a basic narrative in which pragmatic, democratic, individualistic American social life (home), though suffering a major wound from having been attacked by a malevolent force from outside, nevertheless triumphed in its ability to reconstitute itself and not give up on its ideals. The problem with this narrative was that the benign wholesomeness of the social home was not necessarily something that had been interrupted by the traumatic event, but perhaps created momentarily by it in the immediate aftermath. And when that moment passed, it seemed that it was quickly projected onto the mess, violence, and compromise that life had predominantly been before. From my own experience as someone who had been living in Manhattan for nine years at that time, for about two weeks after 9/11, quotidian life in New York City took on some radically uncharacteristic forms of behavior: there was a sudden slowing down and opening up of social life and in many cases human interactions, touchingly, became patiently pragmatic and respectful – in contrast, that is, with the more fragmentary, rough-and-tumble concern that, attractive as it can be, is the city's rather different ethical mode normally. Such an opening up is, indeed, often attendant in the wake of a tragedy. People took time to talk; lunch took on an almost southern languorousness; one felt that one belonged perhaps with others, since others seemed invested in how one felt. Many might argue that, as New Yorkers, they were able to experience this sense of improved belonging, if but under the shadow of a great sadness, for a long time after. Some may argue that life in the city was never the same again. However, in the United States at large, this moment quickly got conscripted by what Douglas Coupland in the early 1990s would have called "Legislated Nostalgia": in other words, a set of practices that essentially "force a body of people to have memories [in this instance of American social life] they do not actually possess."[8] And so in many instances the social to which one could belong was only able to constitute itself as functioning by means of appearing in temporal displacements, within a kind of non-place, the numbed void following a traumatic event, and in a past that, if it could speak, would probably not recognize it. Admittedly, with the Obama administration there was a paradigmatic shift, and the social began to appear in the temporal displacement of the future ("Yes we can!"). But in many cases it has not been able both to appear and sustain itself.

Perhaps, then, we might argue that this absence of the social home in the present proves the point, common to the work of Chantal Mouffe, Ernesto Laclau, and Slavoj Žižek, amongst others, that the social world per se is fundamentally, indeed constitutively, marked by failure. Or in Žižek's phrase – with its ironic echo of Margaret Thatcher's infamous remark, "Society doesn't exist" – that "the Social is always an inconsistent field structured around a constitutive impossibility, traversed by a central 'antagonism.'"[9] Such an antagonism is both fundamentally defining of a particular form of social life (for example, capital in capitalism) and yet, simultaneously, the dissonance that invalidates the social form's ability to function authentically without being structurally reliant on some kind of social violence. And so although in a literal sense we are constantly involved in the seeming home-making labor of trying to form relationships and create attachments, such social negotiations are perhaps understood at best as being in exile from society. Since the social can never fully constitute itself according to it own claims, "every process of identification conferring on us a fixed socio-symbolic identity [a sense of social belonging and home] is ultimately doomed to fail."[10] At worst, they constitute the labor of ideological fantasy, whose function is "to mask [the] inconsistency within fixed socio-symbolic identity and the fact that 'Society doesn't exist,' and thus to compensate us for the failed identification."[11]

In Žižek's analysis, we witness the ideological masking of the social's fundamental inconsistency in what he calls the "sublime object of ideology," a notable example for him being the figure of the Jew in antisemitic discourse. The Jew, as Other, is scripted as the alien element that creates a blockage in the social's attempt to constitute itself as our home. The basic racist script here runs as follows: "If only society were not infected by this foreign element, we would be able to enjoy our social life more fully and completely." But it is not the Other who has robbed us of, in the Lacanian sense, our enjoyment. Rather, the social contract itself, in a purely neutral, formal sense, is reliant on us accepting the "forced choice" of undergoing a kind of symbolic castration: we cannot be outside of the social, and yet by being within it we must give something up and so lack. In the psychoanalytic terms used at the end of this study's first chapter, by entering into society, we give up the excessive enjoyment of (in Lacan, at any rate) the death drive for the censorship of the pleasure principle. The fact that we have no choice about this relinquishment – it being formally as true for democracy as it is for any other social formation – does not, however, allow us to make our peace with the resulting sense of lack, as if we could phlegmatically shrug our shoulders and accept that "that's just the way things are." Žižek's argument is that the pressure (and ability) to enjoy remains. As a result, social formations must find a way of organizing this excessive remnant of enjoyment to their own advantage, for otherwise it might destroy the social formation itself. The obscene enjoyment of racist fixations provides one such means. Outbreaks of racism within, for example, presently existing capitalist social structures are therefore not just aberrations within the system that could be removed by making capitalism function more humanely and democratically. (That was just an idealistic fantasy that reached its apotheosis and then withered during the course of the 1990s.) Rather, they are structurally constitutive; capitalism is reliant upon them. By means of the deflection of the drive onto excessive interest in the enjoyments of the Other, subjects of capitalism are "compensated" for the lack they have assumed as payment for their entry into the social contract itself. Moreover, they are compensated without shaming acknowledgment that capitalism itself is lacking. And so in Lacanian terms, by means of the sublime object of ideology, we seek, in a sense, to protect the big Other from its own inherent failure, as if we were engaging in the not-uncommon practice of protecting a figure of authority from its own impotence.

If we assert that "Society doesn't exist," what kind of home can music have in it? In a famous analysis of Claude Lévi-Strauss's, the facial decorations of Caduveo Indians form a visual text that, as Fredric Jameson puts it, "constitutes a symbolic act, whereby real social contradictions [inequality and conflicts indicative of the failure of the social structure], insurmountable in their own terms, find a purely formal resolution in the aesthetic realm."[12] The Caduveo, as Lévi-Strauss writes, "were never lucky enough to resolve their contradictions. . . . Yet since they were unable to conceptualize or to live this solution directly, they began to dream it, to project it into the imaginary."[13] Here, as Jameson comments, "the aesthetic act is itself ideological, and the production of aesthetic or narrative form is to be seen as an ideological act in its own right, with the function of inventing imaginary or formal 'solutions' to unresolvable social contradictions."[14] In a fantastic historically panoramic passage immediately following, Jameson then points out that if this were the case for the relatively more confined and negotiable precapitalist and even pre-political societies, then how much more true it must be for any societies that have followed.[15]

We might assume that as the factors exacerbating the always-already impossibility of the social multiply, the temptation for music to present an imaginary resolution of fundamental social antagonisms also increases. It is from the foundation of such assumptions that critical musicology has sometimes sought to articulate how certain musical practices (most notably those associated with Western discourses of musical autonomy) have worked, essentially, to paint a smiling face over an ongoing dissonance; the potential for this has already been witnessed in the finale of Mozart's K. 459 piano concerto, discussed in this study's first two chapters. From this perspective, the task of the musicologist faced with music should be "to brush history against the grain,"[16] or to reveal, as Adorno put it, that "the expression of history in things is no other than that of past torment"[17] and thus unmask the obfuscations that were necessary to allow for home to happen.

If "Society doesn't exist," then one way that music has a home within it is by being in exile within it. In Lydia Goehr's terms, music needs to create a "freedom within": "The key to this notion of *freedom* within is the idea that music is immanent and social, but it is not merely or instrumentally social. Rather, it aspires to be resistantly social through its purely musical form."[18] Music thus starts to practice a politics of critique,[19] in which, as Adorno has put it in an aphorism concerning modern dwellings, if one is to have a home then "today we should have to add: it is part of morality not to be at home in one's home."[20] As a critical agent, music does not function according to that aspect of Kramer's project that seeks to attach music to that within society which already exists and can be known. Rather, it points on the one hand toward the possibility of a different social condition; on the other hand, it engages in the paradox of giving voice to that which, at present, cannot be known in the normative sense.[21] Predominantly dialectical, what a critical music values in human belongings is their potential for becoming. Because it is the underlying formal lack in that which has been conceptually determined that allows for such becoming, a critical music therefore aims to encourage as a constitutive feature of human practices the keeping open of the gaps, silences, and fissures that this lack creates. Through a paradoxical exchange, by being exposed to the fact that our concepts are less, we get the magnificence of more, the full presence produced by an absence. Thus, as music moves from practicing the belonging of social collaboration to practicing the becoming of social critique – and so makes the transition from home to exile – it shifts its orientation from its content (how it has been socially determined) to what we can refer to here as its form (meaning, to a degree, as in the previous chapter, the constitutively open structure on which it is both founded, but which also allows for it to exist in excess of its social determinants). And so if our sad-eyed friend disturbs our sense of belonging – robbing us of the certainty that with her help we might have been able to survive as we are within the situation in which we now find ourselves – she nevertheless offers us the hope: that by realizing how our life does not yet live, we might therefore live otherwise. This in part explains the complex paradoxes that enable sad music to make us smile.

But exile is not pure. If Adorno states that "it is part of morality not to be at home in one's home," he is also emphatic that morality should neither be equated with homelessness, nor with giving up one's home.

Regarding the former, "one must nevertheless have possessions, if one is not to sink into that dependence and need which serves the blind perpetuation of property relations." To be homeless is not to be authentically outside of the problem of the Social, but merely to have become the necessary exclusion by which the hegemonic ideological inside is able to perpetuate the validity of its own violent and exclusory forms of social belonging.[22] However, to merely propound a giving up of relations to possessions can lead to a kind of destruction of the potential for relationship formation per se, "a loveless disregard for things which necessarily turns against people too." Such lovelessness is not merely resolved by deciding to opt for possessions again, since such an antithesis to the giving up of possessions "no sooner uttered, [becomes] an ideology for those wishing with a bad conscience to keep what they have."[23] So even though music's exile is laudable for allowing for the possibility of critical distance, it must remain guilty of ownership in order to remain moral.

To be, we must allow ourselves to be tied to possessions – both literally in the sense of objects, but also more broadly, in the sense of other people and what I have referred to earlier as human belongings. On the one hand, we are therefore subject to possessions. But we are also in possession of a piece of equipment, which, if we practice our technique and strategies, can sometimes be used to cut through the ties that keep us fully beholden unto possessions. It might even be employed as part of an act of will against what we are tempted to perceive as the truth residing in the force of our feelings. The name I give to this equipment and our ability to use it is autonomy – the potential of the subject (never easy, straightforward, or guaranteed of success) to make the transition from a being that is, in a neutral sense, subjected, formed from a heteronymous force, to a being that is the agent of an act.[24] If music is to preserve a distance within the social – that critical exile that enables it to resist – then music must, in some sense, be autonomous too.

Autonomy does not therefore denote some kind of narcissistic projection of virile self-sufficiency that works to deny its cultural origins. It acknowledges that there have been parents and homes, and so it acknowledges in a literal sense that we cannot compose, perform, or listen to music without the dwelling of a certain socially oriented time/space symbiosis. However, it cannot condone the domestic ideology that sometimes underlies the attempt to make music at home in the social and so it is ever wary of overprotective parents, and overly contextually grounded musicology. Of course, it is understandable that we should be nervous that our children might attach themselves disastrously to prosthetic parents: bad friends, sinisterly seductive adults, religious cults, and so on. Of course, it is true that it can be beneficial to know who is influencing our music and whose house it is presently playing within, for if we give it free rein and turn our attention away, as if it were completely autonomous, it could wind up in trouble, or cause trouble either for someone else or some other music. But if, as is not completely uncommon, such security measures come with a self-validating assertion that if we eradicate exposure to the identified dangers everything will be fine, then they are then en route to belief systems in which parents and the social are scripted as self-sufficient sources capable of providing children and music with everything they need. Such a lurking belief, particularly when considering contemporary musicology, is somewhat ironic, for it means that in order to deflate musical autonomy, the social must itself be inflated into something autonomous.

Although we (and music) cannot be without having been molded by our parents (the Social), we are not *just* them. It is for such reasons that children and pieces of music are often scripted on the one hand (for example, by Michael Jackson and Ernst Bloch) as a form of hope, the possibility that the future will be different; and yet on the other hand (for example, in *Lord of the Flies* or by Søren Kierkegaard), they are seen as daemonic, for they come from us but neither guarantee nor are reliant upon our continuation. Children, we might say, are the excesses produced by human interactions that, retroactively, turn humans into parents. This explains why parents are often haunted and disturbed, for the source (the child) that has given birth to who they now are (as parents) is something that, through a kind of temporal uncanny, has come after they themselves have been formed. The child is an origin, therefore, that in a sense comes from the future. Likewise, human social life is haunted by music. As a result, the child, like the piece of music, can be thought of as a kind of gap within the economy of mediations; it is a marker of the constitutive (and productive) failure of the parent, in the same way that music, in its critical form of exile, is one of the traces by which we can experience the constitutive failure of the social. Since the child must on some basic psychological level reject the parents in order to come into being as a proper subject, parents must be perceived of as lacking in order to be at all. Regarding music, the lack is illuminated by noting that if the social is a self-supporting system, then why is it, to return to some of Kramer's terms, that we should need music in order that we remain attached to it? Rather than being an esoteric abstraction alienating us from the social, music qua music would appear to be a privileged means of allowing for the possibility of the social in the first place; and so in order for there to be one (social life), there must be two (social life *and* music).

We might attempt to suture such problematic splitting through assertions like Kramer's that "music is our premier embodiment of the drive for attachment."[25] Since music here is merely a manifestation of a necessary feature ("the drive for attachment") for the production of human social life, we cannot properly talk about two. In fact, in this instance, the displacement of the drive for attachment onto music makes music itself into a virtual human, a kind of cyborg, and in doing so, autonomy, like a manifestation of the repressed, starts to return.[26] For music is now somewhat uncannily endowed with a kind of human agency, like Frankenstein's electrically vivified monster. As Kramer's continuation attests, "[Music] works, it grips and grasps us," and so resurrects us from our condition of alienated non-engagement, since this contact is "almost with the electricity of touch."[27] However, ravished into this state of arousal by the musical cyborg that we have created, to what do we then attach ourselves? Unless we are either frigid or too-cool-for-school, we respond reciprocally, and attempt to embrace the music itself – through dance, movement, attentive listening, singing along, or the canceling out of distractions, by closing the eyes or turning down the lights. Admittedly, one might argue that what allows us to get seduced by music is attraction to the traces in the music of the very social life that had initially motivated the music's production. However, it would be debatable to conclude that what keeps us lodged there is merely this content. Something else, however mediated, also comes into play. Otherwise there would be no need for the sometimes embarrassing disorientation occurring when you hit the ground after the music is over, no sobering sense of return after a moment of forgetting, such as we experience when we step out of the concert hall and the malevolent sprite of quotidian concerns resumes its whispering in our ears. And so maybe the reason we seek expression for our socially conditioned selves through such saucy fooling around with music is to create a decoy allowing us to fool around with music. With music, perhaps, social life is just a ruse.

If, as reception history and film music attest, almost anything can attach itself to the same piece of music, then music is also potentially indifferent to human social life, like a dog that stares out blankly from the series of anthropomorphic costumes in which its lonely owner has it dressed. After all, although the making of music is (leaving aside certain animals and computers) done by humans, the resulting musical sounds are no more human in themselves than a chair. In part, people dress up their animals at the prompting of a kind of sociological idealism, to convince themselves that human social life transcends its own constituency. Yet the costumes can also be a means of disavowing the more difficult reality, that some people find being with animals qua animals more life-enhancing than being with people; some people make the same decision regarding music. In both cases human social life is shown to be lacking, for if it were good enough, why would we need to expand its circumference to include animals, or detach ourselves from a wholesome daily dosage of normative human socializing in order to sing songs? Of course, we might ban animals and music. But the imposition of such a law would merely reinforce what has been my presiding point: that the social (music's supposed home) only appears in a functioning form through a process of exclusion. If musicology is therefore to try and continue with its project of keeping music on the side of the social, then, to appropriate Richard Leppert's words, we must allow music to be the Other: "not the Other of silence, but the other of the nonmusic and the antimusic of social relations. Music registers itself as difference, as it were, as an alternative to nonmusical life – nonmusical life meant both as neutral fact of existence and, more to the present concern, as a dystopian reality in which music is, in ironic actuality, virtually inescapable."[28] And so to repeat the point, music must, for political and ethical reasons, have the potential for autonomy.

However, as we are now more than aware, music's autonomy, under the name of "absolute music," has a history, and for some this means that it is a "construct." This fact has been reason enough for many to question whether autonomy can therefore be said to be autonomous. Daniel Chua, for example, writes that "absolutes only have histories when they self-destruct to reveal their false identity. This means that absolute music can only have a history when it is no longer absolute music."[29] By returning now to this history, I argue on the side of children, and so otherwise. History, like parents, has limits.

FROM MIMESIS TO TRANSCENDENCE

Musical autonomy has tended to be located in the complex set of historical forces that led to the waning of the power of mimesis within musical production and discourse about music toward the end of the eighteenth century. With perhaps overly large brush strokes, I now summarize the argument, which many others have meticulously investigated, as follows. Early eighteenth-century aesthetic theorists, particularly the French, placed the arts into a hierarchy, giving priority to those that provided the clearest connection between their signifiers and their signifieds.[30] This can be seen most clearly in Charles Batteux's paradigmatic neoclassical treatise *Les Beaux arts reduits à une même principe* (1746). In the mimetic system, the more obviously representational of the arts – the visual and literary arts – were held in high esteem. Music, especially music without text, was considered to be inferior because of its inability to say and communicate its message clearly and unambiguously. There was even debate as to whether music, by its nature, was capable of saying anything at all, the suspicion being that without the solid support of linguistic meaning, it was merely a set of pleasing yet essentially vapid gestures and effects, rather like a fireworks display.

All this is well known, especially its neat summary in Fontenelle's rather wicked quip, "Sonate, que me veux-tu?" (Sonata, what do you want of me?). Apart from the obvious message that music is ambiguous, Fontenelle's joke implies that music without text is ridiculously artificial. Admittedly, this is in keeping with the idea prevalent in early eighteenth-century aesthetics that both performers and audience members alike should experience the arts as artifacts.[31] Batteux wrote that "if sometimes it happens that the musician or dancer may actually be feeling what he expresses, that is an accidental circumstance which is not at all the intention of the art."[32] To confuse the distinction between art and life is to act without taste; it turns the art into something grotesque and unsavory, "like a painting which is on a living skin and should be on a canvas."[33] Fontenelle's remark, though, is more cutting; it suggests that seriously engaging with a piece of music is as risible as conversing with a chair or a cup.

Eighteenth-century mimetic theorists venerated art that was clearly understandable. For them, the unambiguousness of a tasteful piece of art implied a particular dramatic scenario between the audience and the art – or, as I will refer to them, between the implied *listening subject* and the *musical object*. In this dramatic scenario, the listening subject is characterized as an active observer and the art as a passive object, an artifact. As an artifact, the object obviously has no life separate from the meaning the listening subject assigns to it. It cannot return the listening subject's gaze and achieves meaning only when the listening subject recognizes what it represents. The listening subject is omniscient; she surrounds the artifact with her knowledge of what that artifact represents. As Carl Dahlhaus wrote, "A listener assumes the role of the relaxed spectator, an observer who deigns to judge the likeness or unlikeliness of a description."[34] The listening subject is never consumed by the effect of the art because of a "conception of the character of musical feelings that [is] primarily objective and objectifying."[35] Therefore, "in unprejudiced perception, a melodic motive does not express dullness and transport one into a dull mood, but rather it seems dull in itself."[36]

If mimetic theories of music aimed to resolve the problem of music's potential ambiguity in relationship to meaning (understood in the normative, linguistic, and depictive sense), then around the turn of the nineteenth century and onward it was precisely this ambiguity that started to seem attractive. It has held a certain line of attention ever since, for example, from the Schlegels, Schopenhauer, and Nietzsche through to Adorno and Goehr. From a more ahistorical perspective, the reason for this interest might be adduced from consideration of this truism: that music can seem incredibly meaningful even though we are often at a loss to say, beyond the application of a sometimes rather Neanderthal expressive labeling system, what it actually means. Frequently one hears the report that music has given articulation for a listener to something that had been too profound to be touched by words.[37] Thus, if music is insufficient as a normative form of meaning, then, conversely, music frequently reveals that meaning itself is lacking with regard to what makes life meaningful. If music shows normative meaning to be insufficiently meaningful, and normative meaning, in functioning through communal recognition, is a means of attaching us to what already is, then music shows us that meaningfulness arises not solely from increasing our proximity to the existent, but from the possibility that even from our position inside a historical condition we can expand the relational space between ourselves and what is and so create distance. Thus, Goehr writes that in the nineteenth century, "The idea that a philosopher should become a musician was dependent upon seeing in music, or, rather, in the musician, the capacity to view the world at a distance."[38] This, for example, would explain the strange sense of expansiveness and release that is frequently attendant on musical expression, even when, as for example with melancholic music, the condition to which it refers is one that when experienced for real produces a physiological sensation of weighty incarceration.[39]

Historically, mimesis, broadly conceived, was superseded by a process in which its dramaturgical positioning of listening subject in relationship to musical object was reversed, with the result that the epistemological superiority of mimesis's implied listening subject crumbled. This reversal was achieved by trumping the materialistically oriented linguistic foundations of knowledge in eighteenth-century mimetic theory with cards that had by the early nineteenth century regained considerable force amidst the Western intellectual's deck. As Goehr writes, "The lack of intermediary, concrete, literary or visual content made it possible for instrumental music to rise above the status of a medium to actually embody and become a higher truth."[40] The concept and value of stable musical meaning were ousted by the idea that musical ambiguity is in touch with or even *is* the transcendent: "The suggestion that music carried transcendent meaning led soon enough to the view that instrumental music did more than point to the transcendent. It also embodied it."[41] Thus, in his famous essay of 1813, "Beethoven's Instrumental Music," E. T. A. Hoffman writes that music "is the most romantic of all the arts, one might say the only one that is genuinely romantic, since its only subject matter is infinity."[42] Or, in the words of the young Friedrich Nietzsche, "Language can never adequately render the cosmic symbolism of music, because music stands in symbolic relation to the primordial contradiction and primordial pain in the heart of the primal unity, and therefore symbolizes a sphere which is beyond and prior to all phenomena."[43]

Within this transcendence-oriented discourse, the musical object no longer functioned as the passive receptacle of the listening subject's objectifying aural gaze; in touch with the seemingly unreachable, it could now surpass what had once been the secure locus of power. Musical effects, which because of their lack of inherent semantic meaning had been dismissed as incoherent by Fontenelle, were now a source of almost inconceivable force, possessing the "double quality of a narcotic that both intoxicates and spreads a fog."[44] Unable successfully to rationalize that which music now confronted her with, the implied listening subject tended to be scripted either as experiencing anxiety or fear, or simply as relinquishing herself to being overwhelmed; the elephantine magnitude of her reactions, in turn, became a means of validating the authenticity of the music's transcendence. In a musical environment where, as Hoffman put it, "shining rays of light shoot through the darkness of night and we become aware of giant shadows swaying back and forth moving ever closer around us," not only did the mimetic listening subject's rational orientation equipment essentially no longer function, but, to a certain degree, it was now judged to be profane.[45] For in the same way that the attempt to fully comprehend God is usually considered an act of hubris, so too now with music. As a result, in early nineteenth-century musical discourse, one starts to encounter the uncanny scenario in which listening subjects intuit that the musical object has itself become a knowing subject. At its most extreme, this subjectively transformed musical object simply became terrifying because it was indifferent, like one of Rilke's angels: capable of sustaining itself without the seeming life-giving fuel provided by the listening subject's own aural gaze.[46]

In this fashion, musical autonomy has been shown historically in its state of belonging: at home in paradigmatic nineteenth-century discourses of transcendence and their various afterlives. By contrast, my aim here will be to suggest how it could be located in the condition of the historical movement itself; not at home, but in exile. As a result, it will not be possible to capture autonomy by once again summarizing a broadly defined historical discourse about music, because such a discourse in this instance does not exist in the way that mimesis and transcendence do – however crude they may be in their form here as generalized *epistêmês*. Exile is particularly averse to categorizations; like the law received in Exodus, it eschews the graven image. So this is an autonomy that must be captured, as it were, in its autonomy from discourse. Thus, I will be seeking more to note its effects, the presence of its potentiality and the way that force marks, moves, and even distorts an already existent reality, rather than constituting its own reality per se. In short, I will be concerned with its form – since autonomy, though mediated by content, strictly speaking has no content itself.[47]

Specifically, my argument will be organized around the thesis that one such effect of autonomy between mimesis and transcendence is the instrumental music of the Viennese classics. As a result, attendant at the peripheries of my investigations will be the following potentially provocative historical thesis: that this repertoire – until relatively recently, considered a primary home in which musicology's controlling systems of aesthetic evaluation could be nurtured – had, at least in terms of aesthetic history, no proper home of its own.[48] Or, to draw out the inherent complexities here, to tell the history of this repertoire is in part to show how it is marked by the authentic trace of its founding "inability" to constitute itself in such a way in relation to its original conditions that it would later be possible to fully historicize it. And so, to refer back to an earlier formulation, examination of instrumental music of the Viennese classics helps to articulate the possibility that, like society, "history doesn't exist."

THE UNDEAD

If the Viennese classics are setting out, it is also the case that they haven't yet properly left, for they are dependent to an enormous degree within their historical frame upon the presence of recognizable formal and stylistic musical conventions. Take, for example, musical topoi, which have, since the 1980s, been so regularly a part of musicological discourse regarding this repertoire. Topic implies the possibility that there is some kind of bond linking musical signifiers to extra-musical signifieds. As Harold Powers writes, "Each topic either implies or characterizes a recognizable feature of music from a particular social context. The topics are terminological tags naming kinds and manners of musics familiar to a particular society of musical consumers. They are verbal equivalents for items in a musical vocabulary."[49] Allanbrook makes a similar point: "By recognizing a characteristic style, [the writer] can identify a configuration of notes and rhythms as having a particular stance, modified and clarified, of course, by its role in its movement and by the uses made of it earlier in the piece. In short, he can articulate within certain limits the shared response a particular passage will evoke."[50] Since musical topoi in order to function must allow the implied listening subject the power to be able to both identify them as potentially discreet units of information, and credibly posit the primarily social context that would ground their meanings, their functioning presence would imply that this repertoire was still within the orbit of an essentially mimetic aesthetic worldview.

However, it has long been noted that the situation frequently arises in classical music in which such conventional elements occur in a problematic or incorrect manner. Moreover, an important trait of classical instrumental pieces is that they often appear to be driven to solve such problems, to reinstate the convention in its correct formulation. It is as if the disruption or displacement of a musical convention is the problematic gesture that sets a process of discussion in motion, and the establishment of the accepted use of that convention is the goal toward which the piece is driven. An example of such a process is given by Haydn's String Quartet op. 33, no. 5, discussed in greater detail below. The first movement begins peculiarly with a cadential figure (X in Example 3.1). According to the prevalent behavioral tendencies of classical music, to begin a piece of music with a figure usually reserved for points of closure is to confuse the musical syntax, thus creating a disruption. Admittedly, the problematic opening figure already finds a more proper recasting at the end of the first period of the first movement, and this would seem to suggest that the initial syntactical infelicity is quickly excused.

3.1. Haydn, String Quartet in G, op. 33, no. 5,
1st movement, measures 1–2

However, since the problem of openings and closings in musical syntax pervades not only the rest of the first movement but the quartet overall, we might merely consider this as but a temporary relaxation within an ongoing anxiety regarding the problem of openings and closings in musical syntax that the opening unleashes. Only at the very end of the quartet's finale, when the first movement's problematic opening figure recurs repositioned in its proper syntactical context (X in Example 3.2), can we understand that the problem has achieved a harmonious relationship with its surroundings without compromising its identity.

It would seem that classical conventions in action here exhibit the decidedly human qualities of blundering and rectification: they get drunk, trip up, get back on their feet, try to get sober, and maybe endeavor to learn a lesson in self-improvement from their experiences. As a result, they introduce a somewhat uncanny live element into the otherwise beautiful artifice of the mimetic. It is as if, to return to Batteux's somewhat disgusting image, the music were "like a painting which is on a living skin and should be on a canvas" – undead. The Dresden china shepherdess suddenly picks her nose, wipes it on her floral dress, then reassumes her demure pose. The listening subject is unnerved. So how are we to understand this twitching that disturbs the surface of these conventions' appearances? I argue that it is the effect produced from the presence of autonomy. It is a kind of anamorphic trace marking a constitutive internal gap, or difference, between the handed-down ma-

3.2. Haydn, String Quartet in G, op. 33, no. 5, 4th movement, measures 84–end (106)

teriality of the conventions themselves and a force that, while only able
to exist through embodiment within the conventions, nevertheless is
able to act upon them. To return to the theory of the previous chapter,
it is an excess produced by the forming of the conventions itself. Moreover, it adds another layer of complexity to the claim that this music is
in a kind of historical exile. For historically speaking, the potential for

autonomy would mean that this music, in not yet having fully left the orbit of mimesis, is strangely already on the cusp of entering into the world of the transcendent – the aesthetic paradigm in which, as we have seen, the musical object starts to take on the qualities of being a subject. Classical music therefore appears to us historically in double focus: both post- and pre-factum, on the wane and on the cusp, an old-style material artifact with its feet firmly planted on the social and historical *terra firma* and an elusive and partly dematerialized autonomous entity on the edge of sublimation into the transcendent. It is suspended in a kind of historical exile, and to illustrate how it sustains itself in this condition, I now return to Haydn's op. 33, no. 5 and examine the interplay between (mimetic) conventional expectations and (transcendent) disruptions of those expectations. I start with the scherzo and trio and work my analysis outward from there.

THE PURSUIT OF HAPPINESS

The most striking problem about the opening antecedent and consequent of the scherzo is the hesitant quality of its final cadence, mm. 7–10. By means of the empty measure, m. 8, and the repetition of the dominant chord from the end of m. 7 in m. 9, the resolution onto the tonic is extended by two measures. Mm. 9 and 10 are not only literally separated by the silent measure, but also gesturally differentiated from the preceding material, texturally, dynamically, and registrally. From the robustness of the antecedent we have moved to the lighter realm of this cadence, which seems strangely out of place, as if grafted on from a different piece. Anomalous and slightly unconfident, the cadence does not fulfill its assigned local-level syntactical role of drawing a conclusion and tying up a loose end. Also, when the cadence finally arrives after the silent measure, it bypasses the expected voice-leading resolution onto G as shown in Example 3.3.[51] This resolution had been prepared at the end of the antecedent in violin 1 (mm. 3–4), but only partially fulfilled in the consequent (Example 3.4 shows how the ends of both the antecedent and consequent might have been connected in terms of voice leading). As a result, the final gesture of the opening period has more the quality of a raised eyebrow than an affirmation.

3.3. Haydn, String Quartet in G, op. 33, no. 5,
3rd movement, reworking of measures 7–10

3.4. Haydn, String Quartet in G, op. 33, no. 5, 3rd movement, measures 3–8,
voice leading implications

In the context of the movement's dance-based genre, this rhythmic hitch, created through a two-measure displacement of the expected regular units of measure grouping, is a major generic disruption. This hitch has the ability to draw an implied listening subject into an intimate proximity with the music, with the resulting effect that the music, like an autonomous subject, can start to seem as if it is responding, self-reflexively, to itself. For example, the problem of the cadence in mm. 9–10 could now appear as an attempt by the music to rectify an opposite problem in its antecedent. Like the consequent phrase, the antecedent distorts its role within the dance genre. In contrast with the end of the consequent, though, the antecedent's fault lies in the contraction of material into a regular space, as opposed to the stretching of regular material into an expanded space. The expectation of a recognizable three-beat measure in this dance genre is unfulfilled in the antecedent because the two rhythmic components of motive X (a and b) are compressed into a two-beat unit, X^1 (Example 3.5). This compression is confusing in terms of syntax because the new X (i.e., X^1), grating against the measure line as it stomps up its two-octave range in violin 1, is in fact a liquidation

(a)

(b)

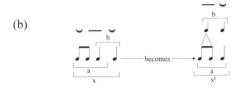

3.5. Haydn, String Quartet in G, op. 33, no. 5, 3rd movement, measures 1–4, rhythmic motives

3.6. Haydn, String Quartet in G, op. 33, no. 5, 3rd movement, measures 1–4, motivic liquidation

of Y from X. (Y is ornamented by a semitone inflection whose rhythm is derived from X; thus, a tentative yet rather unstable relationship between the two is kept in place [Example 3.6].) Liquidation, usually a sign of transition or closure, is at odds with the expository function of the antecedent. As a result, the music is swept up in a drive to the final cadence of the opening period before any material has been suitably presented to justify that dash. Moreover, when the cadence finally arrives, its anomalous quality fails to fulfill the overblown expectations that the attempt to get there too quickly had created. One explanation of this discrepancy is that the final cadence of the first period rectifies the initial brevity of thematic exposition in the antecedent through the introduction of material sufficiently contrastive to be labeled as a belated mini-exposition. Hence the impression of different material. Similarly, the expansion of the consequent phrase can be seen as counteracting the contraction in the antecedent. These two attempts to re-

3.7. Haydn, String Quartet in G, op. 33, no. 5, 3rd movement, measures 17–23

store order, though, overcompensate, and the final cadence still seems unintegrated.

Attempts at rectifying this idiosyncrasy can be seen in two places. The first passage, from the middle section of this movement, starts in m. 16 with a reworking of the problematic opening antecedent, now on the dominant. This reworking then leads into an attempt to rectify the compression of X into the disruptive two-beat liquidating figure of Y in the opening of the movement through the stretching of Y back into the three-beat measure unit of the scherzo's underlying dance genre. While the accompanying instruments crack the whip to the time of the original problematic two-beat unit in mm. 21–22, violin 1 continues the process of expansion with a broad overemphasized retrograde of Y, in which another expansion of Y is embedded (Example 3.7). The second passage, m. 32 at the beginning of the return of the opening period, consists of an expansion of the upbeat to the initial antecedent into a full measure. On a local level, it sounds like running in place. But, by means of this expansion, an attempt is made to assert X as the generating motive of the antecedent and so counteract the emphasis on the liquidation figure (Y) that had initially assumed center stage and confused the expository function of the antecedent in the opening period of the movement. To this effect, the attempt fails because the opening period of the movement is recapitulated without alteration, and Y therefore resumes its initial status, apparently undeterred.

The unaltered recapitulation of the opening period raises a number of difficulties. However formally conventional an exact repetition of the opening passage may be in itself, in the context of this movement's tense interplay between convention and disruption, it smacks of the music's stubborn refusal (or inability) to align itself with conventional expectations. It is a dialectically dense moment, since the fulfillment of a con-

3.8. Haydn, String Quartet in G Major, op. 33, no. 5, 3rd
movement, resolution of end of scherzo in beginning of trio

ventional expectation in this instance sustains a moment of disruption.
Admittedly, a fleeting form of resolution is created on a local level between the end of the first playing of the scherzo and the beginning of the
trio. The two concluding motives of the scherzo are recast here as one
compact unit and both are resolved in terms of the G one might have
wished to hear at the end of the scherzo and at the end of the opening
period (see Example 3.8, in which the bracketed notes are the expected
but unfulfilled resolutions). Thus related, the difference in tone between
these two motives is subsumed under the flow of one melodic line, and
the problem created by the anomalous quality of the final cadence is
temporarily resolved. With the repeat of the scherzo, however, the movement finishes with this unsettling cadence and so we are returned to the
strange state of suspension with which we had begun.

Earlier in this chapter we saw the first movement of this quartet
beginning inappropriately with a cadential figure (Example 3.1) – a kind
of syntactical infelicity, a jumping of the gun, equivalent to the presentation of a conclusion before the proofs. In the first movement, the reper-
cussion of this opening was a general destabilization and disorientation
of the syntax, particularly of cadential closure. But in the following slow
movement, the cadences are clear and correct, as if the problems created by the opening of the previous movement have been resolved. This
interpretation is made credible because the refrain that marks the major
cadences in this movement is motivically derived from the problematic
opening cadential figure of the previous movement (compare x in Example 3.9 with Example 3.1). However, the slow movement, characterized by a consistently elevated *opera seria* tone, ends with a statement of
its basic cadential refrain, which is followed by an anomalous pizzicato

3.9. Haydn, String Quartet in G, op. 33, no. 5, 2nd movement, measures 7–10

that has the quality of a satirical aside. Suddenly, cadential closure seems unstable again. This clownish final gesture creates and emphasizes a set of motivic connections between the ending of the slow movement and the opening of the scherzo (Example 3.10) communicating that the following movement already wields a negative effect. The final gesture of the slow movement is a moment of bad decorum, as when a guest (the scherzo) turns up to a party both far too early and offensively attired, or when somebody finishes off someone else's heart-felt pronouncement with a facetious throwaway remark. The backward seepage of the scherzo's antics into the end of the slow movement also marks an unfortunate return to the syntactical disarray of the first movement. Like the contradictory cadential incipit of the first movement, the scherzo presents itself too soon. Its rush to blurt out its message then provides the catalyst for the unruly momentum of the liquidating dash toward its final cadence.

3.10. Haydn, String Quartet in G, op. 33, no. 5, motivic connections between end of 2nd and beginning of 3rd movements

But the scherzo's sabotage can also be viewed as a comic critique of the pretensions of the slow movement. By chipping the exquisite veneer of the slow movement, the scherzo leads us to recognize that the slow movement's grand mien is not simply an expressive device that communicates that the syntactical mayhem of the first movement has been laid to rest. Rather, bundled up in the slow movement's hauteur is an unpleasantly supercilious attitude that derives from its willful blindness to the true state of affairs within the processes of the quartet thus far. The slow movement pretends that everything has been successfully concluded by striking a slightly tragic and stoical pose that can draw an implied listening subject into an admiring and sympathetic concentration on the slow movement's own sufferings and strengths and so makes her forget the real issues under discussion elsewhere in the world of the quartet. It is as if the slow movement articulates a separate psychological tendency within the personality of the quartet as a whole. Admittedly, it makes a token gesture of taking part in the ongoing logic of the quartet's own self-reflexive considerations by elevating motivic material from the first movement into the realm of tragedy (Example 3.9). But it is essentially self-centered, and so when the scherzo trips it up by stepping on the train of its huge dress as it exits the stage, it is as if we realize that the slow movement's message had been "Let the rest of the quartet eat cake!"

If we keep in mind the slow movement's tendencies toward disavowal, the ending of the scherzo might no longer appear quite as stubborn. Rather, the scherzo's inability to resolve fully can be interpreted as a kind of honesty, a difficult acknowledgment that the repercussions of the syntactical problems unleashed by the quartet's opening movement are still strong enough to hinder successful cadential stabilization, and, thus, that there is still more to do. And indeed, the set of variations that constitute the proceeding finale, with its lightness of tone, can be understood in these terms. Admittedly, for Donald Tovey, for example, the finale's ease of address was unsatisfying: "The finale ... shows that the revival of the divertimento style, though adding important new resources to the string quartet, has its dangers. Three melodic variations and a runaway coda do not make an adequate finale to a quartet with so important a first movement; and the prettiness of Haydn's Siciliana theme is extinguished by comparison with the poetry of that of the finale of Mozart's D minor Quartet, a comparison it has the misfortune to suggest."[52] But Tovey criticizes the finale for failing to produce something it is not set up to achieve. The expansive formal parameters of the first movement cannot be read as simply the product of Haydn's compositional yearning to write an expansive first movement. The particular nature of the first movement is the product of the difficulties it faces in wrestling with the problem with which the quartet as a whole begins. And so to ask that the finale be as long and involved as the first movement is tantamount to requiring that the work begin and end in extreme difficulty, a state of affairs that would seem to contradict the ample evidence that the quartet is trying to bring its own difficulties to rest.

That the variation theme and its subsequent variations are exceedingly regular periodically should not be taken as evidence of a lame deflation of Haydn's compositional inspiration. Rather, the comforting return to regularly placed, stable cadences throughout the variation finale acts as a sedative to the syntactical volatility that had unnerved the characters of the preceding scherzo and the opening movement.[53] It is as if the finale marks the accessing of another psychological trait within the quartet's overall personality, one which, like a voice of reason, presents the syntactically overwhelmed quartet with an exemplum of good syntactical behavior in the form of a regular theme and three undisruptive variations ending in a presto in which, as we have seen, the opening figure of the first movement appears as a cadential figure to a reworking of the variation theme. The ethos of the finale, a gentle and unimposing manner, holds things steady despite the storm of problems that disconcerted the first and third movements' arguments, and drove the slow movement into performative denial and eventual abandonment of the quartet's logical dilemmas. Thus, when the Presto asserts that the problematic opening gesture of the first movement can be resolved into the quartet's concluding statement, it is as if all the other movements can be pictured as willingly standing up to participate in the reconciliation created by the traditional concluding dance. As the curtain falls, the quartet smiles, happy to have been made psychologically whole again.

GHOSTS

Everything about this ending bespeaks of homecoming. All the distorting creases created by the disruptive presence of an autonomous agency appear to have been ironed out. All its wandering about in the no-man's land between mimesis and transcendence is brought to rest at the warm hearth of the conventional, and so too perhaps at the mimetic. The quartet's state of exile in a more confusing, modern world is concluded by an act of grace that allows it to nestle back down into the maternal embrace of the eighteenth century. And so as we look back upon our friend as she is closing the door behind us, she looks at us and smiles.

But does the syntactical regularity created by the finale's theme and variations act as an authentic critical resolution to the complex state of affairs that is left precariously unresolved in the rather shallow breath of the scherzo's concluding cadence? Or does the finale surreptitiously shift modality from a dialectical autonomy – in which the music, as it were, creates a distance between itself and its handed down elements – and into a kind of mildly infantilizing placation? Does not the syntactical regularity, aided by the rhythmic lilt of the pervading sicilienne topic, merely rock the listening subject and the quartet itself into a *feeling* of safety, rather than proving that things have indeed been secured? Perhaps it is seeking to convince us that our autonomy can be reconciled with presently existing states of affairs. Or, even worse, that if we allow our autonomy to manifest itself, it will eventually just reproduce (autonomously, as it were) the already given, as if autonomy could be reduced to merely the conventional wisdom of a kind of common sense. Such a suspicion, for example, haunts Adorno's deep disquiet regarding Beethoven's "Heroic" mode. Of course, our ears are tainted by a traumatic future that we might argue that Haydn's quartet, in its original context, never knew; it is almost a conventional cliché of our time to see ideology in affirmation. Nevertheless, maybe Tovey's judgment of inadequacy is inadvertently resonant with a certain truth about the composition's autonomy. Maybe the quartet attempts to compensate for a failure within the social by dreaming it into the realm of the aesthetic, by projecting it onto the imaginary. This being the case, the quartet is then structurally no different from the face paintings of the Caduveo Indians in Levi-Strauss's famous analysis mentioned earlier.

This line of reasoning, however, is dialectically limited. Admittedly, it has allowed for a force of negation (autonomy) to make its presence felt within the immediacy of conventions, a process that helps to make manifest the structurally inherent lack within what had previously seemed to be the full plenitude of the given. And this, indeed, can be critically productive. But having achieved this, it then freezes the two terms within the structure of a rigid opposition, and in having brought the conceptual movement to a halt, curtails any further negation. Conventions and mimesis get scripted as bad and autonomy and transcendence as good, or visa-versa. The result, predictably, is a kind of academic tennis match in which the aim of each position is merely to win, and the Viennese classics become like a harried child caught in the legal crossfire of a custody contestation. My argument, however, is that this quartet retains its potentiality for autonomy precisely *because* it capitulates in an almost mechanical fashion to the conventional. Thus the potential of a convention to create the possibility, via its autonomy, of becoming something else results less from its openness to a kind of self-pluralization, and more from a certain kind of inward focusing repetition of itself. In this case, I would like to illustrate this point by turning to a discussion to Kant's famous "An Answer to the Question: 'What is Enlightenment?'"

Kant's essay famously begins with an injunction: "*Enlightenment is man's emergence from his self-incurred immaturity. Immaturity* is the inability to use one's own understanding without the guidance of another. This immaturity is *self-incurred* if its cause is not lack of understanding, but lack of resolution and courage to use it without the guidance of another. The motto of enlightenment is therefore: *Sapere aude!* Have the courage to use your *own* understanding."[54] This seems like a relatively standard enlightenment position: if we are to be free, we must relinquish ourselves from the "laziness and cowardice"[55] that keep us bound to figures of authority that we invest with the power to think for us. "Dogmas and formulas, those mechanical instruments for rational use (or rather misuse) of [the individual's] natural endowments, are the ball and chain of his permanent immaturity."[56] Instead we should use our reason in order to establish what it is that we should and should not do. Kant is here asserting autonomy, that which had opened up the gap between classical music's conventions and their disruptive presentations.

For Kant, however, the process of moving toward the actualization of freedom must be tempered by legislative procedures: "A public can only achieve enlightenment slowly. A revolution may well put an end to autocratic despotism and to rapacious or power-seeking oppression, but it will never produce a true reform in ways of thinking. Instead, new prejudices, like the ones they replaced, will serve as a leash to control the great unthinking mass."[57] As he distinguishes later in the essay, we are not living in an enlightened age, but rather in an age of enlightenment,[58] where ritualistic adherence to authority and dogma – Kant associates this primarily with religious doctrine, but one could it expand it to the *ancien régime* in general – must coexist with the use of reason.

This simultaneous existence of faith and reason would seem to be indicative of an insurmountable historical antagonism whose only solution would be the sudden transformative act of revolution – that which Kant has already dismissed. Kant's solution is characteristic of so much of the rest of his philosophical project in that it posits two positions separated by a gap, rather than an all-encompassing theoretical totality fully available to our understanding. Alluding to the political policy of Frederick the Great, Kant argues that in order to become free, "*argue as much as you like and about whatever you like, but obey!*" What this

means is that in our public roles – which Kant defines, rather confus-
ingly, as a place where as people of learning we address "the entire *reading public*" – the "use of man's reason must always be free, and it alone
çan bring about enlightenment among men." Whereas in our private
roles – defined as a "particular *civil* post or office with which [an indi-
vidual] is entrusted"[59] – "it is, of course, impermissible to argue in such
cases; obedience is imperative."[60] So, like the Viennese classics, on the
one hand we are to align ourselves to the given of conventional roles,
while on the other we are to engage in critique of those roles.

Kant's assertion is paradoxical, as can be seen from his formulation
of it in the context of a discussion of the categorical imperative in "What
is Orientation in Thinking?" (1786):

> If reason will not subject itself to the law it gives itself, it will have to bow under
> the yoke of the law which others impose upon it, for without any law whatsoever
> nothing, not even the greatest nonsense, can play its hand for very long. Thus,
> the inevitable consequence of declared lawlessness in thinking (an emancipa-
> tion from restrictions of reason) is that freedom to think is finally lost.[61]

Some might argue that Kant's idea that freedom is no freedom unless it
is forced endlessly to negotiate its own antithesis (for example, the law)
gained sociopsychological validity from the fact that it proved to be historically prophetic – for the eradication of already-existing laws created
by the initial acts of the French Revolution ultimately left the political terrain vulnerable to a return of the repressed of un-freedom in the
form of the Terror. Kant's argument, though, is not merely sociological.
As Onara O' Neill has written, "Kant does not ground reason in actual
consensus or in agreement and standards of any historical community;
he grounds it in the repudiation of principles that preclude the possibility of open-ended interaction and communication."[62] Philosophically,
we might illuminate the truth of the Kantian paradox of freedom by
recasting it (somewhat provocatively) in the characteristically Hegelian
negation of negation.

If freedom is that which resists dogma and conceptual ossification,
then freedom cannot define itself as always resistant to such laws, since
freedom would then have become a dogma (a dogma of anti-dogma),
and at worse it would have reduced its purported critical function to a
meaningless injunction ("always resist dogma"), the mere recognition of

which being the justification that something politically and philosophically valid is happening. To resist the rhetorical stylization of its own lawlessness as if it were a universally valid law, freedom must therefore incorporate law (the negative that had initially been Other to it) back into itself, thus negating the initial negation. Freedom is open-ended, but it can only remain so by being open to the possibility that in order to move it must simultaneously be skewered on static invariants. But in the process of the negation being negated, both the initial term and the reincorporated negative undergo transformation.

In the first stage of a complex reading of Kant's essay, Žižek argues that it is in fact exactly this taking on of the law that allows us to view it as something Other to us that we can then distance ourselves from. This "acceptance of given empirical, 'pathological' (Kant) customs and rules is not some kind of pre-Enlightenment remnant – a remnant of the traditional authoritarian attitude," which Žižek associates with the essentially Baroque universe. Rather, this paradoxical taking on of the law for the purposes of freedom radically reconfigures the authority of Baroque law itself, which "is never experienced as nonsensical and unfounded; on the contrary [pre-Enlightenment] law is always illuminated by the charismatic power of fascination." It is "through this acceptance of the customs and rules of social life, in their nonsensical given character, through acceptance of the fact that 'Law is Law,' we are internally freed from its constraints – the way is open for free theoretical reflection." As a result, laws take on a "given, non-founded character" in our experience of them that "entails in itself a kind of distance from them."[63] Instead of being full, laws become ghostlike, Other to what we would imagine them to be, while still remaining absolutely necessary to the structure that opens up the possibility of freedom. Similarly, the political subject might also be said to become ghostlike, since in order to keep the possibility of her freedom open, she too has had to become Other to what she would imagine herself in her freedom to be: she has to become the subject of the Law.

Žižek proceeds to a more sinister analysis of how our distance from, in Kant's word, the "pathological" aspect of social customs is in effect only made possible by the "traumatic, truth-less, non-sensical character of the internal, moral law itself"; that "we can free ourselves of external social constraints and achieve the maturity proper to the autonomous enlightened subject precisely by submitting to the 'irrational' compulsion of the categorical imperative." Thus, the internalized "moral Law is obscene in so far as it is its form itself which functions as a motivating force driving us to obey its command – that is, in so far as we obey moral Law because it is law and not because of a set of positive reasons."[64] For these reasons, Žižek ultimately sees in Kant's moral philosophy the very structure that binds us to ideology. Žižek's argument is a compellingly disturbing one, but I would like to arrest its progress at the point at which the law and the political subject, at the moment of the negation of the negation, both become ghostlike, since ghosts are transparent and through them we can start to see something other than the meaningless addiction to the form itself of ideological commitment that is Žižek's vision. I would also like to turn back to the ending of Haydn's string quartet.

If, as I have argued, the freedom of autonomy can only be salvaged from rhetorical stylization by taking on its Other, the negative of the law, then it follows that the process in classical music whereby the givens of conventions are disturbed into restlessness by the critical movement of autonomy only resists becoming similarly stylized by the imposition of conventions in their accepted form *and* precisely at the point where resolution has not necessarily been achieved. As in Kant's argument, the quartet can argue as much as it likes, but eventually it must obey – not because the conventions are right and all, but since without that act of knowingly meaningless genuflection (in this case before the law of closure) the work of autonomy would be unable to preserve a "distance from the external 'machine' of social customs"[65] and conventions that keep the possibility of autonomy in effect. The seeming stasis of reconciliation at the end of Haydn's quartet is thus no ideological masking of an underlying disruptive autonomy, but rather the very precondition of that autonomy remaining authentic and not descending into mere gestural simulation. As a result of this paradoxical act of preemptive, meaningless, mechanical closure, the finale of Haydn's op. 33, no. 5, like the distanced law in Kant's formulation, takes on a certain transparent ghostlike quality, which might help us to review Tovey's judgment of inadequacy as inadvertently correct. It is as if having secured the possibility for the moment of its own continuance and autonomous openness in its own present, the quartet then turns toward us by looking through its own final ghostly transparency, as if it were a window onto this once unknown future. It directs its gaze to what at one time did not exist and throws a promise to where we are now. And so smiling, it waits sad-eyed for us to answer.

4

Enchantment

(Mozart, La clemenza di Tito)

THE END OF ABJECTION

Food is frequently disgusting, our relations to it haunted by an almost archaic abjection. Few of us can enjoy our fried egg if we simultaneously keep in mind that it has come out of the feathery end of a chicken. And so a careful set of practices has to be kept in place to keep what appear to be real origins at the distance that constitutes denial. But note, only "appear." Although we are unnerved at the thought that we might get too close to something, that something is often in excess of the literal object of disgust itself or even its origin. Julia Kristeva writes: "When the eyes see or the lips touch that skin on the surface of milk – harmless, thin as a sheet of cigarette paper, pitiful as a nail paring – I experience a gagging sensation and, still further down, spasms in the stomach, the belly; and all the organs shrivel up the body, provoke tears and bile, increase heartbeat, cause forehead and hands to perspire."[1] Yet the milk skin is "harmless." Our paroxystic reactions are thus not merely born out of pragmatic concerns for cleanliness, even though present cultural obsessions with bacteria work hard to convince us that merely the demands of common sense are being fulfilled. A sort of fascination infects our relationship to the abject, as is attested by the ease with which the most flippant of suggestions can magically make the horror suddenly present – as if secretly we want it here, that Other thing from elsewhere. As if secretly, we are enchanted.

Such forms of disgust are distant from aesthetic experience only if we forget the Eucharistic notion of real presence by which the aesthetic has been haunted, at least since the late eighteenth century.[2] Debates concerning the differences between transubstantiation and consubstantiation have been at the source of the most vehement of conflicts within the Christian church. Yet both notions are available for feeling the threat of abjection, for in each case bread and wine are forced into an almost claustrophobic proximity to things that exist seemingly beyond their material limits, the real presence of flesh and blood. In transubstantiation, the substance of the bread and the wine are literally transformed, even though their appearance (their so-called "accidents") remains the same; in consubstantiation, bread and body, wine and blood, coexist. There is a disturbing holographic double-focus that potentially makes the sight of those taking of communion somewhat nasty. Kristeva argues that the feeling of abjection is created by that which threatens the security of the boundaries through which we define ourselves. "It is thus no lack of cleanliness or health that causes abjection but what disturbs identity, system, order. What does not respect borders, positions, rules. The in-between, the ambiguous, the composite" – the body/bread, blood/wine, and those who sit comfortably with the illusion of their intermingling.[3] We are displaced by the sight of the transgression of what to many of us is the grounding perception of literal materiality, and so to allay fears regarding the uncanny sense that there may in fact be something more to things, we react with an excessive materialism often verging on the oxymoron of hysteric pragmatism. We respond to belief by means of an intense *belief* in nonbelief, and so allow perhaps for the repressed that is our desire for belief to return under the guise of our profound revulsion.

It can be likewise with the sight of enchantment created in some by aesthetic experience, particularly of music, which so easily compels its listeners to bodily contortions that are difficult not to interpret as expressions of utter commitment and belief in some kind of real presence emanating from that with which they commune. If we are not in the mood, the state of arousal in which music grips others can be incredibly threatening; the lewd rubbing up of musical materiality to spiritual transcendence, for example, is easily insufferable. Standing at the bar (not moving, unmoved) watching the music's gust propelling our lover about the dance floor like one of the damned in hell, the frame of our experience can easily split in two, leaving us in the nowhere of an anxious suspension between attraction and flight. "How is it that the music's rhythmic thump merely presents itself to me as just that, rhythmic thumping? Why is it that the same inane stuff transforms my lover when it can only incarcerate me in the prison of what I already know myself to be? Why can I not be seduced by the music – am I frigid? And why can my lover so easily make himself available to music – is he a whore? Maybe I could forget myself into being with him and music, a *ménage à trois*. But perhaps it is safer to remain here drinking. I could, of course, placate myself by writing the whole thing off as different strokes, different folks. So my lover's got his place and I've got mine. As I'll remind him. When we get home."

Undoubtedly, the sense of abjection caused in some by the belief in the Other's suspect ability to allow the unrelated into too *close* a proximity is a constituent feature of many forms of violence against the litany of the marginalized (the gay man, the illegal immigrant, the woman, the African American, the lover – there are so many, dancers all).[4] Yet it is far more common to see the dismissal of enchantment politically justified on the opposite grounds: because it creates *distance* and so won't allow things to be close enough. The particularly famous instance, which covers many of this position's themes, is Walter Benjamin's "The Work of Art in the Age of Mechanical Reproduction."[5]

For the Benjamin of this essay, the work of art's ability to enchant has its source in its aura, the seeming presence that its authentic and singular origins exert on its audience. Enchanted artworks are regressive since they work to keep people in their place through the fascination exerted upon them by this presence. In order for its magic to work, the source of this presence must somehow remain withheld and so at a distance. Caught in the double helix of a conflict between the inquisitive forward movement of his desire and the backing-away movement that the taboo against unveiling the secret inspires, the convinced spectator gets riveted to the spot, mesmerized, and so is impotent to act.

For Benjamin here fascism works likewise. The self-alienation of mankind "has reached such a degree that it can experience its own destruction as an aesthetic pleasure of the first order."[6] (It is as if modernity, which had seemed to work to rid the world of myth, has resulted in a situation where people experience their own condition mythologically – as merely spectators of their own fate, of the inevitability of the way things are, as opposed to being agents of history.)[7] And so "This is the situation of politics which Fascism is rendering aesthetic"; it keeps this condition of self-alienation at a distance, so that political agency will remain neutralized. By comparison, "Communism responds by politicizing art";[8] it recognizes "the desire of contemporary masses to bring things 'closer' spatially and humanly" – something which, in part, Benjamin argues can be achieved by means of mechanical reproduction.[9] "Every day the urge grows stronger . . . to get hold of an object . . . to pry an object from its shell, to destroy its aura," to perceive the "sense of the universal equality of things."[10] In a strongly Marxist sense, social equality, Benjamin implies, will result when people have seized the ability (perhaps through an art transformed into revolutionary praxis by mechanical reproduction) to allow all things to come into an equally increased state of proximity. The shattering of a kind of gravitational ordering of objects will act as a catalyst for entry into a relativity of social space. This is one of the reasons why Benjamin in this essay is so interested in cinema. The cameraman, for example, can act like a surgeon who "cuts into the patient's body. . . . He greatly diminishes the *distance* between himself and the patient by penetrating into the patient's body."[11]

It is as if Benjamin sees a radical challenge being thrown down by mechanical reproduction: to liberate oneself by daring to come into contact with everything. And so I am tempted to think of Kant's famous clarion call, "*Sapere aude*" (dare to be wise), which I discussed in the previous chapter. Perhaps Kant and Benjamin are just stages of a larger project that, loosely speaking, we might call Enlightenment, and perhaps we might provocatively reconfigure that project's drive toward the disenchantment of the world as but a crusade to rid the world of abjection, to banish the fear of proximity so that things at last might come together. This being the case, we could also include contemporary musicology, which, over the past decades, has repeatedly sought to show how our experience of the aesthetic – with all its strong feelings that encourage us to talk of spiritual elevation, transcendence, and the liberating sense of expanded horizons – is in fact the product of a closing off, a distancing, the strange collateral gained from our donning of an eyeless mask that allows us to be blind enough to forget. And so musicology demands that we arise from our slumber, wipe abjection from our eyes, and place music once more back amidst the material throng of human meanings. Those who are brave enough to disenchant are awake; they are kept brightly alert by the proximity of things. Those who submit to enchantment are asleep; the world as it recedes into the distance works to close their "gloom-pleased eyes," allowing them, to complete Keats's phrase, to rest in "forgetfulness divine."[12]

But this choice, common enough, is overdetermined and too stark: eyes open or eyes shut. And so to use a phrase to which I will return, it is more of a forced choice, for the only right decision is to choose to turn one's eyes open. But is it really the case that the enchanted Other is so fully consumed by the sleep of his forgetting? In his classic study of play, Johan Huizinga recounts an anecdote told to him by the father of a young boy. The man "found his four-year-old son sitting at the front of a row of chairs, playing 'trains.' As he hugged him the boy said: 'Don't kiss the engine, Daddy, or the carriages won't think it's real.'"[13] Such admissions, as Huizinga concedes, betray "a consciousness of the inferiority of play compared with 'seriousness', a feeling that seems to be something as primary as play itself."[14] It is "only a pretend."[15] Play cannot stretch far enough, and so one has to be terribly careful lest you wake up the toys. Yet this should not lead us to conclude that play is therefore deficient. A mere flickering it might be rather than a solid entity, but that does not prevent it from being so mesmerizing that we are more than happy to forget its spurious status in terms of the real: "Any game can at any time wholly run away with the players."[16] What the anecdote reveals is that enchantment is far more radical than merely the static condition of self-sufficient belief that perverse non-believers, fascinated by the Other, construct their fantasies around. The little boy's enchanted play fearlessly survives in, and is even produced as a result of, its flagrant proximity to its understanding of its own fiction. Children, we might say, have the courage to let distance remain within reach. By comparison, with disenchantment everything can be close *except* for distance. Disenchantment is able to appear brave only because it keeps the one fear that remains insurmountable far away. And as a result, it is haunted by abjections.

This chapter began life many years ago as a perfectly respectable study in disenchantment. I had been interested to investigate the contextual determinants (social and historical) at work in the structures of representation of women in Mozart's *La clemenza di Tito*, specifically regarding the character of Vitellia. I had wanted to illustrate a politically vexing, though far from uncommon paradox: that although Vitellia is the most convincing character in the opera, if not the locus of the opera's success in terms of verisimilitude, she nevertheless is employed to embody a set of ideologically loaded fictions prevalent in the eighteenth century regarding women. Vitellia enchants, and so my goal was to stop this from happening by drawing her musical material back into proximity with its cultural determinants. I was working according to a political praxis that has remained common enough amongst scholars of race, gender, and sexuality: in order to rectify the abuses committed against the marginalized, the cultural products that have been used to circulate and naturalize the repressive discourses that have worked to exclude must be stripped of their seeming naturalness. Vitellia is a cultural puppet. Our job – which I envisioned then in a kind of Brechtian sense – is to reveal the strings.

Such an endeavor can be completely valid; this chapter is not some elaborate call for the cessation of politicized contextual study. Yet I found that fidelity to the very logic of my acts of disenchantment kept leading me back toward enchantment. No doubt, I could have derived a certain deconstructive conclusion from this, enchantment functioning as the excluded but constitutively necessary marker for what Derrida might have called the "originary lack" within the logic of disenchantment's claims to self-sufficiency. But since the same conceptual hollowing out could just as easily have been performed on enchantment, the benefit of such a project seemed predominantly for the claims of deconstruction itself – a worthy cause, perhaps, but not my crusade. Rather, like the child who allows distance to be close, I wanted to be kept in place by the patterns created by the pulsing of enchantment and disenchantment in and out of each other. And so the following three sections of this chapter are an attempt (performative to a degree, by necessity) to recapture some of the movements that that act of concentration revealed. In the later stages of the chapter, I broaden the discussion out in an extreme political way in order to propose why being attendant on this phenomenon has value, and why the effort not to concentrate upon it should give us pause.

ALLEGORICAL VERISIMILITUDE

La clemenza di Tito was first performed in Prague on 6 September 1791 as part of the celebrations for the coronation of the Austro-German emperor Leopold II as king of Bohemia. The venerable libretto, originally written by Metastasio in 1734, had received over sixty settings before Mozart and Caterino Mazzolà, the court poet at Dresden, collaborated to create their two-act version for the festivities. Its plot is organized around the tension between Vitellia and the Roman emperor Titus, whose father had murdered and dethroned Vitellius, Vitellia's father. At the beginning of the opera, Titus is on the point of marrying Berenice, daughter of the king of Judea, and Vitellia, livid with jealousy at the thought that her claims to the throne have been spurned, has coerced Sextus, who is in love with her, to set fire to the capitol and murder Titus. During the course of the first act, Titus recants on his decision to marry Berenice, sends her packing back to Judea, and refocuses his marital plans on the modest and honest Servilia, Sextus's sister, whose hand in marriage Sextus has promised to his friend Annius. Servilia, tormented by Titus's intentions toward her, confesses to the emperor where her true feelings lie, and the ever-clement Titus, touched by her honesty, releases her from the law of his plans and blesses her union with Annius. Servilia's joy is misinterpreted by Vitellia as a sign that Servilia will indeed marry Titus, so she rekindles the flames of her treacherous idea in Sextus's mind. Sextus has scarcely set off to execute the plan before Vitellia learns, too late, that Titus has finally decided to marry her. The first act ends with the capitol in flames and the onlookers shocked at the assumed death of their benign emperor, who, we later learn, has fortuitously escaped harm. The second act is taken up with the unveiling of Sextus's crime, Titus's exoneration of him, and Vitellia's final decision, occurring on the cusp of the opera's conclusion, to confess her seminal role in the whole proceedings. In the final scene, the self-evident meaning of the opera's title prevails, and with no surprises Vitellia is forgiven.

Considering the event for which it was commissioned, the opera invites strongly allegorical interpretation, with Titus as thinly veiled representation of Leopold II and Vitellia's plotted rebellion echoing the fraught political situation in Europe. In particular, as John Rice has written, "the burning of the Capitol at the end of the first act may well have been understood in 1791 as a frightening symbol of the violence with which the Bastille had been attacked just two years before."[17] Following the allegory's logic, the implication is that Leopold II is personally touched by the French Revolution because of the situation in which it placed his sister Marie Antoinette. More generally, the allegory asserts that Enlightenment absolutism's continuation and feasibility are ensured by the presence of Leopold, for seemingly by means only of the magnetic emanations from Titus's magnanimous aura, characters' deviant political behavior is drawn back into moral and civic alignment. Leopold, like Titus, is to be seen as humane, appealing to those who wished to preserve the continuation of the Enlightenment project. (For example, Leopold had abolished torture during his time as Grand Duke of Tuscany.) However, he will not be led to embracing extreme radicalism, which, on the one hand, would have meant Joseph II, Leopold's brother, whose Enlightenment policies Leopold was keen to distance himself from as soon as Joseph had died in February of 1790; on the other hand, the French Revolution itself.

Attractive as this image of flexible enlightened despotism is, it nevertheless draws its convincing glow from the dubious sexual politics that constitutes the allegory's shadow. The rather excessive demand that the opera might have made as a credible reflection of a political reality, particularly to an audience mired in the turmoil of the late eighteenth century, could have been ameliorated by the character of Vitellia. As an unruly and politically dangerous woman, she was easily available for fulfilling sexist fantasies increasingly prevalent within enlightenment thinking in the second half of the eighteenth century, and, in so doing, functions as a locus for the allegory's claims to truth.

This is not to deny the undeniable advances made by women during this period, particularly those arising from a shift in the relationship between ethics and politics that accompanied the transformation and eventual dilution of Absolutism and the *ancien régime*. Absolutism had been a severe solution to the pervasive political catastrophes of the seventeenth century engendered by the Reformation and the resulting split in religious authority. It sought to resolve the crises by means of the figure of the monarch, who was to neutralize the devastating power of the church by recognizing no other authority than God himself, and whose only goal was to stop civil and religious wars. All other concerns – freedom of speech, the articulation of conscience – were considered expendable. Ethics was subordinate to politics. As Reinhart Kosselleck has described it, "There must be a clean break between the internal and the external. . . . External actions are to be submitted to the ruler's judgment and jurisdiction. . . . To survive, the subject must submerge his conscience."[18]

As the destabilizing threats of the seventeenth century receded, absolutism's positioning of morality beneath politics was replaced by morality acting as the foundation for the political. In intellectual history, this shift is articulated with Hobbes being superseded by Locke, whose famous "law of Opinion or Reputation" painted a picture where "citizens no longer defer to the State power alone [but] jointly, they form a society that develops its own moral laws, laws which take their place beside those of the State," and ultimately become the state.[19] With the waning of the older notion that politics constituted the primary location of the ethical, public opinions concerning women began to transform, and instead of being viewed according to the ancient notion that they were violent forces of nature requiring the civilizing discipline of man, women came to be seen as civilizing forces, the ethical agents for producing and sustaining the very autonomous social realms that Locke had envisioned. Particularly in their central roles within the developing cultures of the salons, they became a locus for the Enlightenment's veneration of sociability.[20] In *Clemenza,* this particular inscription of woman finds embodiment most clearly in the character of Servilia.

But to a large degree the ideal of a political world defined from the bottom (ethics) up remained precisely that, an ideal. For example, in many instances the administrative order of absolutism essentially remained in effect, resulting in a situation where whole strata of society could, on the one hand, constitute a public sphere, but on the other, wield almost no legislative clout and so remain politically impotent. Thus, financiers in France were major creditors to the state and so fundamental to its existence, yet not "only did they lack all influence in fiscal matters . . . [but] their capital itself was wholly insecure: time and again a royal fiat would arbitrarily rob them of the gains they had worked and ventured for."[21] Women often found themselves in structurally similar situations. On the one hand, they were lauded as seemingly central to developing social formations and ideals because they were perceived to be endowed with a civilizing capability that could temper the forces of what many (rightly) perceived to be the violent forms of indifference and unrest caused by the rapidly developing structures of capitalism and commerce.[22] But on the other hand, this resulted in them being almost exclusively assigned to a private realm categorically cut off from the very politics that was, and has continued to remain, focused on coercing the world so as to preserve the vested interests of successful capitalists themselves. Neutralized, women could be adored – a fact that we should keep in mind when historians get sentimental over the development of the cult of conjugal love in the eighteenth century.

But even privatized (as it were) women remained a threat, as attested by the increasing appearance during the eighteenth century of qualifications to the basic tenets of the Enlightenment when the question of women and politics was at stake. At the foundation of Enlightenment political discourse as it developed in the later seventeenth century was the notion that all humans are, or have the potential to become, autonomous as a result of being in possession of reason. Already in the first half of the seventeenth century, the dissemination of Descartes's mind-body split had begun to raise the status of women, particularly in salon culture, by removing the body-determinative theories that had traditionally functioned to locate them outside the spheres of intellectual and political action. If, as Cartesian philosophy suggests, women are in the same degree of possession of reason as men, then the autonomous workings of reason itself necessitate that women must have the same access to the political sphere as men. As Mary Wollstonecraft wrote much later in 1792: "Consider . . . whether, when men contend for their freedom, and to be allowed to judge for themselves respecting their own happiness, it be not inconsistent and unjust to subjugate women. . . ? Who made man the exclusive judge, if woman partake with him of the gift of reason?"[23]

Many were made nervous by such proto-feminist thinking and sought to negate it without, nevertheless, appearing to cancel their purported Enlightenment allegiances; scientific discourse, one of the foundations on which Enlightenment discourse had been built, provided an answer. Thomas Laqueur writes that by around 1800 "writers of all sorts were determined to base what they insisted were fundamental differences between the male and female sexes, thus between man and woman, on discoverable biological distinctions, and to express these in a radically different rhetoric."[24] Before the eighteenth century the sexual organs of men and women had been understood primarily in an inversional relationship to each other, rather than as non-commensurate systems.[25] However, if it could be shown that women were, in biological essence, different from men, then it followed that reason was not available to them and so, in recognition of the laws given by nature, they must not be allowed access to the political. As Rousseau never tires of repeating in *Émile, ou de l'éducation* (1762), women should remain in the domestic sphere, suckling children.[26] Rousseau railed against the salons precisely because they were presided over by powerful women readily involving themselves in current political debates; by failing to respect the boundaries of their own nature, such women unleash a force of artifice that then corrupts what should be the natural procedures of politics.

Vitellia could easily have validated such beliefs regarding the destabilizing artifice introduced when women transgress nature and enter the sphere of the political: her natural feminine tendency toward feeling and emotion, untethered to its natural outlet in the domestic sphere, and accompanied by her equally natural feminine lack of reasoning, act to incarcerate her in a miasma of self-involvement. As Rousseau states in *Émile*, "The male is male only at certain moments," whereas "the female is female her whole life" and "everything constantly recalls her sex to her."[27] This was a widely held opinion in the later eighteenth century. Thirteen years later, for example, we see it again in Pierre Roussel's important *Système physique et moral de la femme* (1775): "Woman is not woman only in one place but in every aspect under which she can be envisaged."[28] By comparison, to be rationally autonomous would, in effect, necessitate there being a place within woman that was not woman, and so, interestingly, men could prevail within this discourse because of the assumption that they are somehow able to exit their sex and create an internal distance in relationship to themselves. Seemingly incapable of such self-reflection, Vitellia is blinded by her feminine jealousy and loses sight of her duty toward the political whole; constantly recalled to her own sex, fully determined by her emotional life, she is driven to igniting the flames of an unnecessary political rebellion by disturbing the balance between artifice and nature. The contemporary belief in the existence of ties between radical thinking, such as proto-feminist debate, and the French Revolution would only have authorized this further.[29]

Women in the eighteenth century of course were far from being absent from political action. Dominique Godineau notes that women of the lower classes continued in their traditional roles as making up the first ranks of all public disturbances, such as food riots, religious upheavals, and anti-fiscal and political uprisings.[30] It was the women of Paris who in asserting their ancient rite to petition the king regarding food had set in motion the events of October 1789. Throughout the period, women of the upper classes, particularly those who organized salons, remained vital to the brokering of political relationships and often acted as important political patrons. This was also the century of Catherine II, the "Great," of Russia, and Maria Theresa of Austria. But women in the eighteenth century tended to suffer from a predicament that has been described as "'mixity' without parity."[31] Women's political roles were either predominantly barred from being properly legitimated, or neutralized by being reinscribed into the protective allure of the normative, and so, for many, evidence of the fact that women had political lives often failed to reach the light of day. The French Revolution, for example, not only failed to grant women the full political rights of citizenship, but actively sought to prohibit it: Olympe des Gouges, author of *Declaration of the Rights of Women,* and Claire Lacombe and Pauline Leon, founders of the Société de Citoyennes Républicaines Révolutionnaires, were arrested. Rioting during the revolution invited the age-old claim that women were shrews, and evidence suggest that after rioting people seemed relatively accepting of returning to business and performing usual social roles.[32] I have already touched on Rousseau's rejection of the salons, but it is interesting to note that Wollstonecraft herself shared a not dissimilar disgust. Often enlightened thinkers who believed that women did have genuine rights could still continue asserting that women should be barred from taking part in politics because of a lack of independence and reason.[33] In many instances, women were prepared to justify only the sort of limited roles offered to them. In a direct response to Wollstonecraft's *Vindication*, Laetitia Hawkins, in *Letters on the Female Mind* (1793), wrote that "it cannot, I think, be truly asserted, that the intellectual powers know no difference of sex. Nature certainly intended a distinction. . . . In general, and almost universally, the feminine intellect has less strength and more acuteness. Consequently in our exercise of it we show less perseverance and more vivacity."[34] Maria Theresa's succession to the throne in 1740 gave birth to eight years of war, in no small part because her aggressors continued to believe (wrongly, it transpired) that the twenty-three-year-old woman would be such a weak head of state that her lands would make easy pickings.

The fact that the reality and efficacy of women's political lives tended to be kept out of general circulation could have worked to relinquish many audience members from the responsibility of finding a critical point of reflection in contemporary reality for Vitellia. As a result, the way would have been relatively open for giving free reign to the paranoid projecting onto the allegory of prevalent sexist prejudices, allowing them easily to coalesce into the conviction that "of course that's how a woman *would* act in such a situation." Ironically, therefore, it is precisely the fantasmatic potential of Vitellia to a late eighteenth-century audience that might have grounded the allegory's credibility as verisimilitude; to return to the language of my introduction, *Clemenza*'s ability to enchant is focused around something that, in relationship to reality, retains a distance. In this context, the patchy quality of the Titus portrait might therefore have functioned like the looser attention to detail in the background of a painting: in other words, counterintuitively, as something against which the distance (Vitellia) could then stand out.

THE PARADOXICAL LIFE OF ARTIFICE

When we forget the strings, puppets start magically to move as if by their own volition – this is a common popular trope regarding enchantment. But this notion is not fully applicable in this instance, for this allegory works because part of it (Vitellia) doesn't. Vitellia never manages to appear as fully autonomous; being a woman, something of the puppet must in this particular ideological context remain. So far we have seen that

Vitellia is a *representation* of something that doesn't work. However, I have assumed that the material *mechanics* of her representation have successfully left no perceptible trace of themselves in the final enchanting effect. What I wish to suggest now, however, is that such a disenchanting smudge would have been available to an audience's perceptions. To do so, I turn to Vitellia's famous rondò no. 23, "Non più di fiori."

Alan Tyson's examination of the paper types suggests that this rondò was composed in two stages, the opening *larghetto* being written shortly before the first performance, but the concluding allegro preexisting Mozart's work on the opera.[35] The fact that "Non più di fiori" is sown together from this-and-that may well have threatened to topple its aesthetic appearance into the unintentionally mechanistic. This being the case, it would have challenged Mozart's own aesthetic allegiances, which tended to work according to an attempt to find a balancing point between two principles. On the one hand, like earlier eighteenth-century neoclassicists, Mozart asserts that art should retain its relationship to artifice. Thus, in the famous letter to his father regarding Osmin's rage (26 September 1781) Mozart bluntly states that the "music, even in the most terrible situations, must still give pleasure and never offend the ear, that is, must always remain *music*."[36] On the other hand, Mozart also wished to create the impression that what we are experiencing is more than just an artifice. And so in another letter to his father, this time regarding the subterranean oracular voice in *Idomeneo* (29 November 1780), Mozart writes that "the voice must be terrifying – must penetrate.... The audience must believe it really exists."[37]

Admittedly, there is no binding reason why an aspect of this rondò's compositional history should have communicated itself to a late eighteenth-century audience, particularly since late eighteenth-century *opera seria* practices were pervaded by aria substitution, pasticcio, the primacy of performance and performer, and a generally more pragmatic approach to the theory of artistic production. However, as Rice has pointed out, the compositional history of the music means that Mozart composed the allegro of the rondò with no knowledge of the singer who would eventually perform the role of Vitellia at the first performance, Maria Marchetti Fantozzi. Rice's analysis of the kinds of musics that composers tended to write for Fantozzi's voice suggests that certain passages in

Clemenza would therefore have been very awkward for her to sing. As the letters repeatedly attest, the particularity of specific singers' voices was very much a consideration in Mozart's attempts at creating realistically convincing operatic characters. And so the limits of Fantozzi's voice in relation to the music may well have drawn attention to the limits of the composition's integrity as a coherent artifice capable of creating a credible representational illusion.[38]

These are more pragmatic, contingent concerns. However, "Non più di fiori" also threatens to disenchant itself because of more formalist issues arising from its framing between two particularly successful moments of musical expression: no. 21, "S'altro che lacrime," Servilia's entreaty that Vitellia plead to Titus for Sextus's life,[39] and the opening chorus in honor of Titus, no. 24, "Che del ciel," which starts the final scene.[40] In both cases, the high quality of expression results from the sustaining of the Mozartean balancing act outlined above between the laws of musical artifice and the need for convincing verisimilitude.

Originating in Servilia's sentiments, "S'altro che lacrime" appears effortlessly to find embodiment in Servilia's music and then pass through to Vitellia and us; it is as if its untarnished emotional authenticity has magically made it indifferent to the walls through which it wafts. In a paradox that has often been seen as defining of effective aesthetic enchantment, Servilia seems to erase the material mechanics of her own representation by means of the very song that that representational mechanics creates, as if an artifice were being negated by the very ground of its own artificiality. As a result, the effect of a delicate and almost imperceptible blending is achieved between, on the one hand, nature and the body presenting themselves as if without cultural mediation to our aural gaze, and, on the other hand, the culturally produced artifices of musical technique and style, which are what allows in fact for this presentation to occur. Nature presents itself initially in the subtly etched continuous background of lightly pulsating eighth notes that delicately flow into aural view in the two measures of orchestral introduction, and then, in gentle sinuous fashion, thread their way through the landscape of the musical fabric, every now and again calmly gurgling to the melodic surface of the composition, particularly at the breaks between the vocal phrases and in the brief orchestral coda. It is a musical landscape resting calmly in the cool shadowy half-light between images of soft breezes and quietly rippling brooks. The body makes its presence felt in the form of Servilia's sighs, which emanate from her out into her melodic line and then are delicately echoed in softly padded *fortepianos* and *sforzandos* within the natural landscape of the instrumental backdrop, like a pathetic fallacy.

Such subtle pictorial intimations are framed by and also constitute the culturally grounded compositional artifices. As is typical, the undulating and regular rhythmic background helps the basic underlying rhythmic gesture of the aria to measure itself *out* into the tempo of a minuet – a dance form that, although somewhat outdated in the ballrooms by the end of the eighteenth century, could still be assumed to create the affect of a "noble and pleasing propriety, but joined with simplicity,"[41] as J. G. Sulzer writes. And yet this background simultaneously is measured *into* ordered rational musical perspective by means of the minuet's consistent cycle of three-beat measures. More specifically, however, Servilia's sighs are both coopted into articulating phrase structure and also play an active role in producing subtleties within that structure, helping to annul any hint of vulgarity from its potential four-squareness. In the opening four measures, descending sighing gestures (**a**) occur in the second and fourth measures, both adding eloquence to the divide between the two two-measure units, and modestly drawing our awareness to the motivic relations that link them (Example 4.1). Finally, in mm. 7–10, we are presented with a descending sequence of these sighs, growing out of the melodic pitch contour (**n + o**) of mm. 5–6, and creating a four-measure unit that is more continuously fused in comparison with the more literal two-measure unit orientation characterizing her opening four measures (Example 4.2). The overall impression is of a sensitively flexible, seamless entity, one that appears autonomously to define a boundary and then accept as natural the sense and good taste in not transgressing it. The minuet, after all, is "the queen of all dances . . . the best occasion for displaying everything beautiful and charming in nature which a body is capable of employing."[42] Unity and variety balance each other out in a dance between artifice and the real. Or, as Kant put it, "Art can only be termed beautiful, where we are conscious of its being art, while yet it has the appearance of nature."[43]

4.1. "S'altro che lacrime," measures 3–6, motivic relations

4.2. "S'altro che lacrime," measures 3–10, motivic relations

A similarly convincing focused expression is also created on the other side of Vitellia's aria, in the grandly sublime Handelian chorus "Che del ciel."[44] Here the image that presents its reality to us is of autonomous, free-thinking individuals, drawn magnetically together as if by the natural instinct of a general will into a benign, non-coercive social contract. To return to earlier terms, ethics creates politics from below. Again, a boundary is defined and the law against its transgression seemingly experienced by the protagonists within the representation as benignly beneficial and empowering. The orchestral introduction in the elevated French overture style emanates the authority of its origins in Absolutism's processionals, yet the potentially restrictive formalities that the style might invoke engender the opposite image of spontaneity. The voices of the Roman citizens appear, as if without premeditation, to suddenly coalesce into rhythmically unified choral pronouncement. Entering on the second beat, as if the spectacle they both witness and participate in keeps them momentarily stunned with awe, they then burst into life with their first exclamation, magically inspired simultaneously to sing the same music as if it were all nevertheless unscripted.[45]

The success of both "S'altro che lacrime" and "Che del ciel" arises from their shared tendency toward what appears to have been an easily achieved synthesis, consistency, and homogeneity of musical expression. In contrast, Vitellia's music, sandwiched in between, is all juxtaposition and superimposition, fracture, edge, and seam. Of course, in the world of operatic representation, whose high points have often been constituted by mad scenes for women, it hardly holds water to assert that such surface disarray would, by definition, constitute an effect of distracting artifice. We could even assume the opposite, that the expressive disjuncture of Vitellia's music is in fact what helps to constitute the convincing presence of her emotional state. However, at four points during the rondò, the potential for such disjunction to appear negatively is exacerbated by the somewhat warped character of a musical idea first introduced in the obbligato basset horn part and immediately repeated by Vitellia. With its paper-thin sincerity, weakly sentimental pathos, and rather saccharine and insinuating chromaticism, its effect threatens to fail to transcend the materials from which it is made. It is thus no effect at all, for as Rousseau, for example, states, "Something is 'effective' when the sensation produced seems superior to the means employed in creating it."[46] In Mozart's terms, it remains music, but in too literally a material sense, and so might "offend the ear" and no longer "give pleasure." There is a kind of grotesque literalness to its motivic, phrase, and harmonic structures, which stands it in sharp contrast to the effortless and modestly inconspicuous subtleties of Servilia's melodic material. This is particularly emphatic when (in both mm. 56–60 and 109–113) it is spread across a clodhopping march accompaniment that makes for slightly difficult aural digestion, like curdled frosting atop a stale piece of cake (Example 4.3 is the first occurrence of this theme).

The theme's artifice is emphasized by means of the rondò's rhetorical structure, for in each instance the presentation of the theme is preceded by a grand, accumulative musical sweep, worthy of comparison with the high tragic style Mozart employs for other heroines, for example Donna Anna in "Or sai chi l'onore." Repeatedly, we are led to expect something more elevated than what we get. Admittedly, the effect of bathos then created by the theme's presentation could establish the empathetic relationship between us and Vitellia that the words associated with the theme would seem to solicit: "Chi vedesse il mio dolore / Pur avria di me pieta" (yet he who could see my distress would have pity on me). Yet

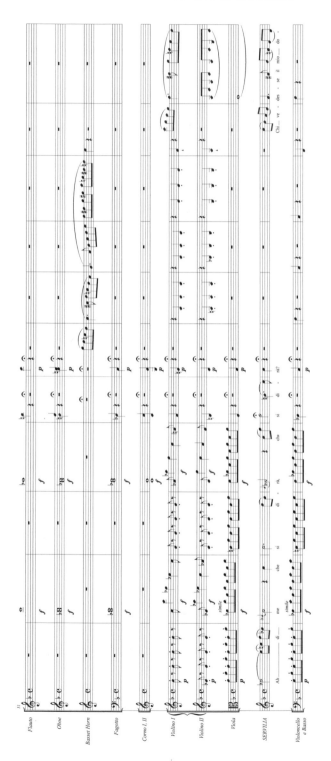

4.3. "Non più di fiori," measures 51–82

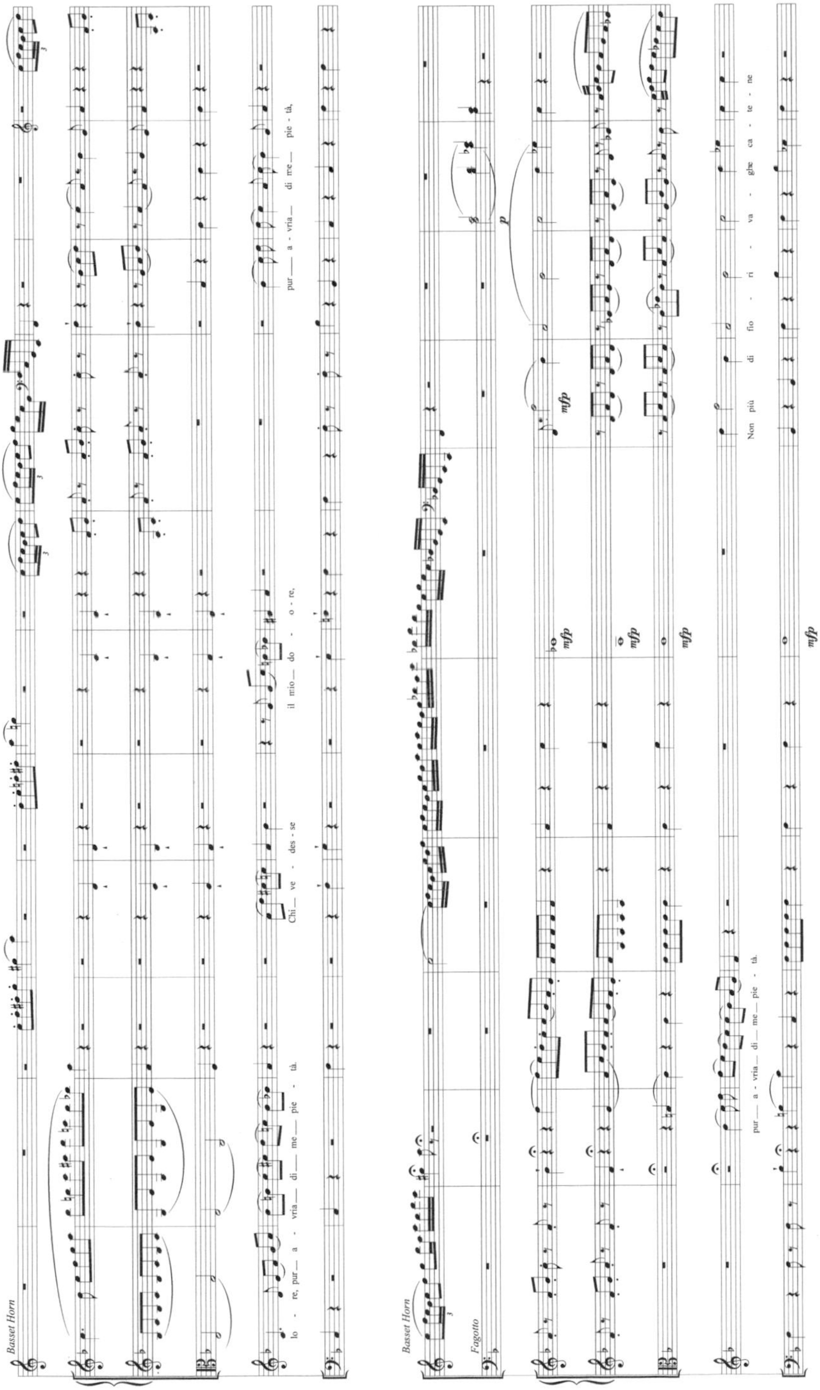
Basset Horn
lo - re, pur__ a - vria__ di__ me__ pie - tà. Chi__ ve - des - se il mio__ do - o - re, pur__ a - vria__ di me__ pie - tà,
Basset Horn
Fagotto
p
mfp
pur__ a - vria__ di__ me__ pie - tà. Non più di fio - ri va - ghe ca - te - ne

if we hear the theme as just pitiful, in the mundane colloquial sense, then the pity it would inspire would not be that of pathos but mean, sneering rejection (as in "I pity you!"). This kind of reading particularly exerts its pressure at the theme's first presentation, where ambiguity exists as to the words to which the theme refers. The theme is first heard in the basset horn, and only then is it grounded by association with the words "Chi vedesse il mio dolore." Therefore, at first the theme could be thought of as an answer to the line of text by which it is preceded: "Ah, di me che si dirà" (Ah, what will be said of me?). The melody provides a sonic analogy to an answer: what will be said is something like this theme, something crudely unsympathetic. It is as if the situation that Vitellia finds herself facing (and indeed, which could result in her own shameful public death) is simply so abject that even the music that should allow us to be convinced of her state of anxious expectation gets crippled. Momentarily, it becomes possible to hear the mechanics of the Vitellia representation in "Non più di fiori" spluttering and stalling. The representation has to be kick-started back into action, and retrained to be convincing. This pedagogical function is performed by the basset horn, which instigates Vitellia's utterances, coaxing her to sing her own music and then celebrating with virtuosic figuration when it appears that the lesson has been learnt and Vitellia has once more reclaimed her elevated, declamatory musical rhetoric with the return of the opening words, "Non più di fiori" (see the whole of Example 4.3).

Against this reading, it could be argued that the contrast here between chromatically saturated melodic expression and simple four-square accompaniment constitutes an effect of stunned tragic shock. And indeed, this kind of melodic writing was soon to become a staple by which such emotions were to be communicated in Italian opera in the first part of the nineteenth century. So the melody can be understood as evidence of the stylistically advanced nature of *Clemenza,* a point that commentators such as Daniel Heartz have urged.[47] However, the historical discourse that predominates in the opera is relatively hostile to progress and the new. Rice, for example, has argued that *Clemenza* was coopted into aiding Leopold's strategic attempts to reinvoke positively the political and cultural atmosphere of the 1760s as a counterfoil to contemporary political tendencies. The 1760s, after all, was a period that many Viennese looked back upon as a golden age before the troubles created by the events of 1789.[48] The minuet of Servilia's aria and the Handelian grandeur of "Che del ciel," both stylistically retrospective, perform an analogous function; this point is underlined by the fact that in each instance the stylistic invocations are aligned with representations of civically correct behavior (Servilia's servility, and the citizen's sublime respect). By comparison, Vitellia's musical arsenal in "Non più di fiori" is oriented strongly toward the present and the future: the rondò form employed in "Non più di fiori" had only recently become fashionable; the basset horn, whose obbligato part in the opera was written for Anton Stadler, was a relatively new invention; and the melodic writing, as noted, was stylistically prophetic. And so within the context of *Clemenza's* presiding historical ideology, the stylistically advanced nature of Vitellia's music would further highlight the potential malfunction of the theme we have been considering. For if Vitellia's rondò breaks a little too easily, it proves itself, in contrast to the enduring qualities of the recent musical past, to be disposable bad composition. And so even though the audience is potentially confronted with aesthetic failure at this moment, the resulting sense of disenchantment can itself be incorporated back into the opera's ability to enchant – at least on the level of its presiding ideological agendas.

AUTONOMY AND THE CONTEXTUAL SUBLIME

Somewhat cynically, we might argue that the act of disenchanting necessitates resisting the passivity of being fully seduced by something in order that one might act upon it more than being acted upon by it. Indeed, without such resistance, it is difficult to imagine any functioning form of critique in relationship to music.[49] But if a cultural product is, as we have just seen, already involved in its own disenchantment, it potentially threatens disenchantment with the embarrassment of appearing comically duped. Confidently, disenchantment strides up to whisk away the illusory veil only to find that it has already started to slip off of its own accord; its intention unexpectedly preempted, disenchantment is left exposed in its redundancy halfway across the hermeneutic stage, the spectacle of its act thus strangely disenchanted. Although Vitellia's little barrel-organ theme can, as I have argued, be made to function within an economy of enchantment, it also has the potential of creating a deliciously spiteful moment of upstaging: a perverse appropriation of the disenchanter's own song before the disenchanter has even had the chance to open her mouth and sing it. It is as if the theme is telling us that there is as much smoke and mirrors required in order to pull off the act of disenchantment as there is for something to enchant in the first place. In *Clemenza* this underlying disorientating joke is capped off by Vitellia's rondò proceeding directly and without break into the following chorus. No time is offered for the distracting artifice of applause, and, thus, no room is made available to contemplate whether what we have just heard may, in fact, have been an artifice. Like Brünnhilde to her immolation pyre, Vitellia runs out of her own disenchanting embrace (if in fact she was ever there anyway) and into the sublime forgetting of the final spectacle; fully reenchanted, she suddenly chooses the magic reality of illusion once more.

Of course, just because the music might make us laugh at disenchantment doesn't mean that disenchantment must leave the stage. Disenchantment could argue, for example, that these aesthetically dissonant moments of artifice in "Non più di fiori" are meant to direct our attention back appreciatively to a seemingly benign moment in eighteenth-century philosophical discourse, one which could then perhaps join company with the other attractive echoes from the past that, as we have already noted, *Clemenza*'s politics puts into circulation. For Diderot, for example, it was perfectly rational to deduce Being from the unambiguous presence of mechanistic artifice. In the *Conversation between Diderot and D'Alembert* (1769), it leads him, hilariously, to articulating exactly how you could come to eat a marble statue, or equate a philosopher with a clavichord.[50] If the illusions of an opera can be fully disenchanted through mechanistic philosophical discourse, then that is nothing to be bemoaned, for so too can we. The musical automata so popular during the eighteenth century were, in part, palliatives against feelings of alienation from the natural world. Thus, when Vitellia is briefly revealed as such we are drawn closer to her, since we are made too. This being the case, the fractures in Vitellia's music are no longer dissonances that disenchant the consoling consonance of operatic illusion, but merely analogous to one side of a normative mid-eighteenth-century mode of perception that ricochets with childlike glee between the presence of Being and its almost magical grounding in a mechanistic causality that is fully available to our understanding. The services of disenchantment are still required, for if puppets were the norm and the distinction between reality and artifice almost moot in the 1760s, then contemporary audiences might still have been prone to being seduced into believing that Vitellia's strings were being pulled by nature – nature functioning here as camouflage for the ideological mechanics. The 1760s, after all, is the decade toward which *Clemenza's* approval is most clearly directed. Disenchantment, thus, still requires disenchantment.

Alternatively, disenchantment might ground her interpretation in the Kantian philosophy of the transcendental subject, which in the 1790s was beginning the process of its influential European dissemination. Contrary to mechanistic assumptions that we are fully determined by nature, Kant asserts that something of us, our status as subject, escapes the necessities of full determination, thus allowing us to hold a viewpoint on how we have been determined. The subject for Kant is in part autonomous, its dignity coming from its ability to separate itself from heteronomy and to live ethically according to how things ought to be, rather than how they are. From this perspective, Vitellia's mechanistic slips can illustrate where she fails to access her own autonomy; they are acknowledgments of her inability to invoke the necessary ethical act of will that would halt the automaton of her actions as they proceed inexorably toward political disaster. This interpretation would substantiate my earlier feminist critique of the questionable aspects of *Clemenza's* representational politics, and so would still necessitate the services of disenchantment.

If it were feeling rather grand, disenchantment might even broaden its contextual horizon to include the overriding sense of instability characterizing the post-1789 era in Europe generally. Indeed, I did a very similar thing in the previous chapter when I located the Viennese classics neither here nor there but in a kind of condition of historical exile suspended between the musical cultures of mimesis and autonomy. After 1789, it was far from certain whether the political upheavals would lead forward into the full realization of Enlightenment freedoms or merely instigate a repressive backlash and a return to the more static and uncritical systems of Baroque despotism. With this in mind, it would be tempting to hear the disorienting slips in *Clemenza* that are instigated by Vitellia's broken theme – from the mechanistic to the transcendent, enchantment to disenchantment, heteronomy and authority to autonomy and freedom – as somehow resonant with the widespread sense of instability. Disenchantment, therefore, would still be required here in order to remind us that Vitellia is functioning as a screen onto which various political anxieties are being projected; it would caution us against delimiting our relations and judgments merely to how we respond to her character.

However, having thus reasserted the import of disenchantment, we do not now have just one Vitellia before us, denuded and in the ideological raw, but three: a Vitellia whose mechanistic orientation indirectly enforces pejorative Enlightenment constructions of women; a Vitellia whose failure to create the illusion of autonomy similarly acts as a negative political indictment on *Clemenza*, working to convince us that women are driven mad by entry into the political sphere; and finally a restless Vitellia, bespeaking the shaky political ground of Europe in the years immediately following 1789. Instead of a narrative of disenchantment, in which the magical seductions of one cultural object are dispelled, we have a Gothic tale in which one seemingly enchanted being has been replaced by three replicants, a trio of Vitellia puppets all moving according to different cultural mechanisms. E. T. A. Hoffman and Edgar Allen Poe loom. Admittedly, we have managed to turn artistic effects into material, into identifiable political, historical, and cultural "stuff." However, the liberating conceptual control that was to be our prize is threatened by the accompanying act of multiplication, and obviously there are many more disenchanted Vitellia puppets that can be produced. We have created a scenario like the sorcerer's apprentice, a nightmare of replication that is only brought to rest when the sorcerer returns and performs a terminating act of magic. So disenchantment has led us into a crisis that can only be concluded by the use of the very thing (magic) that disenchantment was employed to eradicate in the first place. Since at any one time one can only hold a certain amount of readings regarding one cultural object under the controlling power of one's hermeneutic gaze, the object will eventually start to escape us. I have only performed the beginnings of three further disenchantments of Vitellia, but, as musicology now acknowledges, any cultural object can undergo an almost infinite amount of cultural and historical contextualizations. Like the stars in the sky, contexts can easily induce a sense of sublimity, as if the cultural object itself in its singularity nevertheless has acquired the ability to exceed us. As our autonomy in the face of the object starts to wither, the object itself can start to appear as autonomous in our place. Vitellia now conceptualizes us? I argue yes. But many in the academy have been politically motivated to answer with an emphatic no.

THE DISENCHANTED SUBJECT

Musicology of recent decades has worked exceedingly hard to make our engagements with music open up (to human social life, meaning, context, plurality) rather than to focus in (on the autonomous, the enchanting, the separate). To reassert the enchanted autonomy of the object would not just be a blow to a present methodological predilection within the discipline, but to a whole political and ethical project that has worked by tacit assumption: that if music is to be opened out by disenchantment, that is only because we ourselves must be too. Following the lead in part of the essentially linguistic revolutions of postwar continental theory, musicology has sought to disperse the self-sufficient bourgeois autonomy of the subject. From the linguistic perspective this has led to a profound questioning of the assumption that, in effect, we are the light that shines through the words, and thus that we are deep. Continental theory has asserted otherwise; we are flat; the postmodern celebration of surface that I examined in chapter 1 is part and parcel of this assertion. For language precedes us; our words have passed through a potentially infinite number of mouths; abjectly, the regurgitated is always in our throat. Language is exterior to us, Other, and that realization can puncture the fullness of our being with a disenchanting prick, leaving us as but flaccid rubbery swatches of wrinkled color, embarrassed at the memory that once we believed we were taught with the magic ability to float and enchant.

Melancholy and its constrictions are indeed often attendant on these kinds of thoughts. Yet so too is a newly found sense of space and release. For although our linguistic interpolation deflates the puffed-up chest of our autonomy, it also offers us the possibility, if we can get over the shame of no longer being completely self-sufficient, of getting something for nothing – of play rather than work. We are reimbursed for the Fall through a kind of secularized grace. In a similar vein to the material unconscious that I articulated in chapter 2, an autonomous force within language haunts our attempts at static self-containment with an ever-fecund possibility of more. Slavish observance of cultural, political, and subjective injunctions strives at making the molecular structures of language freeze and meanings stabilize. Yet with the addition of but a little warmth, the connections become fluid again and our statements crash, with the iceberg's ecstatic fall, into an ocean swarming with differential others, the infinite deferrals of sound and sense in which then we float and swim, unburdened of the sinking weight of having to be one. At least since the later nineteenth century when, famously, Mallarmé broke the contract between words and external reference and Rimbaud split open the fiction of the first-person singular, stating "Je est un autre," there has been a continuous stream of projects whose intention has been to make us melt: from the automatic writing of the Surrealists to the acrobatic wordplay of Lacan's seminar; from Heidegger's etymological meditations, where "Die Sprache spricht," through Derrida's *différance;* from Joyce's babelic torrent to Cage's linguistic chance operations – a brave new world of epiphanies devoid of God. Moreover, this has been accompanied by a certain revisionist zeal, a project to unmask the seeming stability that had characterized human language life before this revolution and to reveal the robust swarming that fragile appearances had worked so hard to keep from view. We have always been language animals and so the seeming singularity of our cultural products have always been but gateways to journeys along a path of infinite junctions. Vitellia is a post-structuralist martyr *avant la lettre,* a wriggling revolt amidst an authoritarian fossil. Unlike the servile Servilia, that simpering schoolgirl who always tries to hold it together, Vitellia, vital and hot, plays truant from frigid social roleplaying in the name of melting – even if, as it finally transpires, she must forgo applause and in silence suffer Handelian punishments as her reward.

But if we are now, as it were, like satyrs dancing in front of the ancient Ark, it is also the case that, as George Steiner puts it, "the dancers know that the Ark is empty," and so there is nothing in there except the de-individuating sea of differentials.[51] In the name of consistency, we satyrs must then accept our own inherent emptiness and Vitellia's, too. Ergo, we are not authentically enchanted by her, since the intimation of a real presence that would authorize the assumption must be delusional: there must be the presence of some*thing,* singular, not something's immediate dispersal into everything else. At best, what we have is the Mallarmé-like paradox of a real absence. If Vitellia's revolution is indeed a proto-post-structuralist one, then it must be done in the name of a particularly postmodern kind of subject, one that, in comparison with the subject of modernity, has learned to live with this absence.

The subject of modernity was not so much a disenchanted being as the agency that enacted disenchantment. It removed the barriers created by enchantment and so transformed nature into material stuff that could be understood and hence made vulnerable through instrumental reason to being exploited for the sake of increased human happiness and material well-being. However, this modern subject never had the faith to be fully faithless, and so enchantment was retained on some level. In order to sustain the feeling that its domination over nature was secure, the modern subject felt that it had to preserve itself from the threat of what might happen if its own disenchanting gaze, in a moment of auto-sadistic self-reflection, should turn back upon itself and so transform it into a merely material object, which, like nature, could then be dominated and exploited. Disenchantment had already had considerable success in performing this maneuver on sovereignty during the course of the seventeenth and eighteenth centuries, and so such fears were not groundless. Even though heads might be cut off, crowns still had to be worn. The subject had to remain sovereign, its innermost core magically protected within an enchanted circle. Music was one of the means by which this sleight of hand was to be achieved.

This is Daniel Chua's basic argument in his virtuosic *Absolute Music and the Construction of Meaning.* Faced increasingly with a possible void within subjectivity, modernity turns to music and constructs a paradoxical discourse in which music's semantic vagueness is no longer a marker of its insufficiency but the sign by which the presence of a higher meaning, trumping petty linguistic specificity, can be accessed.

Through music's inability to mean in a normative sense, meaning, in its broader metaphysical sense, was guaranteed, and the disenchanter, thus, could still appear to itself and others as enchanted. Deep in his heart was the very thing that music seemed to point toward beyond the clouds. Through the authority of the feelings engendered by reverberations and resonances between himself and music, he could validate the proximity, even identity, between the interior of his subjectivity and the metaphysical exterior beyond normal existence. There was a certain redemptive political collateral to be gained from the sudden electric shock between these two seemingly polarized positions. For if the undoubted disappointments and disasters of broken quotidian life could momentarily be avoided through music, as if the aesthetic created a bridge between the interior and the beyond, then that could give fuel to the utopian hope that present conditions could be negated and that humanity might sublate itself into a higher state of grace.[52]

But humanity never did. As many in musicology have argued, if the history of the twentieth century is anything to go by, Utopia, preserved like an enchanted fly in the disenchanted world of modernity, has been successful at creating nothing but human atrocities. Totalitarian regimes are driven on utopian gas; if you want to bring such horrors to cessation, then cut off the fuel supply. Chua's argument against utopic enchantment works according to a kind of amused squeamishness, poking fun at the hyperbolic nature of absolute music's claims (in Romanticism) and the somewhat agonized indulgence of the bathos that some (mainly Adorno) have felt regarding its failure to fulfill them after the negative turn taken by the French Revolution: "The endless negations and negotiations of Utopia can be a tedious business." For Chua, it is as if a basic commonsense understanding of the limited shelf life of human emotions will eventually trump such higher ideals: "It does not take long for eschatological desire to sink into procrastination; *kairos* soon dissipates into *ennui*." After all, "for how long can the aesthetic stall the end before it wears itself out and resigns its fate to the everyday?"[53] And so, for example, "Romanticism fizzles out and flops into the lethargy of post-apocalyptic depression, and betrays its own ideals."[54]

We should note that Chua's argument here is a strongly behavioralist one, and for all the comic brilliance of its theoretical *aperçus*, its solution – even with its strongly theological flavorings – frequently concurs with predominant musicological positions within the academy. It constitutes the basics of what I would call postmodern disenchantment: instead of trying to preserve the possibility of an enchanted real presence by endlessly attempting to resuture the divide between the autonomous subject and the metaphysical beyond, we should, once and for all, just let the bridge collapse and let ourselves fall into the "real" world in between which we have been so keen to avoid. Thus, in the Biedermeier world after the Congress of Vienna, "by dispensing with the absolute, music returned from theory back into social praxis in which songs, both with and without words, became the harmonic structure for an honest, stable bourgeois life. . . . Life goes on and society elaborates. . . . Music returns to normal."[55] Chua's remark is in part tongue in cheek and he is careful not to make an ideal out of "the Biedermeier world of sausages, beer and kitsch."[56] But his conclusion is, nevertheless, a call for a life lived within more modest parameters. Our music is made by us, and thus there is no need for us to call upon a kind of secularized religious attitude in order to justify the effect that it can create. The fact that we can articulate – through sociological, contextual, historical, and anthropological practices – many of the reasons for why it does the things to us it does should not dispel those things, as if knowing were a kind of profanity. To act in such a fashion is to lack the faith to be faithless; it is to turn one's back on the possibility of being fully emancipated finally into human finitude; it is to fail to stand in the space that is lit neither by sovereignty nor God, but by us, by humans. To reassert enchantment would be to negate the emergence, at last, of a truly human politics. And so at stake here is a claim regarding what constitutes the human.

For postmodern disenchantment, the human is in part revealed through an act of deconstitution, by pulling out the metaphysical plug in the enchanted dam of subjectivity and letting the aforementioned immanent differential torrent of language flood forth into the arid plane. As a result, the human is no longer constituted by a proprietorial stance in which it holds onto the content of "who it is," but becomes becoming itself, an endless flowing forth, a richness birthed from a void. Like Vitellia, our inscriptions slip and slide; like the Haydn string quartet discussed in the previous chapter, our statements cannot rest. Our music moves us because it moves and will not be still. However, like the painterly paradox of too much color, where the canvas is so chromatically varied it starts to seem grey, this act of deconstitution also threatens the human with a boredom verging on despair and madness. And so while acknowledging the euphoric dispersal at the center of our being, postmodern disenchantment has also tended to direct our attention toward the virtues, to appropriate McClary's phrase, of conventional wisdom.[57] We have needed to travel forth, but we have also needed homes, and homes cannot be built solely from travel; the desert is endlessly on the move, which is why you shouldn't build a house in the sands. Our dispersal has had to be counterweighted by a fusion, a coming together into identifiable, repeatable *social* patterns that (hopefully) have been formed through accumulated wisdom over time to provide us with the sense of belonging needed to survive the anything we could be. As bell hooks has recently argued, we have needed place, both literally and metaphorically.[58]

An understanding of the mixture of deconstitution and belonging in the postmodern human could be salutary for the creation of a kind of behavioral pragmatism: faced with the death of the old guarantors of human meaning, the subject must confront the polarities of its own constitution and so establish the means by which they must be organized so as to maximize good mental health. However, we could politicize this maneuver by pointing out the similarity between our own potential, via our linguistic inscription, for dispersal and the endless melting into air to which the force of capitalism makes all aspects of human life vulnerable, to nod toward Engels and Marx.[59] The danger here lies in the fact that our own ability to melt, to return to an earlier metaphor of mine, might simply make us indistinguishable from the more frightening melting of capitalism itself, thus eradicating any effective boundary of resistance between us and it.[60] Admittedly, there was a period in the late 1970s when, for example, theorists associated with the collectively oriented French journal *Tel quel* celebrated the resonance between the seemingly pluralizing conditions created by capitalism in the United States and their own project to promote a literary revolution through the kinds of radical linguistic dispersals found in the work of writers such as Bataille, Joyce, and Artaud. But, as Cornel West, amongst many others, has continued to argue, unmediated exposure to market forces and their attendant mentalities has been the cause of a kind of deadening nihilism, a "monumental collapse of meaning, hope, and love." It has led to "a form of sleepwalking from womb to tomb, with the majority of citizens content to focus on private careers and be distracted with stimulating amusements."[61] It has worked to neutralize political life in the United States. As a solution to this, West, much like bell hooks, has urged for the political value of belonging, the weaving together of a community by means of love, to use his characteristic imagery.[62]

Keeping this in mind, we might thus assert that Vitellia's charge into the seeming mausoleum of Absolutism at the end of *La clemenza di Tito* is no more to be mourned than the stabilization of musical conventions at the end of Haydn's op.33, no. 5, discussed in the previous chapter. The reliability of the theme and variations form in the final movement of the Haydn had appeared, at first, as unexpectedly neutralizing after the endless dialogic disruptions of the first three movements. However, it ultimately transpired that this seeming anomaly was in fact dialectically erudite, and that it was precisely through the negation of the dialogue provided by rest that the possibility of dialogue's own survival was guaranteed. Likewise, Vitellia doesn't capitulate; she is just wise enough to have the modesty to acknowledge when she needs to relinquish her transgressions to belonging, and so she gives up on the possibility of being the everything offered by her dispersals and focuses on saner forms of social participation.

POST-IDEOLOGICAL HAPPINESS

If the postmodern disenchanted subject results from a balancing act between falling away and coming together, fission and fusion, it therefore necessitates marginalizing (sometimes rejecting, *tout court*) the specific singularity of the autonomous individual and its particular agency – a source from which enchantment is often authorized. For both polarities of the disenchanted subject are different faces of a singular drive toward particular forms of the many: the former toward the many of multifariousness, the infinite array of endlessly transforming differences; the latter toward the more focused many of the community that has organized itself around a set of conventionalized practices. Undoubtedly, faced

with our own attempts stubbornly to remain in sole ownership of ourselves, there is much to be admired about giving it up. As the perverse
economy of miserliness illustrates, by keeping what you think you have
solely for yourself you can end up with the feeling that you have nothing
at all. There is little that unclots our being quite so effectively as being
made to fall apart with laughter (fission) or to concentrate our focus away
from ourselves and onto some kind of group activity (fusion). Promot-
ing a release of tension, such activities can easily make us happy, and we
might argue that one of the functions of postmodernism's project of fully
disenchanting the subject is to create such a possibility, by encouraging
the heroic autonomous subject of modernity to become a more humble,
modest, playful thing. Again, Vitellia is inspirational, for she apparently
relinquishes herself from the awful death-drive of her self-involvement
and opts for the pleasure principle of the good life.[63]

But there is a potential danger with this project. As certain symptoms of the contemporary world show, the reorganization of human life
around the perspectival focal point of, note, a *certain* notion of happiness
has worked to transform "giving it up," the relinquishment of individual
autonomy, into an ideological injunction. And this is paradoxical, for the
postmodern disenchanted subject has often been presented as if it were
thoroughly congruent with the production, sustaining, and maintenance
of the kind of *post*-ideological world epitomized famously in Francis
Fukuyama's early *The End of History and the Last Man*.

Fukuyama's argument had been that with the end of European communism we finally left behind the epoch of grand political causes that
had begun with the French Revolution (in effect, Utopia), and so were
then free to enter the "Post-Communist Condition," a world in which we
could sensibly understand that the forms of late capitalism, with perhaps
a little tweaking here and there, could be reconciled with the furthering
of a kind of global democratic cosmopolitanism.[64] At the ground level,
this new post-ideological cosmopolitanism would work by means of the
endless dialogue and negotiation between, essentially, postmodern disenchanted subjects who have accepted the humble limitations of human
finitude and so concern themselves with pragmatic concerns brought
to attention by the here-and-now – that is, rather than being distracted
by the impossible beyond-and-never of the transformative revolution-

ary politics of modernity, which postmodernists sometimes reject as totalitarian. The endlessness within the dialogue would bespeak of the fact that with the demise of Utopia the human project becomes constitutively open, and this openness resonates harmoniously with the infinite dispersals constituting one pole of the postmodern disenchanted subject's orientation. The construction of the subject and the construction of the politics coincide. Conversely, the dialogue within the endlessness bespeaks of the need for reconciliations, however temporary, as a means of stabilizing the resultant transformations so that they can become livable. Again, there is a coincidence of political and subject constructions, political stabilizations here corresponding to the opposite pole of the postmodern disenchanted subject, its orientation toward belonging. The message, therefore, would seem to be that if we are now either working toward, or have in part achieved, a post-ideological world, that is because we are post-ideological subjects. Part and whole have ultimately coincided in a benevolent way, communicating to us that we have seemingly chosen to be free (open and endless) to belong (dialogue and rest). Moreover, if the forms of late capitalism are, as Fukuyama had then argued, what allow for this coincidence that opens up the possibility of our choice, then it too is post-ideological. So we have chosen to be free to belong to late capitalism.

But what if our endless, post-ideological dialogue were to lead us to the choice of being free to belong to something *other* than late capitalism? A pro-forma "happy" post-ideological answer would be that if we chose such, we would be choosing to give up the right to choice, and so in the name of choice we have to not make that choice. This being the case, post-ideological life then deflates somewhat into being the product of having accepted what Lacanians might call a "forced choice" – of having to accept the choice of the already existing frame of the economy.[65] As Žižek writes, the community to which a subject belongs states the following, that "you have freedom to choose, but on condition that you choose the right thing . . . If you make the wrong choice, you lose freedom of choice itself." In other words, "the subject must freely choose the community to which he already belongs, independent of his choice – *he must choose what is already given to him.*" And so: "The point is that he is never actually in a position to choose."[66]

Tautologically, choice only comes into focus within the frame of human agency when we are presented with a situation where there is the possibility of choosing. When it is immediately deemed obvious which thing we (ought to) want, we are dealing with a situation that is focused more around either coercion, or something akin to desire, attraction, or perhaps even instinct. What threatens within the happy politics of the so-called post-ideological world, therefore, is that politics starts to be organized around a particularly postmodern oxymoron, which I call instinctual choice. In instinctual choice, decisions are no longer organized around an initial act of will residing in the autonomy of a particular individual agency resisting the immediacy of certain instinctual gratifications in the name of opening up a space for something other that, as of yet, does not exist. For postmodern musicological discourse, such "heroic" restraint is viewed as self-denying, even as a source of gross ethical abuse and totalitarian indifference. In the post-ideological world, agency is now directed primarily toward resisting the forces that would try to dissuade us from committing ourselves to removing the debilitating barriers that stand between us and our instinctual gratifications. We train ourselves to open up a space that will allow for our immediacy in relationship to what *already* exists.

There are, of course, situations where fighting to allow the human access to its instinctual choices can be liberating and politically productive. For example, in most instances a gay man does not in any obvious way choose to be sexually aroused by men. The politics that fights for the rights of gay men is often, therefore, a particular instance of politics being made in the name of allowing for safety to be created around the public acknowledgment of activities that certain humans have, to a degree, *not* chosen. Queer politics, in short, has asserted that sexuality is attraction, not distraction; it is neither a choice nor an addiction that disenables one from making the "right" choice. A similarly structured political discourse can also be seen in the "coming out" phenomena amongst First World Western composers in the 1970s and 1980s. Fighting against what some have seen as the indoctrination created by dogmatic, postwar modernist aesthetic ideology, many composers started composing their music in accordance with the music they were (instinctually) attracted toward, rather than continuing to struggle to sustain fidelity to what they perceived as an increasingly constrictive and forced modernist "choice."

Talking of the spirit of 1968, the British composer Robin Holloway has said, "Things were absolutely forbidden."[67] As a result, when Holloway in 1970 wrote his Schumann-inspired piece, *Scenes from Schumann*, he felt "anxious, guilty and confused. And when the Festival people wanted to see a movement in advance, I posted it off with shame. I felt as if I'd committed some kind of crime."[68] Holloway states that he felt barred from "basically everything that I loved most: what seemed to me essential to the very nature of music, which was something that bubbled and flowed forth and gave simple pleasure."[69] In other words, not something chosen so much as something instinctually felt; for Holloway, composition without prohibition amounts to a kind of homage to one's desires, as if the composer were transforming from a human agency that makes choices into part of the flow of nature itself: "One turns like a grateful plant towards all kinds of very contrasted composers who excite and please one, and pays them for what one takes in the form of a stylistic or technical homage."[70] In the case of David Del Tredici, the logic of instinctual choice is made even more unambiguous: his coming out as a homosexual man being presented as practically synonymous with his turn as a composer to tonality.

But this happy politics, founded as it is on the liberating oxymoron of instinctual choice, easily gets caught up in something else. For example, in a recent and important book on comedy, the Slovenian philosopher Alenka Zupančič questions the common postwar, First World belief that true ideology, contrary to the practices of liberal society, functions solely by means of the unambiguous dogmatic force of oppression. Rather, the happiness produced by "ironic distance and laughter often function as an internal condition of all true ideology," because ideology "has a firm hold on us precisely where we feel most free and autonomous."[71] As Lacanian psychoanalysis argues, our feelings (or affects) are not signifiers, and so, with the notable exception for Lacan of anxiety, they can easily lie. Thus, what we feel to be a protective distance from oppressive control can quite easily transpire to be the motor of control itself. For Zupančič, it is this potentially deceptive lure attendant on affect that has allowed for the contemporary ideological conscription of happiness, whose primary and spectacularly pervasive symptom is the rise of what she calls a "bio-morality (as well as a morality of feelings and emotions)."[72] This new morality works by creating a "short-circuit between the immediate feelings/sensations and the moral value," which we might understand as follows.[73]

At one time, fighting to allow for a deregulation of the prohibitions barring certain groups from their instinctual choices could function as a form of political dissent; the moral judgment was directed primarily toward the offenses committed by hegemonic power structures. Those liberated to make their instinctual choices were maybe now happy to be able to do so, but that happiness did not necessarily morally script them for themselves as any more good or bad than they had been before – although it may well have politically scripted themselves in a better light. By contrast, in the "post-ideological" environment beginning in the early 1990s, what starts to develop is a situation in which subjects now strive at being able to view themselves as good *as a result* of managing to have made themselves happy for being free to act on their instinctual choices. Instinctual choice has, therefore, now been instrumentalized within a certain scene of the super-ego; it is a means by which the subject attempts to relinquish itself from guilt, rather than the means by which it refuses repressive hegemonic power. It is like the archetypical bad New Year's Eve party, whereby if one is unable to have a good time, then one quickly feels that one only has oneself to blame. And so one either leaves – in ideological terms, one excludes oneself from the event – or one tries to hide that part of oneself that might betray one's inherent badness. To conflate two colloquialisms, one gives it up in order to get over it, and in some party situations this is perhaps a good thing.

However, as many a testament of rape shows, not every party is organized around the Good. For example, we might say that in the terms of the contemporary bio-moral universe, the good gay man is he who has made himself happy through his liberated sexual life.[74] But we could take this further and argue that the increased presence of images of gay (and predominantly white) men comes from the fact that as the notion of homosexual acts becomes in certain media locations less shocking (i.e., less of a hindrance to the accumulation of capital), gay men have become a decidedly useful means of successfully keeping in circulation the ideological short-circuit between goodness and happiness, between ethics and feelings. Moreover, since what allows for the circulation of this ideological rhetoric is essentially capitalism itself, the following message is often attendant: that by politically liberating marginalized groups so that they can step out of the shadows of censorship and into the bright light of circulation within the existent economic form, we are allowing them to transform themselves into the happy good. This, in turn, creates another effective set of short circuits: because the happy, bio-moral goodness of the gay man arises from the oxymoron of his instinctual choice, and because that instinctual choice can be happily made to reside within the economy, then the presently existing form of the economy must be our instinctual choice also.

Capitalism starts to be conflated with biology, as, for example, the highly successful show *Queer Eye for the Straight Guy* attested. Here instinctual and economic lives interpenetrated and gay men appeared as commodities that can tell us how to purchase other commodities. It was as if a common premodern and non-Western inscription of the gay man as shaman now returned: gay men, scripted as instinctual beings – the shaman, after all, can speak to animals and understand the language of the trees – come out of their domain at the peripheries of the community and perform the necessary acts of medicinal magic (retail therapy) that allows the ideologically centralized "straight guy" to realign himself with the nature surrounding him and within him. In short, through gay men (amongst others) capitalism can appear as nature. It is part of a contemporary tendency in which, in Zupančič's words, "our present socioeconomic reality is increasingly being presented as an immediate *natural* fact, or fact of nature, and thus a fact to which we can only try and adapt as successfully as possible" – through the help of gay men, for example.[75]

But capitalism, obviously, is not nature, and this explains why a kind of super-egoic structure is necessitated in order to keep us contained within the illusion that we should, "by nature," be happy. As Zupančič puts it, "The unhappy and the unsuccessful are somehow [perceived now as] corrupt already on the level of their bare life," as if they were in fact a different race.[76] Therefore, post-ideological happiness is a vital constituent of a new contemporary racism, one which no longer tends to

"socialize biological features," thus translating them into the sociosymbolic order, but, rather, "tends to 'naturalize' the differences and features
produced by the sociosymbolic order" itself – as if, for example, disparity
in the distribution of wealth and the unhappiness it brings to the poor
were a sign of "human differences" resulting from a failure of some to
adapt to nature.[77] The seeming predominant *individual* orientation of
post-ideological happiness around the attempt to create an immediacy
of relationship to our instinctual gratifications is, therefore, deceptive,
since post-ideological happiness is frequently constitutive today of a certain ideologically loaded *social* bond. Moreover, this social bond can be
made to function most effectively when its participants have adapted
their coordinates in terms of the polarities of the disenchanted subject of
postmodernity. For as I have stated above, the functioning of this kind of
subject necessitates a marginalization and even rejection of the specific
singularity of the autonomous individual and its particular agency – in
other words, a defusing of the very force that might effectively resist, and
so say no to, contemporary forms of happiness.

Since this kind of autonomy is a source from which enchantment is
often authorized, we can now start to see how the gesture of disenchantment – seemingly at the foundation of any ideological unmasking – can
itself start to work ideologically. Thus, at this particular historical moment, enchantment potentially returns as ideologically redemptive. If
Vitellia retains fragments of this ability, then, like Haydn's op. 33, no. 5,
perhaps she too waits, both triumphant and sad-eyed, for us to answer.
The fact that, as we have seen, such enchantment only flickers in and
out of possibility – as strategic grace and slippage within the paradoxes
of music's worldly inscriptions – should remind us that, far from being a
pompous form of smug posturing, autonomy is in fact a moment of risk
that sometimes must be seized.

5

Forgetting

(Edward Said)

I started this book by saying no to yes, and out of fidelity to no-saying, I would like to end by saying no to no. But as a result of this consistency of procedure, this book will no longer be consistent. So if there is any conclusion to my investigation, it has already occurred, and what you are now reading is, in effect, an argument that is happening after the end. This does not mean that nothing heretofore will find echo in what happens next. Even if we decide not to talk with our friend about the awful concert we have just attended, it nevertheless casts a certain shadow over our drinks and chat afterward. I am well aware that if you have gotten this far, you may have already had to listen to some quite bad music that might be difficult to forget. It all seemed necessary, even if only time will ultimately tell. But in the meantime, I'd like to indulge in the pleasure and privilege of just being in something different for a moment – precisely, in fact, in order to investigate indifference. So I break the pattern of the rest of this book, which had worked out its philosophical and political arguments around readings of pieces of late eighteenth-century music, and move closer to the present to consider that remarkable and controversial figure of the post-1968 intellectual landscape, Edward Said, who died in 2003. Specifically, I will be concerned with the question of Said's late style, and how it might help us to understand the place for Said of the West-Eastern Divan workshop and orchestra, the project that Said found himself engaged with as a result of his friendship with the conductor Daniel Barenboim and which he often claimed was the most important one of his life.

But if I break the pattern regarding content, I also set my thinking *en route* to breaking the pattern with form, too. For the majority of my arguments so far have been brought into focus by means of a critical perspective founded on the assumed values of a kind of dialectical opening up of music, both in excess of, and also away from, the assumed already-given of human practices and their meanings. My acts of no-saying have thus been less concerned with pruning and more with the possibilities of increased foliation, expansion rather than contraction. Now, however, they will start veering toward a kind of intense and focused form of saying yes to one relatively circumscribed thing, in this instance, musical performance. And as with love – which, we should remember, is constituted by an almost violent sustaining of the choice of one specific object at the expense of the almost infinite array of all the others – this involves, however momentarily, an outrageously indifferent no to everything else, a no that can be almost completely undisturbed by the restless movement of dialectical mediation that characterizes negation proper.

This being the case, one might wonder why Said's late style would be of interest. After all, the general consensus that continues to develop regarding Said's late thinking is that here, more than in any other period in his life – when he could easily break intellectual allegiances and affiliations (to Foucualt, for example) if they threatened to transform into unproductive orthodoxy – the late period was organized around a borderline identification-relationship to one intellectual figure, Theodor Adorno.[1] Famously, in an interview published in *Ha-aretz* in Tel Aviv in 2000, Said even claimed that he was "the only true follower of Adorno."[2] There are many reasons for why the identification would work, not least among them being the profound importance of exile as metaphor and reality for both thinkers; but one of the most compelling is politics. As Moustafa Bayoumi has sensitively articulated, there exists a profound resonance between Said's late perception of the antagonistic deadlock of Israeli-Palestinian relations in the wake of the failure of the Oslo Accords and Adorno's similarly grim perception of late capitalist modernity in general.[3] Indeed, Said's discourse frequently starts speaking fluent Adorno when the topic is on the table. To take but one example: "This is a dialectical conflict. But there is no possible synthesis. In this case, I don't think it's possible to ride out the dialectical contradictions. There is no way I know to reconcile the messianic-driven and Holocaust-driven impulse of the Zionists with the Palestinian impulse to stay on the land. These are fundamentally different impulses. This is why I think the essence of the conflict is its irreconcilability."[4] For the late Said, like Adorno, one must inhabit irreconcilability, make one's home in that nowhere place through the practice of a negative dialectics. Although my study has been far from an extended application of Adorno, negative dialectics, particularly in the third chapter ("Exile"), have never been far away. So why choose Said as a means of moving elsewhere?

In part, to illustrate that if there were signs of something other than Adorno in late Said, then that means that at his death Said had still not arrived. To put pressure on this dissonance and make the fit miss, one retains a certain fidelity to that seemingly inextinguishable intellectual force of exile that, by all accounts, vivified Said to his very end. As I articulate below, for the late Said the search for reconciliation necessitated a refusal of reconciliation, even if, as my own reading tacitly suggests, it produced traces of resistance to the refusal of reconciliation (Adorno) itself. But I also pursue the traces of these tendencies by mildly displacing an invitation given by Said. In the preface to one of his finest late productions, the published conversations with Barenboim, *Parallels and Paradoxes: Explorations in Music and Society* (2003), which I discuss at length, he states that he and Barenboim through dialogue were searching for a certain whole with regard to how music, culture, and politics function in relationship to each other in the modern world. However, "What that whole is, I am happy to say, neither of us can fully state, but we ask our readers, our friends, to join us in trying to find out. After all, these are conversations not treatises, and it is the nature of conversation at its best to be engrossing for everyone involved, as well as from time to time to take even the speaker by surprise."[5] Madly, since he is dead, this final chapter is therefore an attempt to keep Said surprised, and I wonder if that is not the highest compliment one can pay a writer: to show how where they stopped remains fecund.

FROM ONE TO TWO

I would like to begin by considering in detail an interview between Said and the feminist psychoanalytic scholar Jacqueline Rose that first appeared in a volume of the *Jewish Quarterly* in the late 1990s under the title "Returning to Ourselves." The greater part of the interview is concerned with Said's research and political activism regarding the Palestinian question; its initially purported function – at least from Rose's perspective as a Jew conducting it for a publication centered on Jewish issues – was to create "an opportunity for you [Said] to reply to some of the criticisms, not to say misrepresentations, that on occasion you rather dramatically seem to provoke."[6] Rose starts by setting herself up in a relation of difference to Said: "I'm here as a Jewish woman and a feminist with a long-standing commitment to psychoanalytic thinking and, let's face it, none of these epithets could be said to apply to you."[7] But Rose's establishment of a distinction immediately transpires in a following sentence as a means of forging a link: "I'm therefore also hoping that we will have a chance to demonstrate the possibility of undreamt-of forms of dialogue across what have often seemed to be insurmountable barriers of historical difference."[8] The function of the interview now shifts from the judicial (allowing Said the space to defend himself against criticism) to the transformative. Through a kind of microcosmic political logic, Rose implies that if this local-level acknowledgment of each other's difference can open up the possibilities of something that can traverse the "insurmountable barriers" created by difference itself, then maybe there is still hope for a solution to the Israeli-Palestinian conflict.

With laudable sensitivity to the ethical complexities and dangers attendant on their project, Rose and Said set out to defend the attempt of trying to establish the particularity of their own positions and those of Israelis and Palestinians. The goal of this project, as the interview's published title attests, is to allow for some kind of return to ourselves. For Palestinians, the majority of whom live in exile, this for Said means "a return to history, so that we understand what exactly happened, why it happened and who we are. That we are a people from that land, maybe not living there, but with important claims and roots."[9] More broadly, in the background of the interview, one sees a continual configuring of a certain possibility with regard to the metaphor of home. Rather than home being founded on the narcissism of a flatteringly delusional self-identification – always a seductive threat when difference is at stake – the interview insists that our homes must be created in full knowledge of what the facts and truths of our own historical, cultural, and political inscriptions and culpabilities entail. It admits that home seeks the definition of a certain enclosure; but Said's and Rose's utopian aspirations make them question whether that can only be achieved by employing a costly police force to keep others out and residents ignorantly within. This kind of ethics with regard to the conceptualization of home was consistently sustained in Said's work throughout his career, as for example in his vehement criticism of all forms of nationalism.[10]

Unsurprisingly, the body of this interview is allergic to Manichaean-ism, rapidly discharging histamine at its merest suggestion. Said, for example, admits to having spent "a long time criticizing Israel and Israelis"; nevertheless, "one must say that Palestinians have a lot to answer for."[11] Indeed, the interview is littered with anecdotal snapshots that repeatedly undermine possibilities of easily equating the clichéd expectations aroused by difference with the realities of different lives, even with regard to Said and Rose themselves. When Said asserts that "it's very hard to find anybody [in the United States] who's Jewish who doesn't identify with Israel," Rose immediately cuts him off: "I know lots, Edward, I know lots of Jews in the United States who don't identify with Israel. We speak to different people. Clearly we do."[12] The force of her injunction against Said's cliché is given weight by the fact that she has just acknowledged how American Jews themselves can be prone to a similarly crude and unproductive reductionism. She recounts the frankly depressing story of how a distinguished literary critic at Yale University where she had been giving a lecture asked her over lunch whether she had any Jewish blood in her. Rose says she replied that "as far as I knew I had only 'Jewish blood' in me."[13] In response to Rose's own question as to why the critic had asked such a question in the first place, the critic replied: "Because we thought you were Jewish, and then we realized you couldn't be, because in your lecture you cited Edward Said."[14]

It is as if the interview had been organized around a refusal of censorship with regard to the particulars that can dissonantly mar the hoped-for conceptual consonance of identified differences. And as the above examples attest, the result in part of this insistence on a kind of infinite particularity is, paradoxically, an increasing interpenetration of the constituent features of each position within the dichotomy, and, therefore, a dissolution of difference per se. Emergent in the dialogue, then, is an incipient ethics organized around the notion of sameness. Remaining consistent with the micro-to-macro political aspirations of the dialogue, this subtle muddying of the distinctions between Rose and Said, Jew and Palestinian, finds resonance in Said's assertion that a solution to the conflict will not be found by attempting to separate the two peoples. "I'm one of the few people who says that our history as Palestinians today is so inextricably bound up with that of Jews that the whole idea of separation, which is what the peace process [in particular the Oslo Accords] is all about – to have a separate Palestinian thing and separate Jewish thing – is doomed. It can't possibly work."[15] There is nothing glibly idealistic fueling Said's statement, nor of contradiction – even though, under a page later, he admits that even though he himself has frequently felt a great affinity with Jews, "there is a deep – and I say this with great sorrow as perhaps the hardest thing to accept – irreconcilability between Arab and Jew which in my generation will not be overcome."[16] Rather, it is that for Said astute and rigorous attention to the historical, cultural, and political facts that constitute the respective differences of Israelis and Palestinians means that their political fates cannot be fully differentiated, even though, simultaneously, they cannot be reconciled either. The continuing antagonism leaves the politics of difference at work here in an awkward state of suspension; nevertheless, it seems that the only way forward when faced with this differential problematic is to retain fidelity to difference itself. And for Said that in part means a kind of Enlightenment fidelity to the truth to be found in facts.[17] As he states: "I believe in facts and very often the facts get abused, or left out, or embroidered or hidden or forgotten."[18] Similarly: "I think Officials always lie. . . . It is therefore the role of the intellectual, at least as I see it, to keep challenging them, to name names and cite facts."[19] One must never forget – neither what has been, nor what continues to remain the case.

By the time we get toward the end of the interview, this characteristically Saidian practice has accumulated considerable force. So it is noteworthy that on the cusp of conclusion, Rose, as the person asking the questions, resists the temptation to draw the threads together neatly into the tight knot of some kind of final affirmation. It could be argued that such a turning away from the expected is congruent with the ethics and politics in which she and Said have just been involved, a practice that, as we have seen, resists taking up residence in anything that can be too easily identified with – even if, as is the case here, it would be an identification with not identifying. Rose's final swerve can therefore be viewed strategically (dialectically even) in a manner that would link it with the kinds of conclusions reached in earlier chapters of this book: in chapter 3, for example, we witnessed the finale of a Haydn string quartet capitulating to the law of convention precisely in order to keep open the possibility of critical resistance to the law – the seeming arrival at home actualizing, on the contrary, the continuing possibility of a productive exile.

Indeed, it appears that it is precisely such a dialectical paradox that Rose is expecting when in her final question she directs the discussion toward Said's more recent work. Rose here refers to a lecture she heard Said give at the Collège de France on Mozart's operas, a lecture that had struck her because it had introduced a new figure into Said's intellectual concerns: death.[20] As the interview attests, Said's work, particularly under the aegis of the term "worldliness," has always been primarily concerned with a rigorous situating of human action and production within its social and historical contexts, if, admittedly, in their constantly shifting, complex states. By contrast, with this new work it seems to Rose that Said now asserts that "what Mozart understood about death casts its shadow back across the pretensions, the false and killing certainties of social norms and conventional human arrangements."[21] Death, therefore, is in excess of the normative ground on which Said's politics has stood and acted from. And so Rose asks: "How can [this] kind of insight be linked into the kind of political vision and hopes you have for the future?"[22] Her question remains consistent with both Said's and her own position throughout the interview: that by insisting on the particularities that constitute a difference (in this case that a discourse on death dissonantly coexists with a presiding discourse on truth in Said's work) we might find the means of forging a link and creating a consonance.

Said's blunt answer brings such hopes to a halt marking their limit: "I don't think it can."[23]

Death, it would seem, is so absolute a difference as to be beyond redemptive mediation by human social, cultural and political life. So different, in fact, that it constitutes a kind of purely formal *indifference,* which, through its complete lack of concern for the particularity of who we are, casts a shadow over us that makes us shudder. In comparison with the products of our human interactions, which are made, death simply is. As Said says, "It's there."[24] The fact that we can, to appropriate one of Said's characteristically Gramscian terms, "elaborate" upon it nevertheless has no effect upon it itself, and so its presence makes what we have made (our elaborations) somewhat irrelevant. "It is basically almost Schopenhauerian," Said states; "there's a kind of indistinguishable, seething, endlessly transforming mass into which we are going"[25] – not only us ("we") but also the very politics that has shaped so much of Said's life.

Said admits that his own intellectual turn toward the contemplation of death is far from uninfluenced by personal circumstance; by the time of this interview, he had already been diagnosed with the leukemia that on 25 September 2003 would take his life. Indeed, the theme of death, along with that of late style generally, haunts the writings of Said's final decade – although, we should note, as Mariam C. Said, Said's wife, reminds us in her foreword to the posthumously published *On Late Style,* the roots of Said's investigations go back to the late 1980s, and so precede his diagnosis.[26] But if, on the one hand, death seems to place a limit on the forming of connections, and so cannot, for example, be dialogically reconciled with the politics that Said has just been propounding with Rose; on the other hand, for Said that does not mean that death is only of relevance to those like himself who have at last been condemned terminally to its shadow. There is no strongly sustained allegiance to either Heidegger or Nietzsche in Said's work, although the Nietzschean notion of the "untimely" is recurrent in *On Late Style.* Nevertheless, it is as if in the last years of his life, Said starts formulating a proposition for a new mode of being in the world, a kind of being-toward-death. It is not unlike Heideggerian *Dasein;* but its characteristic feature, contrary to Heidegger's desire for us to remember and be astounded once more by

the being of being, is the not unrelated idea of *forgetting*. In other words, it
is oriented toward a somewhat Nietzschean negation of the fundamental
injunction of Said's political praxis, which continued to assert that human social and political life could only be improved by ever-vigilant and
sophisticated forms of *remembering* .

In Said's remarkable final statement in this interview, it appears first
as if interest in forgetting is being born out of the particularity of Said's
undeniable anger regarding what he perceived as the political failure of
the Israeli-Palestinian peace process. Said had been a member of the
Palestinian National Council from 1977 to 1991, but he became highly
critical of (and as a result ostracized from) the Palestinian Liberation Organization, particularly as a result of his disagreements regarding their
support of Iraq in the Gulf War of 1991 and their acceptance of the 1994
Oslo Accords, which Said considered a betrayal of the Palestinian cause.

But present also is the sense of a more widespread political despair.

> I've become very, very impatient with the idea and the whole project of identity:
> the idea, which produced great interest in the United States in the 1960s and
> which is also present in the return to Islam in the Arab world and elsewhere, that
> people should really focus on themselves and where they come from, their roots,
> and find out about their ancestors. . . . This strikes me as colossally boring and to-
> tally off the mark. I think that's the last thing that we should be thinking about.[27]

Familiar here is Said's long-term distaste for the intoxications of mono-
lithic forms of belonging, such as the aforementioned nationalism. But
while Said was deeply suspicious of the kinds of mythologies that might
arise from a people's attempt to identify with where they came from, he
denied neither that you could establish such things nor that such information could be used effectively for political purposes. If he had done
so, it would then have been impossible for him to articulate a history for
the Palestinian people in order to argue, as he tirelessly did in the torrent of political journalism he wrote, that they had a claim to the land of
which they were being dispossessed. And so if we keep this in mind, the
particular quality of the despair changes hue. For it is as if the terminally
sick Said, looking back, sees himself partially located in the very landscape of the problem he is critiquing. If we argue that we are dealing here
with Said's own late style, then we should note that there is nothing of
autumnal reconciliation in evidence, no benign final point of perspective

attained from which a global validation of a life's work can come clearly into view.[28] Rather than a conclusive One, we get a traumatic Two, as if Said is confronted with the necessity not of closure, but rather, to use his own terms, of another beginning.[29]

As a result, new to this interview's ending is the presence of a force that seems to warp the surface of the formulations that then follow, disenabling them from cohering into a unitary plane that can then effectively reflect what we have come to expect as Said's characteristic credos:

> What's much more interesting is to try to reach out beyond identity to something else, whatever that is. It may be death. It may be an altered state of consciousness that puts you in touch with others more than one normally is. It may be just a state of forgetfulness which, at some point, I think is what we all need – to forget.[30]

The passage begins confidently enough, and when first I read it I expected that by reaching "out beyond identity" Said was simply going to arrive once more back at the densely historicized and contextualized world of facts, truth, and their attendant ethics and politics. But his outstretched hand finds no content solid enough to grasp, just "something else, whatever that is." There is nothing more than the presence of a void, "death," which passes like a cold draft through the spread fingers, making the next sentence briefly seek warming consolation in the slightly ghostly image of some utopian community yet to come: "An altered state of consciousness that puts you in touch with others more than one normally is." But like wisps of cloud in the breeze, the image disperses before it can politically coagulate into project, polemic, or manifesto. Indeed, by the end of the final sentence it is as if politics itself, shamed by the realization of its own immodesty, withdraws to the peripheries, head bent in the face of the fact that perhaps we have now reached a certain limit point within the human project and so all that is left is the acknowledgment of the bald, almost existential fact: that at some point what we all need to do is to forget.

FROM KNOWING TO DOING

If the import of Said's remarks is to be made productively available to my study as it draws toward its end, it will be necessary not to muffle

some of the loaded overtones (potentially Nietzschean) of his concluding infinitive: "to forget." As I will be understanding it here, forgetting is
not an embarrassing oversight (as in "I forgot your name") or, tragically,
the varying degrees of amnesia, a pathological inability to remember.
Nor is it a practice of avoidance whereby we carry on as if normal while
consciously circumventing some potentially disturbing and disruptive
thing – such as when we try to avoid the livid gaze of the homeless person
on the subway for fear that her poverty might draw to our attention the
gross injustices on which our own security has been built. If we have
forgotten, then things, at least while we forget, do not remain the same,
since forgetting is a kind of act of substitution rather than the creation
of an unacknowledged lack. We get caught up by means of excitations
into something else, the mass and force of which, by means of a kind of
physics of human attention, pushes our previous forms of inscription
toward certain peripheries from which they can no longer so easily fully
constitute our being as normally they do. To the degree that forgetting
proves that what we had been beholden to is not all (since we can become
consumed by something else), forgetting can produce acts of negation,
and so is congruent in part with the theoretical orientation of this study.
However, forgetting per se is not dialectical, and so to turn toward it at
this point is, in effect, to bifurcate this study in a manner not without
analogy with the splitting in Said's late work that I have just discussed.
Indeed, this is precisely why Said's work is attractive for this final chapter.
The negations created by forgetting are at best collateral, unintended
moments of grace.

   In the sometimes loosely dialectical procedures that I have employed in this book, singular positions have been revealed as being incapable of effectively dominating a conceptual field; something else makes
its presence felt, disrupting the unity of the first position and disturbing
its initially self-confident stasis into a less certain condition of restlessness. Although neither the original nor subsequent position can fully
constitute itself, both positions nevertheless remain visible within the
conceptual landscape and, as a result, create the impression of a kind of
simultaneous if wonky double focus. This kind of structure is not unlike
the dialectical model that Lydia Goehr uses under the name of "doubling" in *The Quest for Voice*.[31] For example, the opening sections of this

study's first chapter ("Veils") elaborated upon what I called the politics of the mirror – a conceptualization of political space that asserts that the particularity and fluidity of differences can be effectively contained within coherently beneficent social structures. However, over the course of that chapter's conclusion and the two subsequent chapters ("Dreams" and "Exile"), that position became increasingly untenable in the face of illustrations of differences' abilities to exceed their assigned positions within a structure. Neither of the positions was able to fully cancel out the other, and yet neither was the possibility of some kind of liberal compromise available. What remained was a tension field epitomized by the finale of Haydn's op. 33, no. 5: the inextricable superimposition of the comforts arising from a job well done atop the shudder created by the indelible presence of what still remains unsaid. Without wishing to be glib regarding profound differences in content and political stakes, Haydn's movement is formally homologous with Said's vision of Israelis and Palestinians: the inextricable interdependence of their histories means that there can be no two-state option; yet their historical reality is, at present, one of irresolvable conflict. Truth is here upheld through a refusal to forget the reality of this antagonism, through a kind of tarrying with the negative, to appropriate Hegel's famous formulation.[32] This is how those scholars reading through the optic of Adorno have viewed the late Said, as a practice of dialectical suspension.

If we take truth to be the product attained from the difficult and real work of attempting to establish what actually constitutes what has been and is, then forgetting is radical (and tricky) precisely because it is not *grounded* in such things. Said's fact- and truth-oriented practice starts from the premise that we need to be able to sustain a simultaneously wide-angled and detailed view of what exists within a certain politically problematic situation; similarly, dialectics, for all its concern with becoming, must work immanently out from provisional understandings of what is already existent. By comparison, forgetting seeks to close its aperture intensely upon the doing of one particularly focused and concentrated thing that transpires neither to be reliant on the pressing terms of what is already known about a situation, nor (and perhaps most importantly) that interested in them. Crudely put, if truth (dialectical or not) is concerned with allowing for knowledge of the existent, for-

getting is concerned with allowing for the existence of doing through
an indifference to knowledge. Through bearing witness to the traces
of such notions, and also the repercussions of what is revealed when
we put pressure on them, we set Said off in a somewhat different direction to Adorno – however inspiring as a model of dissonant intellectual
autonomy he evidently remained to Said from the mid-1990s onward,
in the wake of the failure of the Oslo Accords and in the face of death.[33]

As a form of closing off, forgetting is of course rife with dangers,
and Said is far from always promulgating what he himself at other times
encourages.[34] There is the obvious concern regarding what potentially
negative repercussions might be attendant on partaking in an aesthetic
practice that could easily veer toward encouraging a kind of active stu-
pidity, or worse. After all, as Said on frequent occasions would state – in
this example, in his acceptance speech on receiving the Prince of Astur-
ias Award for Concord in Spain in 2002 – "Ignorance is not a strategy for
sustained survival."[35] Even Nietzsche, the great philosopher of forgetting, admits that forgetting "is the condition in which one is the least capable of being just."[36] Paradoxically, however, what is also problematic is
how the intoxicating force of a forgetting activity can seduce us into confusing its doing for knowing. It is, after all, exceedingly easy to get caught
up into a kind of narcissistic and slightly puritanical affective economy,
whereby we can only justify the magnificence of the feelings produced
in us by our activities and their attendant excitations if we can convince
ourselves that the affective magnitude is somehow a reflection of the
degree to which the activity is relevant and puts us in connection with
an increased circumference of significance. The problem with forgetting
arises not only when we allow it to produce ignorance, but also when we
are not vigilant about keeping it ignorant enough. For forgetting to be a
value, it must actually forget – be singular, dwell in a kind of indifferent
autonomy that cares little about extending its claims beyond the parameters of its own enclave. Once the potentially fatal equating of feeling
with significance is in place, the radical self-containment of forgetting is
easily negated by the force of the desire that seeks to ascribe meaning. As
a result, what then threatens is that the potentially radical opening up to
something else, which is produced from the closing off of forgetting, will
be neutralized by being reinscribed into what already exists. As I argue

later, this is one of the potential problems with Barenboim's discourse in the conversations with Said. Nevertheless, in certain situations, for example that of Israeli-Palestinian relations – a situation that, with a tentative nod toward Walter Benjamin, we might characterize as "dialectics at a standstill" – the violent impotence of the terms available, even within the situation's present truth, perhaps necessitate the risky implantation of such a practice. After all, as practically every new depressing news story about the area illustrates, the channels through which productive knowledge exchange might occur have, as a result of both deliberate sabotage and mortifying unforeseen repercussions, long since ceased to function. And so in a certain sense, we might productively think of the orchestra along the lines that Said and Barenboim sometimes take, as a form of experimental music, an attempt to see if forgetting might not be a productive alternative.

OUTSIDE IN THE STATE OF EMERGENCY

Since I have just invoked Benjamin, we can remind ourselves of one of his most (even over-) quoted statements, since it will help us to focus further on what seems to be radical about Said's position, at least for contemporary musicology. The quotation comes from the eighth of the "Theses on the Philosophy of History":

> The tradition of the oppressed teaches us that the "state of emergency" in which we live is not the exception but the rule. We must attain to a conception of history that is in keeping with this insight. Then we shall clearly realize that it is our task to bring about a real state of emergency, and this will improve our position in the struggle against Fascism.[37]

Faced with the world in which we live – which for the majority of the world's inhabitants is at least as desperate as when Benjamin was writing – we must produce an appropriate way of knowing ("we must attain to a conception of history in keeping with this insight") in order to make our political actions more effective. The passage is consumed by its prevailing injunction, which, ignoring the attractive high-pitched urgency of the rhetoric, is familiar to most traditional left-wing political projects: that our theories and actions are to be valued according to their success in effecting large-scale structural changes. To give a characteristic recent example, Alain Badiou has asserted that politics is "less the demand of a social fraction or community to be integrated into the existing order than something which touches on a transformation of that order as a whole."[38] But in Said's late work, alongside the continuation of his calls for active intervention, as in the late *Humanism and Democratic Criticism* (2004), there emerges a strongly articulated line in which what is valued in a response to the "state of emergency" is the refusal to assume that anything broadly transformative is being accomplished. Such indifference to the call to action becomes, for Said, a form of defiance and, notably, nearly all his examples in this regard are concerned with aesthetic activity. So we might argue that what happens in Said's late investigations into lateness is that the logic of political action is, in part, superseded by a new logic of the aesthetic, the particularity of whose mode of functioning and significance Said died in the process of working through.

There is the distinct feeling in this work of the excitement following on a revelation, as if Said has been suddenly made aware of something that had been present but never properly understood. And so he attempts to make up for lost time by voraciously consuming a varied feast of different courses including, amongst others, Genet, Adorno, Cavafy, Gould, late Beethoven, Euripides, and Mozart. The poignancy of the fact that the project was left unfinished at his death is in part canceled out by the youthful vigor of the act of consumption itself; and the fact that the meal was never completed means that the force behind the hunger was never brought to cessation and, thus, can be fancifully imagined to continue even though Said has gone. Perhaps hunger, in and of itself, has survived beyond embodiment within the hungry person, as if it could exist in excess of its seemingly definitive functionality, as if it had become a movement that moves for the sake of movement itself. Such a statement is stained by poetic conceit, even though it is meaningful from the psychoanalytic perspective of the drive. Yet it is congruent with what Said considers a primary characteristic and value of late works: their orientation toward a movement that, while not aimless, is nevertheless without goal.[39] Lateness provides us with the paradox of a kind of telos-free logic.

But what is the value here for human subjects as they attempt to produce functioning forms of social and political life? The images that most immediately come to mind when I think of humans acting in accordance with such a self-referential movement are frightening and frequently oriented either toward metaphors of machinery or concern humans' interactions with machines. I think of the searing inhuman intensity of road rage in which, as a result of coming into relationship with machines that make movement more efficiently rapid, the human subject can transform into a kind of machine itself, one whose function is simply to move as rapidly as possible without hindrance, irrespective of whether or not there is anything pressing to reach. In fact, the horror of these scenes is precisely given by the fact that in most instances the intensity of the rage is inversionally proportional to the degree to which there is in fact nowhere significant to go. So the phenomenon insinuates the question: where *are* we all going in these catastrophic stages of capitalist modernity? Should one be so bold as to draw the conclusion that when there is nowhere to go we can no longer be human? On a political level, the late Said seemed frequently to be asserting that there was nowhere left for Israelis and Palestinians to go, that the terms that presently defined the situation had reached a state of deadlock. So does that mean that they have now entered into a movement for movement's sake, into a kind of inhuman rage that seeks no result apart from fidelity to each party's respective forms of self-referential continuation?

Said offers no comforting advice, and is quite prepared to admit of an impersonal force propelling human actions that is disturbingly autonomous of the human decision to act itself. In Mozart, for example, Said sees the attempt "to embody an abstract force that drives people by means of agents (in *Così fan tutte*) or sheer energy (in *Don Giovanni*) without the reflective consent of their mind or will in most instances."[40] But Said's vision of such self-referential movement can be clearly distinguished from road rage and impotent political fury because it offers no promise of identification. In *Così*, what Alfonso "devises for the two pairs of lovers is a game in which human identity is shown to be protean, unstable, and undifferentiated as anything in the actual word."[41] The conclusion of the opera "opens up a troubling vista of numerous further substitutions, with no tie, no identity, no idea of stability or constancy left undisturbed. . . . The lovers will go on finding other partners, since the rhetoric of love and the representation of desire have lost their anchors in a fundamentally unchanging order of Being."[42] As a result, shockingly, in Said's hands *Così* starts to look remarkably similar to the late works of Jean Genet, for "it is always the propulsive force driving him and his characters that Genet's work delivers most accurately, not the correctness or the content of what is said, or how the characters think or feel."[43] Carrying on the inadvertent analogies, for Said, the greatness of Genet's play *Les paravents* "is its deliberate and logical dismantling not just of French identity – France as empire, as power, as history – but of the very notion of identity itself."[44] And to conclude, Said asserts that the Absolute, for Genet, "is perceptible neither in the form of human identity nor as a personified deity but precisely in what after everything is said and done will not settle down, will not be incorporated or domesticated."[45] In lateness, then, the movement is fueled by incinerating any sense of arrival. As Said notes, Genet had described *Les paravents* as a "*poetic deflagration,* an artificially started and hastened chemical fire whose purpose is to light up the landscape as it turns all identities into combustible things."[46] By comparison, the movement of road rage is fueled by the desperate attempt to defend the authority of the place on which one stands; to create an absolute identity out of the moment of fury through an endless repetition of its gesture. Road rage is a manic incantation performed in the name of eternity, an appalling denial of the fact that it too must die.[47] Its inhumanity emerges from its *commitment* to what it perceives as the ground of its own position. In lateness, by comparison, the strangely inhuman quality of a Glenn Gould, for example, arises from a certain indifference to grounding per se. As Said writes, "In nearly every sense Gould did not belong, whether as son, citizen, member of his community of pianists, musician, or thinker."[48]

But if the human has become indifferent to its normative grounds (in the form of identity, location, home, belief, property, meaning, family, community, and so on), what is it now doing? The question is an important one, particularly for contemporary musicology, which continues to devote the larger portion of its labors to scripting the human as fully preoccupied with such concerns. The telos-free movement of lateness, incinerating all grounds it traverses, is reminiscent of what Lacanian psychoanalysis would term the discourse of the hysteric. And so perhaps the function of the Saidian late subject is to merely snap back relentlessly, "That's not it!"[49] The writings of Adorno, for example, often seem close to such hysteric negation, as Said suggests: "Modernity was a fallen, unredeemed reality, and new music, as much as Adorno's own philosophic practice, took its task to be a ceaselessly demonstrated reminder of that reality."[50] However, Said does not imprison the dynamic of lateness in a parasitic cycle of negative reaction formation: "Were this reminder to be simply a repeated *no* or *this will not do,* late style and philosophy would be totally uninteresting and repetitive."[51] For Said negation – which can easily imply voiding, hollowing out, and making less – must, paradoxically, be full: "There must be a *constructive* element above all, which animates the procedure."[52] Returning to the previous paragraph, although Gould's life could be read as a kind of "repeated *no* or *this will not do*" to what normatively constitutes human life in the West, this did not preclude him from having somewhere to stand, since "everything about him bespoke the alienated detachment of a man making his abode, if he had one, in his performances rather than in conventional dwelling."[53]

We have to be very careful here with regard to how we let the word "conventional" affect our understanding; it is laden with too many binary temptations that can easily seduce us into scripting "performances" oppositionally as *un*conventional dwellings, or, even worse, as part of the essentially conservative adolescent world of provocative transgressions. Said is indeed courting with the difficult business of articulating how something can constitute a genuine outside without running aground on various forms of impotent escapism or ideological exclusion. The radical nature of the project in the context of Said's own oeuvre is underlined by reminding ourselves that the book, *Orientalism,* that brought Said to prominence, and to which he remained most consistently identified, was predominantly organized around a vehement critique of the violent cultural and political work performed by Western constructions of the outside. As Said frequently reminds us through, for example, reference to Conrad's *Heart of Darkness,* what is presented as outside is often a function for sustaining the existence of a thoroughly centralized and hegemonic inside.[54] The tragedy and bathos of adolescent outsideness, for example, arises from the inordinate degree to which it is performed *for* the Other; its provocation being as much a means of remaining the object of the adult gaze in the no-man's land between childhood and full-citizenship as it is a means of constructing an autonomous route into such adult life. As I say, in many cases it seems easily conservative, as is attested by the relative normality of a troubled youth laying the foundations for a thoroughly non-disruptive adulthood. Indeed, critics have suggested that Said himself, particularly in his role as a Palestinian political commentator, had something of a taste for being the object of his "enemy's" gaze.

The condition of being outside is therefore uncomfortably close to being a symptom of an addiction to, or even just the pragmatic need of, being visible. And so the practices that allow one to constitute oneself as outside are frequently more means than end: payments made to an economy that then allows one to circulate rather than pure forms of activity performed for their own sakes.[55] Yet it is precisely this ease with which the outside can get negatively reinscribed that helps to contextualize what is striking about what Said articulates. For through lateness he is proposing what can be described as an *invisible* outside, an outside arising from the studied attempt *not* to be seen. The most obvious candidate from Said's line up is again Gould, who famously removed himself from the public spectacle of the concert hall and receded into the secret gloom of the recording studio.[56] In its broader, metaphorical sense, an outside is "invisible" when it can no longer be understood only in terms of the inside. Even the hysteric's mode of refusal is too dependent and thus provides the inside with too many flattering opportunities to see the effects of its own power being replicated. Rather, to return to the imagery of the first two chapters, the invisibility of an outside results from its lack of mirrored surfaces; it is cut off from us by its thick covering veil. However, unlike classical fugal counterpoint, for example, it is not yet asleep or dreaming into view the uncanny excesses that the mirror seeks to censor. It is more disturbing, for the invisible outside exists in a nowhere space between the mirror of reflection and the sleep of uncanny dreams. Like forgetting, it is awake; yet covered by a veil, it is part blind. Context-deaf, it is verging on the autistic, and participates in few of the intersubjective reflective practices that have so often been valued in postmodern definitions of human subjectivity. Unlike adolescence, it performs for itself, is indifferent, returns no gaze.

So, for example, "to locate [the poet] Cavafy in late-nineteenth-century and early-twentieth-century Egypt," as any literary historian would normally do, "is to be struck by how utterly his work fails to take note of the modern Arab world."[57] As Said states in a different context, "Late style is *in*, but oddly *apart* from the present."[58] Temporally, with Cavafy everything that is most present has receded furthest away. As result, a clearing is created into which the past floods in the form of memories of Cavafy's own past homosexual encounters and also ancient Hellenistic and Byzantine history, particularly of Alexandria, the city the adult Cavafy almost never left. "The time of the poem, which is never sustained for more than a few instants, is always outside and alongside the real present, which Cavafy treats only as a subjective passage into the past."[59] We should note, however, that this endlessly present past has none of the melancholy grandeur of Romanticism, or the mythological epiphanies of modernists such as Joyce or Eliot. Rather than expanding the horizon of the poetry's projected sense of its own significance, Cavafy's temporal displacements seem to contract it. "In Cavafy," as Said writes, "the future does not occur." The poetry is oriented, rather, toward an "internalized, narrow world of limited expectations than that of grandiose projects constantly betrayed or traduced."[60] Particularly with the poems set in the ancient past, there can often be a sense of almost pointless expenditure of effort, resulting in a poetry of high artifice and cool restraint that, nevertheless, seems indifferent to the suggestion that it might be relevant. I have sometimes had the impression while reading Cavafy that I am overhearing careful reconstructions of periphery conversations from some historical backwater that are indifferent to whether or not they have anything to offer me regarding my own life now.

Drawn to such oddly impotent qualities, it is unsurprising that Said turns also to late Strauss, whose works, like Cavafy's, are similarly marked by a potentially ineffectual, even decadent temporal predilection toward the past. In Strauss's case we are dealing with the eighteenth century, which from *Der Rosenkavalier* onward dominates so many of his endeavors. In comparison with Cavafy, Said implies that the tendencies toward irrelevance are exacerbated in Strauss, since the eighteenth century appears less in terms of its content (for instance, as a source of historical interest) and more for its formal potential as a metaphoric means for discussing relatively self-contained and delimited aesthetic questions. *Capriccio*, for example, has "retreated inward, so to speak, to an intramural level: the dramatic conflict is over whether in lyrical music the words or the music are more important."[61] It is as if the more appalling the surrounding historical conditions became during the 1930s and 1940s, the more Strauss concerns himself with almost pedantic elaborations on the virtues of the craft of music qua music. Again: *Capriccio* is "almost perversely circumscribed, as if to make the point overly plain that the composer is interested only in these relatively small-scale matters, not in anything more significant."[62]

Critical eyebrows have frequently been raised regarding Strauss's tendency toward a questionable historical myopia. Keeping in mind a certain modernist form of praxis, which politically validates the rebarbative as the most appropriate aesthetic response to the horrors of modernity, it is indeed particularly difficult not to conflate the seeming decadence of Strauss's gesture with political complicities of the worst order. Strauss's late music "makes none of the emotional claims it should. . . . It is smoothly polished, technically perfect, worldly, and at ease *as music* in an entirely musical world."[63] Drawing on Adorno's critique, Said admits that Strauss's ability to "spin measure after measure of assured, even eloquent music in this regressive manner" is "downright embarrassing: he shows little sign of anguish or discomfort." If we keep in mind the "appalling depredations of Germany during the war," the situation verges on the insufferable.[64] In the court of moral outrage regarding Strauss, one would imagine that Said has a seat on the prosecution bench. Yet Said remains standing, and the slightly perplexing nature of his gesture, a late style gesture if ever there was one, is accentuated by contrasting it with the more familiar image of his performances as public intellectual, berating his audience from the stage for their failure to be informed about the political realities of the wretched of this earth. In *On Late Style,* it is far from clear what he is up to politically and ethically, and so it is as if Said now stands in a relationship of invisible outsideness to himself, as if he is starting to forget Said – a seeming contradiction that Rachel Beckles Willson, to take a musicological example, finds highly questionable.[65]

Of course, in Said's own *political* terms, Strauss is guilty, and at the very least one might expect Said to mediate the comfy hermetic enclosure of Strauss's late works, with their musically fitted carpet, with some of the harsher realities of life on the cold stone floor of history. Precedent for such a procedure is, after all, to be found, among other places, in Said's infamous reading of Jane Austen's *Mansfield Park,* a reading that, relatively unacknowledged by the director, nevertheless deeply impacted Patricia Rozema's unorthodox 2005 film adaptation of the novel.[66] In effect, Said subjected the novel to a historical and political psychoanalysis, so that the seemingly self-enclosed, domestic consciousness of Austen's representation of trials and tribulations in the world of the late eighteenth-century British landed gentry is subjected to a violent confrontation with its obscene unconscious: the horrific inhuman violence of the slave trade in Antigua, the economic ground on which the particular Western comforts rest. Such a duality is not completely avoided in Said's reading of Strauss. In *Capriccio,* Said notes the alternation between "passages of the most exquisite, thoroughly harmonized lyricism and long passages or turbulent or capricious or sardonic activity,"[67] an alternation that defines the final moments of the opera with its "particular effect of sustaining a traditional line and yet also allowing us to hear the interruptions of the outside world."[68] But what overwhelmingly draws his attention and inspires admiration is, to continue the psychoanalytic theme, the relative absence of symptoms. Although Strauss's late works are "escapist in theme, reflective and disengaged in tone," they are "above all written with a kind of distilled and rarefied technical mastery that is quite amazing." Instead of seeking to find the chink in the musical armor through which the compromising, dark night of history might be espied, Said demands that "one ought to concentrate on the sheer difficulty of what Strauss attempts," on the sheer uncompromised beauty of the armor itself.[69] Said draws us toward a radical conclusion: that we celebrate Strauss's success in using aesthetic activity as a means of temporarily dissolving the existence and influence of what, with a nod toward Fredric Jameson, we might refer to as a historical and political unconscious.[70] This is an argument against depth, and so potentially complicit with the very political celebration of surface that this study had negated as its first dialectic move in the opening chapter. But whereas the postmodern politics of the mirror celebrates surface in the name of making visible who we already are, Said's analysis of late Strauss inches toward a new kind of human: one that can productively forget (in the sense already

outlined) the truth of the existent by means of the demands made upon
its concentration by the technical abilities required to sustain what seem
to be impossible aesthetic tasks. In the potentially privileged moments
when this kind of human can productively step forth, the political conditions are not so much negated as momentarily halted, like cars at a
railway crossing, immobile while another force charges across its path.
The question is: To what end?

MA FIN EST MON COMMENCEMENT

In the wake of Said's death, a number of scholars have tried to trace
out a new kind of politics from the tension that exists in his late work
between what we might broadly call humanism and Adorno-inspired
forms of dialectical suspension. But the evident fascination Said had for
the figures addressed in *On Late Style* complicates this project. For one
of the primary tendencies linking these figures together is their strange
ability in the face of situations that seem to demand immediate political
response and the taking of sides to resist the temptation to flinch into
action. Said's late-style theory can work to preserve and articulate what
we might call the respective singularities of art and politics. Nevertheless, the question of how the potential indifference between these two
categories might be of import for situations demanding political transformation haunts Said's contemporaneous work with Barenboim in the
founding stages of the West-Eastern Divan Workshop and Orchestra.

This is perhaps surprising, since on both the conceptual level of
discourse and the pragmatic level of activity and scheduling, the West-
Eastern Divan project started out by working with an experimental fuzz-
iness regarding the musical and the political. The fact that the residen-
tial workshops interlaced, cheek-by-jowl, the more normative musical
rehearsal periods of a youth orchestra with discussion groups oriented
around loaded political issues concerning territory and identity seems to
have been a means of encouraging mutual contagion and metamorphosis
between the two parameters that would undermine the sustaining of
their respective singularities.[71] There is perhaps a productive homology
to be noted here with Said's aforementioned notion of the inextricabil-
ity of relations between Jews and Palestinians. However, by considering

some of the basic terms first in an abstract way, we can then move back toward the discourse and question whether or not it is this production of a potential hybridity that is fundamental to the project.

Take, for example, the word "workshop." A workshop is both a place and also a kind of intensive educational program whose primary focus we might broadly describe as *technê:* participation in the activity and craft of forms of doing and making that are not, by necessity, instigated by either *a priori* metaphysical truths or *a posteriori* questions of ethics and politics. A workshop is a zone, both spatial and mental, that is not fully contained by *epistêmê,* the world of knowledge and truth – especially not in the culturally, politically, and historically loaded ways in which Said tended to understand such things. At its fundamental level, one can argue that the only end the West-Eastern Divan Workshop must achieve is the formal one of clearing open a "workshop" space (at the time of this writing, located primarily in Pilas, near Seville in Spain) in which young and primarily Middle-Eastern musicians can come together in order to develop their skills as orchestral performers. Once the workshop itself is completed the participants are then part of the West-Eastern Divan Orchestra, which usually then goes on tour. So the workshop can be thought of as practical training, and it is given a certain mode of articulation by the formal pressures exerted upon it by the fact that it has to produce concerts. Its aim is to make an orchestra. If one were then to ask the question, "What is the purpose of the West-Eastern Divan Orchestra?" the first answer must be a similarly tautological and singular one: "To be an orchestra." The failure of the orchestra to produce political transformation through the development of, for example, increased "knowledge of the other" (a leitmotiv in much of the more official documentary footage on the orchestra) would be disappointing. But its attainment is essentially grace, not structurally fundamental – even if, as Willson's interesting thoughts on the commodity implications of the orchestra attest, the sustaining of its Utopian political aura is not unhelpful in its endeavors at sustaining funding.[72] For the West-Eastern Divan Orchestra, its end is in its beginning; an orchestra must be an orchestra.[73]

To continue for the moment at a degree of abstraction from documentary or ethnographic engagement, we can note a certain resonance here with the weirdly seductive hermeticism of Gertrude Stein's most famous line, first found in *Sacred Enemy* (1913), "Rose is a rose is a rose is a rose." The sheer blankness of Stein's repetition goes nowhere, a fact that she herself exacerbated by having it engraved in a ring (round and round and round and round) at the head of her own personal stationary. But like many minimal exercises in the seemingly puritanical *subtraction* of content (in which a rose initially seems less as a result of not being allowed to be qualified by comparison), the effect is potentially to open the rose up, allowing the noun-bud to bloom by means of the mantra into a sublimity of possibilities. Alternatively, the repetition can be read comically, as a schoolmarmish bit of discipline: four raps on the knuckles to keep us concentrated on the rose in front of us and to stop us from staring out the window into a world where roses have spawned an infinite variety of semantic vegetation. We are being schooled in the virtues of *not* being distracted, in the possibilities that are granted us from practicing the discipline of focusing in on one thing. So many of the values that circulate successfully in the postmodern academy are concerned with the idea of opening up: it is fundamental, for example, to revisionist approaches to the canon, to interdisciplinarity, to the whole now vast scholarly field that practices respect in the face of the Other, even to musical performance (and even by Goehr, who these days is no postmodernist).[74] But Stein's mantra can speak otherwise: cut things out, narrow things down, close things off. In effect, say yes, with great excitement, passion and all the rest; but say it to one thing only.

Repeatedly in the published conversations between Said and Barenboim, successful musical performance and particularly orchestral performance are likewise understood as necessitating such a *discipline of subtraction*. The conversations are, by definition, marked productively by a certain improvisatory quality. Nevertheless, it is possible tentatively to formulate this discipline as being constituted by a two-part process in which a necessary act of dropping and relinquishment is then followed by a subsequent act of grasping and preservation.

For example, Said talks of the incredible tensions between the performers that accompanied the opening days of the very first workshop – in other words, before there was any intuition of the sometimes phenomenal, even teary-eyed, success into which the project would subsequently transform. These tensions were not simply isolated to those between Israelis and Palestinians, which, after all, are far from being the only difficulties faced by a region that had a long and complex colonial history and so continues to suffer the disastrous postcolonial after-effects of colonialism's indifferent geographical acts of carving up. For example, the relationships between Palestinians and the countries that housed them after their expulsion in 1948 (primarily Jordan, Syria, and Lebanon) remain complicated, for although Arab nations would often vehemently support the Palestinian cause in the forums of international politics, they were far from always being the best of hosts. And so "there were some Arabs who didn't care for other Arabs as well as Israelis who cordially disliked other Israelis."[75] However, for Said, it was "amazing to watch Daniel drill this basically resistant group into shape," for as a result of the imposition of his discipline one could "witness the group, despite the tensions of the first week or ten days, turn themselves into a real orchestra."[76] The underlying controlling metaphor here seems to be a military one, and so the discourse taps into a venerable theme, for the connection between the idea of the orchestra and the idea of organized armed forces is almost as old as orchestras are themselves.[77] But this is an army without politics: "In my opinion, what you saw had no political overtones at all." Rather, "one set of identities was superseded by another set," as in fact is the case in the initial stages of military training: "There was an Israeli group, and a Russian group, and a Syrian group, a Lebanese group, a Palestinian group, and a group of Palestinian Israelis" – a dissonant assemblage of differentiations. However, "all of them suddenly became cellists and violinists playing the same piece in the same orchestra under the same conductor."[78] In other words, they had to interrupt the normal functioning of their political and cultural inscriptions, and, to a degree, let the clothing by which they are usually identified drop to the floor in order to adopt a certain uniform(ity). In order for an orchestra to be an orchestra, they had to concentrate more on holding onto music rather than to their respective notions of themselves.[79] Their status as subjects of *epistêmê* (who they conceived themselves to be) had to be replaced (or at the very least somewhat displaced) by their status as subjects of *technê*, beings organized around a focused attempt to preserve their ability to perform successfully. Obviously, their epistemic identity is not permanently erased. Nevertheless, as with what we saw happen in chapter 2, when the cultural inscriptions of fugal counterpoint hit the material unconscious of musical form, such identity must come into contact with the materiality of something else, at least for the duration of performing, and that contact produces an excess that on a certain level is simply indifferent to those identities.

Said presents this transformation from *epistêmê* to *technê* in primarily formal terms. However, isomorphic with his reading of late Strauss, where the magnificence of a technical feat of composition is tinged by the threat of how easily the concentration needed to sustain it could have been distracted by contemporary political concerns, this discipline of subtraction is easily threatened by a return of content and, therefore, by a potential transformation back into meaning-oriented discourse. We might start by noting that accompanying the achievement of becoming subjects of *technê* are the seeds of a self-reflexive critique in which an initial form of belonging (for example, being someone from Egypt) is inadvertently revealed to the subject of that belonging as less because another position (for example, being an oboe player in an orchestra) is attractive enough to instigate a temporary defection from it. The transformation thus contains a potential shock, since the first position, the one that is given up, is the one that in certain situations would be most pragmatically oriented toward what seems absolutely necessary in order to sustain the acceptable conditions for one's existence, particularly, one should note, for certain members of the West-Eastern Divan Orchestra. The second position, by comparison, can easily seem peripheral at best to the kinds of politicized life situations that many of the young musicians sometimes face. One could imagine a line of thinking that would find the act of ceasing to defend one's identity as a legitimate subject of one's territory in order to play in an orchestra (moreover, with people who, in a situation of war, could quite feasibly be the direct aggressors of that territory) to be at best a rather foolhardy bit of decadence, perhaps even a form of complicity. Again, we are back with the problems surrounding late Strauss.

Such concerns might help us to read the disturbing scene in the Knesset in Paul Smaczny's award-winning film about the West-Eastern Divan, *Knowledge Is the Beginning*. Here Barenboim receives the 2004 Wolf Foundation Prize, and his acceptance speech quotes from the founding constitution of the State of Israel in order to condemn Israel's continuing development of the settlements and Israel's military agendas. Afterward, there is a brief interview with Menahem Alexenburg, a member of the Wolf Foundation Council, who had held up a sign at the end of the ceremony replicating a reworked version of the infamous sign over the gates of Auschwitz, now reading "Musik macht Frei." He states that "you don't make peace with people who want to kill you, you make war with them." Since the Arab nations want "to destroy Israel as an independent Jewish state," Barenboim's call for a cessation of present military policy in favor of acts of communion like the West-East Divan means that "he's a party to helping that problem." As a means of ironically undermining this remark, the documentary then quietly cuts to the young musicians frolicking around in a swimming pool in between rehearsals, evidently indifferent to working out how to obliterate Israel.

Alexenburg's employment of the figure of Auschwitz as part of a rhetorical gambit to clinch the coherence of his remark is unpalatable. This remains the case even when one acknowledges that it is indisputable that there have been repeated large-scale refusals by Arab nations to accept the legitimacy of the State of Israel, refusals that have, since the founding of the state itself in 1948, frequently erupted into hostilities. Ironically, however, he inadvertently touches upon a key tenet of Barenboim's philosophy regarding musical performance: that in order for music of a truly powerful intensity to come into being, the musicians must to a degree relinquish or become indifferent to guaranteeing in a broad sense their own *extramusical securities*. At times, this line of reasoning could be accused of leading Barenboim's discourse uncomfortably close to a logic of sacrifice in which nonmusical life must suffer in order for music to prevail, and so we are faced once more with the grim irony of an inadvertent resonance with Alexenburg's condemnation of a situation in which he feels that the so-called freedom of music has been purchased at a potential cost to life.

But however questionable Barenboim's position might or might not be as a prescription or ethic, it does, nevertheless, contain a certain truth, the full repercussions of which Barenboim himself is perhaps not completely prepared to take on board. For it is undoubtedly true that when dire social and political circumstances have little to offer people in terms of living, music can seem like a preferable place to take up residence.[80] And if your time is not taken up with tending to the preservation of your comforts (since you don't have any), then perhaps you're going to keep your musical house in better order. I am reminded here of the time I lived in New Orleans, repeatedly a contender for the poorest, most violent city in the United States. In the weeks leading up to Mardi Gras, when there are frequent parades, I became fixated by the endless procession of marching bands from inner-city high schools, an ensemble type for which I'd had no previous interest and have retained little desire to hear since leaving the city. I retain a distinct memory of a level of precision in the coordination and integration of ensembles that I have almost never heard in any other musical forum, and a resulting focus of sound and affect that was mesmerizing in its intensity. A similar point is made by Barenboim regarding the Berlin Staatskapelle, which, admitting that it is not the best orchestra in the world, Barenboim nevertheless considers unique with regard to its musical ethic, its "natural way of standing in front of this music with a mixture of a sense of awe and a great sense of active courage."[81] One of the reasons Barenboim gives for this is that the orchestra functioned within a totalitarian condition for sixty years, through the Nazi era and then that of East German communism. As if in answer to a hypothetical Alexenburg, he quickly states: "This certainly does not justify the need for a totalitarian regime."[82] Nevertheless, Ara Guzelimian, who was also involved in these discussions, summarizes Barenboim's remarks by stating that "there's a much greater urgency to the existence of an orchestra in such circumstances."[83] The statement is also applicable to the West-Eastern Divan Orchestra.

What could the prevalence of these potentially disturbing equations between broken social life and intensely focused performance tell us about music? In part, they bespeak of music's potential indifference, since they show that good music is not reliant on the presence of the Good in order to come into being. Most of us have known our fair share of fine musicians who were as prone to being as ghastly in their day-to-day nonmusical lives as anyone else: homophobic, racist, sexist, manipulative, crass, spectacularly insensitive, indulgent. Music is disturbingly indifferent as to whom she invites to the feast; she cares only that manners are good when she presides at the head of the table. As I have already stated, by adopting the status of subjects of *technê,* musicians potentially make an inadvertent critique of the social inscriptions they are prepared to discard; *epistêmê,* we might assert, is produced as collateral, or, to make recourse to the philosopher Bernard Williams's famous phrase, as the result of a kind of moral luck.[84] But there is no necessary reason to assume that this critique, even if the musicians formulate it consciously for themselves, will therefore produce any kind of reciprocal desire to act any differently and thereby to change the world that has now been revealed as less. So even though meaning and content may be immanent, they can remain dormant to the point of impotency. The revelation that one's social world is less than first one thought could just as easily make one as indifferent as music itself, encouraging one to adopt the wily ways of addicts, maximizing the possibilities of obtaining a musical fix by reducing one's social responsibilities to the absolute bare minimum necessary to support one's appetite.

It is a mundane example, but it is quite possible for me to accrue absolutely no bruises to my conscience when I happily turn to the piano in my office and completely forgo responsible attendance to a student's problem that is weeping quietly at me from the sad shadows of my email account. Moreover, it would be wrong to say that what I am describing here is simply avoidance. Avoidance is prevailed over by the desire to *disengage* from something. We slink around the peripheries of what we are meant to be doing, hoping to avoid its condemning gaze, and so, of course, neither do it nor anything else apart from producing symptoms, such as surfing the Internet, skimming the pages of a magazine, or hoping that the great depth and soft recess of the chair in the coffee shop will be sufficient enough effectively to shield us. Avoidance is a state of uncomfortable suspension, a scene of guilt, in which it is difficult to stand up straight since we are weighed down by our inability to escape the Law. By comparison, the kinds of ethical sacrifices that musical performance can so easily encourage are motivated by a quest for something that will allow us to *engage more,* and the need for that degree of engagement can easily override the attractions of the virtue of responsibility. A lovely illustration of this point, if from a different field, is provided by Hans Ulrich Gumbrecht in his discussion of the swimmer and Olympic gold medalist Pablo Morales, who, after having retired, returned to competitive life and won another gold medal. Asked why he had bothered to do so, "without hesitation, Morales replied that he had made this astonishing effort because he was addicted to the feeling of 'being lost in focused intensity.'"[85] There is nothing inherently ethical in this. At times, the repercussions are profoundly selfish, and one wonders if members of the West-Eastern Divan Orchestra have been accused as such when they announced with whom they were going to perform.[86] After all, many of them have attested to the fact that what encouraged them to audition in the first place was the chance to participate in the elevated *musical* experience that playing in an orchestra conducted by Barenboim would provide. Some confess that they had assumed that they would be able to shield themselves from the things they had heard word about regarding how their participation might transform them *ethically* or *politically*.[87]

Barenboim's position would seem to be congruent with the idea of musical singularity, particularly considering that his statements in the dialogues are seemingly often more formalist than Said's. For example, when Said makes a series of virtuoso critical leaps – comparing the musical issues they have been talking about with, in turn, Homer's *Iliad*, questions of exile, and then the modernist literary tradition of Joyce, Proust, and Eliot – Barenboim terminates the infectious process: "There is a limit to these associations. . . . Words such as redemption, glory, or revolution, whatever it is, bring with them the danger of then using the music, even on a subconscious level, as a description of these ideas." Immediately he follows this with a credo that would not be out of place coming from a Hanslick or Schenker: "I think that the true expression of absolute music has to be found in the world of sound and sound relations themselves."[88] Nevertheless, Barenboim's insistence on the musical in music is frequently undercut by the appendage of a short-circuit back to nonmusical content; and as in the logic of repression, content then floods back in with a force that has been magnified by the attempt to keep it at bay. His discussion of his theories regarding the "phenomenology of sound" provide a good case in point.

Sound, for Barenboim, is understood in relationship to the silence to which it is drawn.[89] "I often compare it to the law of gravity; in the same way that objects are drawn to the ground, so are sounds drawn to silence."[90] Playing music thus becomes a means, in essence, of keeping sound afloat: "You have a whole dimension of physical inevitabilities, which as a musician you try to defy" – primarily in order to sustain the credibility of a certain aesthetic illusion.[91] But these provocative phenomenological propositions, which are oriented more toward *technê,* immediately leap to ethical conclusions: "This is why courage is an integral part of making music. . . . The sheer act of making music is an act of courage since you are trying to defy many of the physical laws of nature."[92] In part, we are still dealing with the basic structure of the discipline of subtraction: for the musicians must here relinquish themselves from the nonmusical phenomenology of sound, in which sound sinks back into silence, and grasp onto music's anti-gravitational attempt to make sound float. But that process is now brought into being not because the musicians, through a technique of concentration, have the ability to narrow themselves down in order to perform, but because, in comparison with those who are not musical, they are already more: they have courage. Of course, one of the paradoxes of Barenboim's formulation is that in order to have this more, the musicians have to have made their lives less. The logic of a heroic sacrifice remains tangible throughout his argument. To be a good performer, music must exist "as a way of life," as opposed to professionalism, which makes "music as a means of life."[93] The argument is that being distracted by the possibility of having more in terms of nonmusical possessions, the professional will compromise the music, and once that happens music's purpose, for Barenboim, will have been lost. For Barenboim as much as Said, compromise is what politicians practice: "A politician can only work and do good if he masters the art of compromise." By comparison, "the artist's expression is only determined by his total refusal to compromise in anything – the element of courage." But in a situation like the one in existence between Israel and the Palestinians, the political art of compromise will not be enough: "A conflict of this nature will not be solved only through political means, through economic means or through arrangements." Rather, "it requires the courage of everybody to use, as it were, artistic solutions."[94] For Barenboim, musical performance must refuse to compromise so that it can preserve the courage necessary to supplement the failure of the political. If we were to ask once more, "What is the purpose of the West-Eastern Divan Orchestra?" the answer from Barenboim, though structurally the same as when first we asked, is now stained by content: it is to create for politics the courage that is always already immanent to the performance of music. So its end is in its beginning, too.

BEFORE THE BEGINNING

That it is frequently necessary for us to engage with politics when talking about music seems undeniable, almost pro forma. In musicology, it is now taken for granted that music and politics are either in close proximity or mutually create each other. There is no purely autonomous musical moment; musical material is always mediated. But the fact that the music/politics trope can be verified and legitimated by the venerable standards and practices of historical and cultural academic research does not mean that its circulation within discourse can only be explained merely by the force of its arguments, even if these are seemingly indisputable. If that were the case, we would have to assume that historical and cultural research practices can obtain the very autonomy from mediation that they deny for music, and so they would be contradictory in their own terms. If the relationship of music to politics can be historically and contextually verified, likewise the emergence of the relationship of the music/politics trope in cultural and academic discourse and practice can be historically and contextually qualified. And this opens up a space in which we might ask: What function does the music/politics trope perform? To what needs does it respond?

Such questions are pertinent with regard to Barenboim because in his more sober moments he comfortably gravitates toward assertions of music's potential autonomy from politics. To take a characteristic statement: "The West-Eastern Divan Orchestra is of course incapable of bringing peace to the Middle East. We are musicians, not politicians."[95] Repeatedly in interviews Barenboim will state that his activities are musical, not political. For example, by defying Israeli law and going to play a recital in Ramallah, he claims simply to be opening up a musical space within the political; his musical practices are not unlike late Strauss's as understood by Said. As a result, when the figure of the political emerges in his discourse, it sometimes has the overdetermined quality of a symptom manifesting itself from out of a politically loaded unconscious space.

(By comparison, although the development of the music/politics trope in musicology can and should be subjected to interrogation by its own terms, it was nevertheless drawn into musicological discourse relatively consciously; politics was nurtured in order to compensate for a growing unease with the unacknowledged and potentially negative cultural work that musical autonomy as a figure was perceived as performing.)[96] Take, for example, the problematic issue of the declaration against the 2006 Israel-Hezbollah war that Barenboim and Mariam Said wrote and ultimately had printed in the programs of the West-Eastern Divan Orchestra that season.[97] Admittedly, the musicians did get to rewrite the document. Further, one can argue that the document articulates more a humanitarian than a political position. Nevertheless, for the not inconsiderable amount of the musicians who were unhappy with the statement, even in its final form, it meant that continuing to perform with the orchestra during that season necessitated submitting to what they perceived to be an act that politically misrepresented them. As an aside, the fact that most of the musicians did remain illustrates once more how attraction to musical activity itself can override consciously held ethical and political positions and responsibilities. More pressing is the huge flock of questions that this act unleashes regarding many of the points with which this chapter has already engaged.

How can we correlate Barenboim's undeniably political cooption here of a musical event with his claims elsewhere that he seeks the possibility of something positive through the preservation of the music/politics distinction? Does not Barenboim once more inadvertently justify Alexenburg, who had criticized him for using the cultural event of the Wolf Prize ceremony as a means of making a political statement? At the beginning of this chapter, we saw how Said, through the acknowledgment of forgetting, death, and aesthetic lateness, had the integrity to allow for the consistency of his own intellectual/political project to be split into a more problematic and unwieldy antagonism. But with Barenboim are we not seeing a darker and less attractive reflection of this in the form of an unacknowledged contradiction? Instead of allowing for the possibility that aesthetic activity might productively blot out the forms of knowledge on which our politics are based, Barenboim threatens to overwhelm the aesthetic itself. Ironically, considering his unambiguous attraction toward Beethoven and the heroic trope, it is as if Barenboim had lost his nerve and lacked the suitable defiance (to return once more to Said's terms for Strauss) necessary to stick with the difficult experimentalism of forgetting. Are some of Barenboim's seemingly courageous political gestures – such as the 2006 antiwar declaration, or his speech at the Wolf Prize ceremony, whose potentially melancholic heroics the documentary *Knowledge Is the Beginning* helps to foster by intercutting the scene with Barenboim's Jerusalem performance of the first movement of Beethoven's *Moonlight* Sonata – are not these perhaps signs of weakness? Or evidence of a lack of discipline with regard to the self-restraint needed in order to keep music as music, politics as politics? To return to an earlier formulation, has Barenboim himself not been seduced into confusing affective force for significance or even signification? The negatively loaded context provided by Middle-Eastern politics potentially helps to increase the intensity of the West-Eastern Divan Orchestra's performances, precisely since they succeed in spite of it. But is it really the case that the intensity of such performances therefore creates the ground of causality from out of which Barenboim's particular political vision can then blossom forth as an authentic effect? Music is terribly naughty, and is more than happy to convince us of all sorts of things, true or otherwise. So we might productively entertain a certain Copernican inversion here: that it is not that music's own content finds resonance with our own, or that music's content inspires the development of our own, but rather that music encourages us to engage with content so that we will be suitably inspired to produce good (effective) music. Politics might be just a metaphorical fuel source by which music gets us to jump-start her into action. Barenboim might merely be a dupe of a certain cunning of musical reason, to appropriate a famous Hegelian metaphor.

For the record, it is important to note that it is not being argued that music could not necessarily do anything transformative within the situation of Middle Eastern politics. The argument is not even to question Barenboim's own understanding of and stance toward the political situation, particularly with regard to Israel's ongoing wall-building project and its relationship to the expansion of Israeli settlements. Rather, my above set of questions and hypotheses are an attempt to give some impression of how potentially overly inculcated Barenboim's position is with various kinds of economies that are easily contradictory or even self-defeating in terms of his purported aim to enact transformation. In short, I wonder if his act of conflating music and politics might be an inadvertent means of *stopping* anything political from happening. And indeed, I raise this question for any situation where the politicization of a potentially nonpolitical field is presented as a political act, including musicology, too. Maybe music is able to do something *not* because it is political per se, but precisely because it is not. And if this is indeed the case, then maybe we need to reconsider what it is that allows for something else to occur, to question the somewhat literal-minded character that sometimes pervades in our musicological models of causality.

It is for these reasons that I characterize the emergence of the music/politics trope in Barenboim's discourse as symptomatic. For one way of viewing the symptom psychoanalytically is as a dual-functioning structure: on the one hand enlightening and progressive, since it returns us in a certain form to the traumatic origins of how we are presently inscribed, and so potentially instigates the desire for things to be otherwise; and yet on the other hand obfuscatory and conservative, since a key feature of symptoms is that they encourage (or simply are) forms of behavior, such as acting out, which merely work to reinscribe us through a self-defeating economy back into our structural delimitations. By politicizing music, we productively draw attention to the frightening degree to which we have been determined; to return to earlier terminology, we question the possibility of an outside (such as musical autonomy, for example), or even show how the positing of such an outside can precisely function to keep hegemonic structures in place. This, perhaps, raises our political awareness and encourages us to do something. However, by attempting to turn the force of political determinations back on themselves (against the determinations of the Other, as it were) through suturing music and politics together as a kind of weapon, we then strangely shoot ourselves in the foot. What I say here is not an argument against art having political content; it is, however, a deep suspicion regarding whether it is the political content within an aesthetic medium (for example, Barenboim's "courage" in music) that constitutes or is capable of producing its possible political act. If the negative forces of the political are as ubiquitous today as they undoubtedly are, then to assume that the political content of something like music is going to counteract them strikes me, frankly, as a somewhat indulgent form of fetishistic disavowal: in other words, the intense politicization of music functions precisely to mask from ourselves the genuine degree of our political impotence within present structures; in the same way, perverts' overdetermined eroticizations of big toes, to take a famous example, masks the horror of their own castration within the Symbolic. For some, there may well be something powerfully affecting about the idea of the West-Eastern Divan Orchestra attempting, for example, to say no to certain actions of the Israeli government; it perhaps also contains an ironic reversal, since one of the forms that the Israeli state's own self-narrativization has taken is of this tiny place defending itself against enormous odds, David versus Goliath. But the idea that this act of no-saying is going to change the incredible sophistication and strength of the force to which it is addressed is delusional, and so works (deliberately so in terms of the logic of the symptom) to make the problem less. This, in turn, encourages increasingly ineffective strategy. As with hysteric and teenage acts of refusal, this no is already included within the economy it seeks to break. And so it is en route to being a yes. This is why, to return to this chapter's opening, we should sometimes say no to no – or in Said's phrase, forget; or in the terms of this chapter, perform music; defuse the power of *epistêmê* by depriving it of ground; clear open the space in the midst of our identifications (in the form, for example, of the rehearsal or the concert) to allow for the exercise of *technê*.

Knowledge is the beginning – this is the title of the best-known documentary on the West-Eastern Divan Orchestra and also, seemingly, the most consistent ethical claim made within its discourse: the situation in the Middle East, particularly regarding the relationship between Israel and Palestinians, cannot be resolved by the present military deadlock; only through the dissolving of the political barriers that keep different peoples apart, through an increased "knowledge of the Other" can a solution, as of yet unknown, be found – such is the argument. However, powerful and even necessary as "Knowledge Is the Beginning" may be as a title, it is ideological and thus exclusory. For what the West-Eastern Divan Orchestra's discourse in one of its forms potentially shows us is that in order for there to be this beginning there must be something else, something before the beginning, as it were. Perhaps this is the true insight of Said's late phase, and thus the tragedy of his death is exacerbated by the fact that it curtailed the ability of such ideas to effectively develop within the West-Eastern Divan's discourses and curb the seductions to which Barenboim is increasingly prone. Thus, it is not so much as a result of an increased knowledge of each other that the musicians can then play; the orchestra's resultant music is not necessarily an expression of some achieved ethical state of beatitude, even though it is, in my experience, almost upsettingly tempting when watching the well-known documentary footage to perceive it as such. Rather, by means of entering a zone of potential indifference to who they all are – a zone that in one of its manifestations goes under the name "music" – a space for the possibility of knowledge is created. In short, *music* is the beginning.

Said notes: "I will never forget the look of amazement on the part of the Israeli musicians during the first movement of Beethoven's Seventh where the oboist plays a very exposed A major scale. They all turned around to watch an Egyptian student play a perfect A major scale on the oboe."[98] The point seems to be that the Israelis did not believe that an Egyptian could be so musical;[99] in other words, being musical for them had denoted an identification, a form of knowledge that had been removed when they saw an Egyptian play with such facility. Moreover, rather than this loss of identification being compensated by a kind of inverted colonialism (that all great musicians are therefore honorary Israelis), what it potentially instigated was the realization that something (performing music) that can seem incredibly important for an Israeli might be something that is not Israeli at all. For sure, it is maybe only in the context of an Israeli upbringing that an Israeli might come to be performing Western classics. Nevertheless, to malappropriate a story of Bertrand Russell, it is not Israelis all the way down – and most importantly, nor is it anybody else. For Said and Barenboim (when he is not seduced by content) it is as a result of such a confrontation with a gap in the cultural chain that knowledge, potentially, can begin. Talking of a Syrian and an Israeli cellist sharing a music stand, Barenboim states: "They were trying to do something together, something about which they both cared, about which they were both passionate. Well, having achieved that one note, they already can't look at each other the same way, because they have shared a common experience"[100] – not just a musical one, but also, for a moment, the experience of not having to protect their respective identities from their inherent lacks, of not *just* being who they are. And so if there is any conclusion to be suggested from music at this temporary stopping point in my engagements, it is as follows: that sometimes the highest form of ethics starts with an act of betrayal.

NOTES

PREFACE: A NO-MUSIC

An earlier version of this chapter appeared as "Postmodern Mozart and the Politics of the Mirror," in *Mozart Studies*, edited by Simon P. Keefe (Cambridge: Cambridge University Press, 2006), 214–242. Reprinted with permission.

1. Susan McClary, *Conventional Wisdom: The Content of Musical Form* (Berkeley: University of California Press, 2000), 169. Here, in the final sentence of the last page of this book, McClary claims that "Western musician have always been reveling in the rubble." "Reveling in the rubble" is her metaphor for the essentially postmodern notion that art is produced out of the preexisting musical materials and conventions in which any composer or performer is located.

2. For a more extensive analysis of the themes covered in the following political sketch, see my "Music after All," *Journal of the American Musicological Society* 62 (Spring 2009): 145–203.

3. For a magnificently damning and succinct critique of Blair, see Tony Judt's "The Gnome in the Garden: Tony Blair and Britain's 'Heritage,'" *New York Review of Books* (July 2001), reprinted in *Reappraisals: Reflections on the Forgotten Twentieth Century* (New York: Penguin Press, 2008), 219–32.

4. Maire Jaanus Kurrik, *Literature and Negation* (New York: Columbia University Press, 1979).

5. Berthold Hoeckner, *Programming the Absolute: Nineteenth-Century German Music and the Hermeneutics of the Moment* (Princeton, N.J.: Princeton University Press, 2002); Alastair Williams, *New Music and the Claims of Modernity* (Aldershot: Ashgate, 1997); Michael Spitzer, *Music as Philosophy: Adorno and Beethoven's Late Style* (Bloomington: Indiana University Press, 2006); Lydia Goehr, *Elective Affinities: Musical Essays on the History of Aesthetic Theory* (New York: Columbia University Press, 2008); Daniel K. L. Chua, *Absolute Music and the Construction of Meaning* (Cambridge: Cambridge University Press, 1999), and *The "Galitzin" Quartets of Beethoven: Opp. 127, 132, 130* (Princeton, N.J.: Princeton University Press, 1995); Richard Leppert, "Music 'Pushed to the Edge of Existence' (Adorno, Listening, and the Question of Hope)," *Cultural Critique* 60 (Spring 2005): 92–133; Martin Scherzinger, "Feminine/Feminist? In Quest of Names with No Experiences (Yet)," in *Postmodern Music/Postmodern Thought*, edited by Judith Lochhead and Joseph Auner (New York: Routledge, 2002), 141–73.

6. Ernesto Laclau and Chantal Mouffe, *Hegemony and Socialist Strategy:*

Towards a Radical Democratic Politics (London: Verso, 1985).

7. In the development of this line of thought, I am indebted to an illuminating conversation with Andrea Spain, whose ideas have remained with me.

8. I have elaborated at great length on this theme in my "Music after All."

1. VEILS (MOZART, PIANO CONCERTO K. 459, FINALE)

1. Jacques Derrida, *Specters of Marx: The State of the Debt, the Work of Mourning, and the New International,* translated by Peggy Kamuf (New York: Routledge, 1994), 85.

2. The American artist Jeff Koons (born 1955) has been greatly influenced by pop art in seeking inspiration and materials from the world of commodities and popular culture. However, unlike some pop artists, Koons has, in general, been relatively uncritical of this sphere, claiming, like many other postmodernists, that it contains a necessary and useful euphoria and fecundity. Particularly in the later 1980s, Koons was prone to recasting iconic images of high art in materials that then worked to transform those images into seemingly mass produced items of kitsch. A good example is Koon's 1986 shiny stainless steel reworking of Bernini's Louis XIV, which, like a Mirror Mozart, transforms a moment of representation into a reflective surface that then represents us.

3. The idea that the exploration of depth could involve danger was notably prevalent in the work of E. T. A. Hoffmann, for example in his tale *Die Bergwerke zu Falun* (The Mines of Falun), discussed by Holly Watkins in "From the Mine to the Shrine: The Critical Origins of Musical Depth," *19th Century Music* 27 (2004): 179–207.

4. Wye J. Allanbrook, "Theorizing the Comic Surface," in *Music in the Mirror:*

Reflections on the History of Music Theory Literature for the 21st Century, edited by Andreas Giger and Thomas J. Mathiesen (Lincoln: University of Nebraska Press, 2002), 195.

5. E. T. A. Hoffmann, "Beethoven's Instrumental Music," in *Source Readings in Music History: Volume 6: The Nineteenth Century,* edited by Ruth A. Solie (New York: Norton, 1998), 153.

6. Susan Sontag, "Against Interpretation," in *A Susan Sontag Reader* (London: Penguin, 1983), 104.

7. See Terry Eagleton, *The Ideology of the Aesthetic* (Oxford: Basil Blackwell, 1990), 227.

8. For an excellent early survey and critique of the anti-hermeneutic impulse of postmodern thought, see Fredric Jameson, "On Interpretation: Literature as a Socially Symbolic Act," in *The Political Unconscious: Narrative as a Socially Symbolic Act* (Ithaca, N.Y.: Cornell University Press, 1981), 17–102.

9. The key texts here are their two-volume reassessment of the legacy of Freud and Marx: *Anti Oedipus: Capitalism and Schizophrenia,* translated by Robert Hurley, Helen R. Lane, and Mark Seem (Minneapolis: University of Minnesota Press, 1983), and *A Thousand Plateaus: Capitalism and Schizophrenia,* translated by Brian Massumi (Minneapolis: University of Minnesota Press, 1987).

10. Alfred Schnittke, "Polystylistic Tendencies in Modern Music" (ca. 1971), in *A Schnittke Reader,* edited by Alexander Ivashkin, translated by John Goodliffe (Bloomington: Indiana University Press, 2002), 90.

11. Robert Fink, "Going Flat: Post-Hierarchical Music Theory and the Musical Surface," in *Rethinking Music,* edited by Nicholas Cook and Mark Everist (Oxford: Oxford University Press, 1999), 114.

12. Ibid., 127.

13. McClary, "Reveling in the Rubble: The Postmodern Condition," in *Conventional Wisdom*, 139–69.

14. Schnittke, "Polystylistic Tendencies in Modern Music," 90.

15. Wye J. Allanbrook, "A Millennial Mozart?" *Mozart Society of America Newsletter* 3 (1999): 2 and 4.

16. V. Kofi Agawu, *Playing with Signs: A Semiotic Interpretation of Classic Music* (Princeton, N.J.: Princeton University Press, 1991), 30; Leonard Ratner, *Classic Music: Expression, Form and Style* (New York: Schirmer, 1980), 9.

17. Wye J. Allanbrook, *Rhythmic Gesture in Mozart* (Chicago: University of Chicago Press, 1983), 194.

18. Allanbrook, "A Millennial Mozart?," 2.

19. Allanbrook, "Theorizing the Comic Surface," 203. Allanbrook's analysis of K. 332 originally appeared in "'Two Threads through the Labyrinth: Topic and Process in the First Movements of K. 332 and K. 333," in *Convention in Eighteenth- and Nineteenth-Century Music: Essays in Honor of Leonard G. Ratner*, edited by Allanbrook, Janet M. Levy, and William P. Mahrt (Stuyvesant, N.Y.: Pendragon Press, 1992), 125–71.

20. Allanbrook, "Theorizing the Comic Surface," 203.

21. Ibid.

22. Allanbrook, "A Millennial Mozart?," 4.

23. Allanbrook, "Theorizing the Comic Surface," 214. To emphasize her point, Allanbrook then cites Ferdinand de Saussure's *Course in General Linguistics*, a seminal text in structural linguistics, on which the whole "linguistic turn" of (post)modern theory and philosophy was founded.

24. See Hayden White, "The Irrational and the Problem of Historical Knowledge in the Enlightenment," in *Tropics of Discourse: Essays in Cultural Criticism* (Baltimore: Johns Hopkins University Press, 1978), 135–50.

25. In defining learned style, I have followed Elaine Sisman's guidelines: "'learned style' should be used to refer to specific textures of the elevated Baroque"; and "strict or fugal style, under the more general rubric of 'learned style,' can be identified as a topic, in that fugal, canonic, alla breve, and *stile legato* procedures represent a defined, recognizable older style within the *galant* style of the later eighteenth century. And since 'galant style' generally meant 'free composition' in that period, it is a useful term against which to place in relief the drama of archaic or elevated references." See Sisman, "Genre, Gesture, and Meaning in Mozart's 'Prague' Symphony," in *Mozart Studies 2*, edited by Cliff Eisen (Oxford: Oxford University Press, 1997), 64 and 49.

26. Georg Albrechtsberger, *Gründliche Anweisung zur Composition* (Leipzig, 1790), 171. Admittedly, one should be wary of assuming that fugal counterpoint was always scripted in this way. As David Yearsley's historically intricate *Bach and the Meanings of Counterpoint* (Cambridge: Cambridge University Press, 2002) shows, even in the first half of the eighteenth century, fugal counterpoint was capable of participating in an array of potential meanings far wider than the merely authoritarian and imposing.

27. For example, see Jean-Jacques Rousseau, "Fugue," in *Dictionnaire de Musique* (Paris, 1768), 221–22; and Johann Adolph Scheibe, in *The New Bach Reader: A Life of Johann Sebastian Bach in Letters and Documents*, edited by Christoph Wolff et al. (New York: Norton, 1998), 337–53. For an excellent interpretation of Scheibe's critique see Yearsley, *Bach and the Meanings of Counterpoint*, chapter 3, "Bach's Taste for Pork and Canary," 93–127.

28. Given in Warren Kirkendale, *Fugue and Fugato in Rococo and Classical Chamber Music*, translated by Kirkendale and Margaret Bent (Durham, N.C.: Duke University Press, 1979), 181.

29. Ibid., 150.

30. Review of Charles Dumonchau, *Trois Sonates et trois Fugues pour le Pianoforte, dans le Style de Haydn, Mozart et Clementi, Oeuvr. 30*, in *Allgemeine Musikalische Zeitung* 11 (1808–09), col. 716; translated in Kirkendale, *Fugue and Fugato*, 150.

31. Daube, *Der musikalische Dilettant*, vol. 2 (Vienna, 1773); cited in Kirkendale, *Fugue and Fugato*, 189n31.

32. Sisman, "Genre, Gesture, and Meaning," 47.

33. Anton Reicha, *Traité de haute composition musicale* (Paris, 1824–26), 2:233, trans. in Kirkendale, *Fugue and Fugato*, 196.

34. Kirkendale, *Fugue and Fugato*, 189. It is true that André's retort to Spazier's criticisms was that it is "as ignorant as it is arrogant to consider every imitative figure as a fugue" (Johann Anton André, *Vierstimmige Fuge nebst deren Entwurf, und den allgemeinen Regeln über die Fuge. 52tes Werk* [Offenbach, 1827], cited in Kirkendale, *Fugue and Fugato*, 190). But as André, according to Kirkendale, was the first writer to give us any kind of extensive definition of the interpolated fugal exposition, we should probably interpret his indignation at Spazier's grouping together of imitation and fugal techniques as a personal issue rather than as representative of widely held beliefs of the time.

35. For a stunning analysis of these issues, worked out in terms of the writings of de Sade, see Theodor W. Adorno and Max Horkheimer, "Juliette or Enlightenment and Morality," in *Dialectic of Enlightenment*, translated by John Cumming (New York: Continuum, 1972), 81–119. I have also found the following useful: Michael Free-man, "Human Rights and the Corruption of Governments, 1789–1989," and Onara O'Neill, "Enlightenment as Autonomy: Kant's Vindication of Reason," both in *The Enlightenment and Its Shadows*, edited by Peter Hulme and Mudmilla Jordanova (London: Routledge, 1990), 163–83 and 184–99, respectively.

36. One of the clearest eighteenth-century expositions of this ideal is to be found in Jean le Rond d'Alembert's *Preliminary Discourse to the Encyclopedia of Diderot* (1751), translated by Richard N. Schwab (Bloomington: Indiana University Press, 1963).

37. Charles Rosen, *The Classical Style: Haydn, Mozart, Beethoven* (New York: Schirmer, 1972), 226.

38. Ibid., 227.

39. Cuthbert Girdlestone, *Mozart and His Piano Concertos* (New York: Schirmer, 1958), 291.

40. Rosen, *The Classical Style*, 226–27.

41. Simon P. Keefe, *Mozart's Piano Concertos: Dramatic Dialogue in the Age of Enlightenment* (Rochester, N.Y.: Boydell, 2001), 174.

42. Allanbrook, "Comic Issues in Mozart's Piano Concertos," in *Mozart Piano Concertos: Text, Context, Interpretation*, edited by Neal Zaslaw (Ann Arbor: University of Michigan Press, 1996), 85.

43. Ibid., 86.

44. This ending has been discussed at length by Allanbrook, ibid., 92–94.

45. On the different types of fugal subjects see Kirkendale, *Fugue and Fugato*, 89–134.

46. The frequent paring of fugal counterpoint with the harmonic instability of developmental procedures in classical instrumental works from the 1770s onward helps to give credibility to this last point. I discuss this point in the following chapter.

47. Elaine Sisman, *Mozart's 'Jupiter' Symphony* (Cambridge: Cambridge University Press, 1993), 70–71.

48. Jean-François Lyotard, *The Post-modern Condition: A Report on Knowledge*, translated by Geoff Bennington and Brian Massumi, foreword by Fredric Jameson (Minneapolis: University of Minnesota Press, 1984).

49. Allanbrook, "Theorizing the Comic Surface," 215.

50. Fredric Jameson, *Postmodernism, or The Cultural Logic of Late Capitalism* (Durham, N.C.: Duke University Press, 1991), 42.

51. Allanbrook, "Comic Issues in Mozart's Piano Concertos," 101.

52. Keefe, *Mozart's Piano Concertos*, 149.

53. Sigmund Freud, *The Interpretation of Dreams*, in *Standard Edition of the Complete Psychological Works of Sigmund Freud*, vol. 5, translated and edited by James Strachey in collaboration with Anna Freud (London: Hogarth Press and the Institute of Psycho-Analysis; New York: Norton, 1953–74), 574.

54. Lacan writes that the real/Other is "something strange to me, although it is at the heart of me": Jacques Lacan, *The Seminar. Book VII. The Ethics of Psychoanalysis, 1959–60*, translated by Dennis Porter (London: Routledge: 1992), 71.

55. I have investigated the respective political and ethical values of the sublime and the beautiful in my "Garden Disputes: Postmodern Beauty and the Sublime Neighbor (A Response to Judith Lochhead)," *Women and Music* 12 (2008): 75–86.

56. Lyotard, *The Postmodern Condition*, 72.

2. DREAMS (FUGAL COUNTERPOINT)

1. Mikhail Bakhtin, *Rabelais and His World*, trans. Hélène Iswolsky (Bloomington: Indiana University Press, 1984).

2. Carolyn Abbate, "Music – Drastic or Gnostic?" *Critical Inquiry* 30 (Spring 2004), 524.

3. Ibid., 518.

4. Slavoj Žižek, *The Sublime Object of Ideology* (London: Verso, 1989), 12, Žižek's emphasis.

5. Ibid., 13.

6. Jacques Lacan, *The Seminar. Book II. The Ego in Freud's Theory and in the Technique of Psychoanalysis, 1954–55*, translated by Sylvanna Tomaselli (New York: Norton; Cambridge: Cambridge University Press, 1988), 141, my emphasis. Indeed, the musical skills required by the analyst are frequently noted by Lacan: "We learn that analysis consists in playing on all the many staves of the score that speech constitutes in the registers of language, and on which overdetermination depends, which has no meaning except in that order." From Lacan's 1957 paper "The Instance of the Letter in the Unconscious, or Reason since Freud," quoted in Malcolm Bowie, *Lacan* (Cambridge, Mass: Harvard University Press, 1991), 66.

7. Most notably in "Negotiating the Music-Theory/African-Music Nexus: A Political Critique of Ethnomusicological Anti-formalism and a Strategic Analysis of the Harmonic Patterning of the Shona Mbira Song 'Nyamaopa,'" *Perspectives of New Music* 39 (2001): 5–117.

8. " Les fugues, en général, rendent la musique plus bruyante qu'agréable . . . dans toute fugue, la confusion de mélodie et de modulation est en même-temps ce qu'il y a de plus à craindre at de plus difficile à éviter; et le plaisir que donne ce genre de Musique étant toujours médiocre, on peut dire qu'une belle fugue est l'ingrat chef-d'œuvre d'un bon harmoniste." Rousseau, "Fugue," *Dictionnaire de Musique* (Paris, 1768), 221–22, my translation.

9. "Une unité successive qui se rapporte au sujet, et par laquelle toutes les parties, bien liées, composent un seul tout, dont on apperçoit l'ensemble et tous les rapports." Ibid., 536.

10. "Mais à peine en ai-je écouté la suite, pendant quelques minutes, que mon attention se relâche, le bruit m'étourdit peu-à-peu; bientôt il me lasse, et je suis enfin ennuyé de n'entendre que les accords." Ibid., 536.

11. Heinrich Koch, *Musikalisches Lexicon* (Frankfurt am Main, 1802), 1451–52, translated in Ratner, *Classic Music*, 23.

12. *Allgemeine Geschichte der Musik* (Leipzig, 1788, 1801), 1:47–48. Translation adapted from Hosler, *Changing Aesthetics of Instrumental Music in 18th Century Germany* (Ann Arbor, Mich.: UMI Research Press, 1981), 185–86. In fact, Koch quotes Forkel's passage in his article on fugue in *Musikalisches Lexicon*, 612–13.

13. Georg Joseph Vogler, *System für den Fugenbau* (Offenbach, 1811), translated in Neal Zaslaw, *Mozart's Symphonies: Context, Performance Practice, Reception* (Oxford: Clarendon Press, 1989), 544.

14. Admittedly, Forkel does mention the dynamic quality of fugal counterpoint; he also hints at the possibility of confusion. Any intimations of anxiety that could arise from these experiences, though, are swept out of the way by the joyously exuberant thrust of his interpretation:

Is not this variegated leading and weaving of voices, which together make a pleasant but manifold harmony, which seem to be going by different routes to one and the same goal, and which as Luther says, en route warmly greet and embrace each other so sweetly that those who have only slight understanding of such music must be quite perplexed and think that nothing in the world is stranger than such a song, embellished with many voices – is this not, this multifarious and artful weaving, an accurate representation of nature, is this not the most perfect expres-

sion of the multiply modified feelings of all the members of a people, feelings which first gradually arise, but then pour themselves out in a universal stream?

Allgemeine Geschichte der Musik (Leipzig, 1788, 1801), 1:47–48, translated in Hosler, *Changing Aesthetics of Instrumental Music,* 186.

15. *Musikalisches Lexicon,* translated by Ratner, *Classic Music,* 23.

16. Forkel's interpretation seems to be particularly suitable for such massive fugal structures as the C-sharp minor fugue from Book 1 of *The Well-Tempered Clavier.*

17. As Floyd K. and Margaret G. Grave have written, "Along with its allegiance to the *stile antico,* Vogler's sacred ideal embraced the technique of fugal polyphony. He proposed that fugal writing be understood as the exclusive property of the church, capable of powerful expression when combined with a sacred text, and he applauded the effectiveness of the great choral fugues of Handel." *In Praise of Harmony: The Teachings of Abbé Georg Joseph Vogler* (Lincoln: University of Nebraska Press, 1987), 127.

18. Theodor Adorno, "Bach Defended against His Devotees," in *Prisms,* translated by Samuel and Shierry Weber (Cambridge, Mass.: MIT Press, 1981), 133–46; David Yearsley, *Bach and the Meanings of Counterpoint* (Cambridge: Cambridge University Press, 2002).

19. *Musikalisches Lexicon,* 1451–52, translated in Ratner, *Classic Music,* 23.

20. *Musikalisches Lexicon,* 1453, translated by Ratner, *Classic Music,* 23.

21. Ratner, *Classic Music,* 262.

22. Kirkendale writes that "it is evident from the large number of fugal finales that Haydn was by no means the first composer to use them, as Noé believed, seeing this as the principal achievement of

Haydn's fugal output" (*Fugue and Fugato*, 57). The scholarly work that Kirkendale is criticizing is Günther von Noé's "Die Fuge bei Joseph Haydn" (Ph.D. diss., Vienna, 1954). For a table of fugal finales in Viennese chamber music, see Kirkendale, *Fugue and Fugato*, 58, 59.

23. James Webster, *Haydn's "Farewell" Symphony and the Idea of Classical Style: Through-Composition and Cyclic Integration in His Instrumental Music* (Cambridge: Cambridge University Press, 1991), 184.

24. Kirkendale, *Fugue and Fugato*, 76.

25. Albrechtsberger, *Gründliche Anweisung zur Composition*, 172, translated in Kirkendale, *Fugue and Fugato*, 76. A "galant" interpretation of the finale of Haydn's op. 20, no. 2 is strengthened by the fact that the predominant fugal subject in the movement – the one that starts the movement off – is dance derived. (Rather strangely, Ratner refers to it as a "passepied-gigue" [*Classic Music*, 264].) Yet the lightness and grace of tone and expression that one might see this gigue subject creating are also potentially deceptive. As with the piano dynamic marking, which I discuss below, the gigue subject can be viewed as masklike: it is a distraction that attempts to camouflage the irreconcilable syntactical conflict on which the movement is founded. For an alternative interpretation of the "galant" in op. 20, no. 2, see Carl Dahlhaus, *Analysis and Value Judgement*, translated by Siegmund Levarie (New York: Pendragon, 1983), 66–71. Webster, *Haydn's "Farewell" Symphony and the Idea of Classical Style*, has argued that the quartet as a whole "progresses from counterpoint (admixed with the galant) and tradition (never self-sufficient), to the galant and sonata style" (299); "The fugues in Op. 20 do not stand for traditional musical culture as opposed to the galant; they conclude works in both styles" (300).

26. A similar interpretation might be made of the fugal finale to Haydn's String Quartet op. 50, no. 4 in F-sharp minor (1787).

27. Translated in Zaslaw, *Mozart's Symphonies*, 544.

28. Hans Keller, *The Great Haydn Quartets: Their Interpretation* (London: Dent, 1986), 45.

29. Dahlhaus, *Analysis and Value Judgement*, 69.

30. The classic instance of an interpretation of the op. 20 quartets as defective is to be found in Adolf Sandberger, "Zur Geschichte des Haydnschen Streichquartetts," *Altbayerische Monatsschrift* 2 (1900): 41–64, rev., reprinted in Sandberger, *Ausgewählte Aufsätze zur Musikgeschichte*, vol. 1 (Munich: Drei Masken, 1921), 224–65. Problems with Sandberger's thesis are discussed in Dahlhaus, *Analysis and Value Judgement*, 67–71, and in the excellent "Historiographical Conclusion" to Webster's *Haydn's "Farewell" Symphony*, 341–47.

31. Webster, *Haydn's "Farewell" Symphony*, 296.

32. Keller, *The Great Haydn Quartets*, 101.

33. Webster, *Haydn's "Farewell" Symphony*, 300. Although the finale of Haydn's op. 20, no. 2, is undeniably radical, fugal finales were, nevertheless, relatively common in the early 1770s.

34. Beethoven also used relatively self-contained and extensive passages of fugal counterpoint for entire sections of movements in his later instrumental works. Examples include the middle section of the slow movement of the String Quartet in F Minor, *Quartetto Serioso*, op. 95 (1810), and the development section of the finale of the Piano Sonata in A Major, op. 101 (1816).

35. Robert N. Freeman, "Johann Georg Albrechtsberger," in *New Grove Dictionary of Music and Musicians*, 2: 224.

36. Cited in translation in Kirkendale, *Fugue and Fugato*, 195.

37. Jacqueline Waeber, "Jean-Jacques Rousseau's 'unité de mélodie,'" *Journal of the American Musicological Society* 62 (Spring 2009), 135.

38. Webster, *Haydn's "Farewell" Symphony*, 183.

39. Mark Evan Bonds touches upon this issue in his essay "Haydn's 'Cours complet de la composition' and the Sturm und Drang," in *Haydn Studies*, edited by W. Dean Sutcliffe (Cambridge: Cambridge University Press, 1998), 152–76. See also Webster, *Haydn's "Farewell" Symphony*, esp. 183–85.

40. Webster, *Haydn's "Farewell" Symphony*, 185.

41. For example, see A. Peter Brown, "The Sublime, the Beautiful, and the Ornamental: English Aesthetic Currents and Haydn's London Symphonies," in *Studies in Music History, Presented to H. C. Robbins Landon on His Seventieth Birthday*, edited by Otto Biba and David Wyn Jones (London: Thames and Hudson, 1996), 44–71. Although Brown doesn't actually conceive fugal writing in the finales of Haydn's London Symphonies as a "problem," he nonetheless sees it as a means of giving the finales added weight.

42. Scholars frequently term the passage in the development section of Beethoven's *Eroica* Symphony (1803) starting in m. 236 as a fugato. This passage is important because it instigates the move toward the massive crisis in the movement, which in turn leads to the so-called "new theme" starting in m. 284. Similarly, the fugato in the first movement of op. 59, no. 1 leads toward the climax on the diminished seventh chord starting in m. 210, which marks the beginning of the transition to the recapitulation. However, the fugato in the first movement of the *Eroica* is only 6 measures long, and 6

measures out of a movement of 610 hardly counts as extensive.

43. Joseph Kerman, *The Beethoven Quartets* (New York: Norton, 1966), 98. Similarly, with respect to the first movement of op. 59, no. 1, László Somfai has stated in a conference discussion group that "to have continuity in an immensely long development [Beethoven] soon realized that counterpoint could be utilized. This probably parallels the change in the size of sonata form": *The String Quartets of Haydn, Mozart, and Beethoven: Studies of the Autograph Manuscripts. A Conference at Isham Memorial Library, March 15–17, 1979*, edited by Christoph Wolff (Cambridge, Mass.: Harvard University Press, 1980), 275.

44. As Richard Kramer has pointed out, this passage caused Beethoven considerable difficulties: "'Der Organische der Fuge': On the Autograph of Beethoven's Quartet in F Major, Opus 59 No. 1," in Wolff, ed., *The String Quartets of Haydn, Mozart, and Beethoven*, 223–65.

45. Haydn had begun to incorporate fugal counterpoint into the development sections of the sonata-allegros of his string quartets in the previous year in the first movements of op. 50, no. 2 in C Major and no. 3 in E-flat Major (1787).

46. Other examples of multimovement works by Haydn that start with some kind of set of variations in a slow tempo include the Piano Sonatas in G Major, Hob. XVI/40 (1784), in D Major, Hob. XVI/42 (1784), and in C Major, Hob. XVI/48 (1789), and the String Quartets op. 2, no. 6 in B-flat Major (late 1750s), op. 9, no. 5 in B-flat Major (1768–70), op. 17, no. 3 in E-flat Major (1771), and op. 76, no. 5 in D Major and no. 6 in E-flat Major (1797).

47. One might also argue that the monothematicism of the second movement sonata-allegro – again, hardly unusual in Haydn – is in this instance marked as a kind of negative effect of the continuing

influence of the opening variations. Of course, the second movement manages to modulate to and solidly establish new keys; nevertheless, like a variation movement, it keeps returning to the same thematic material. This being the case, the sense of movement created by the establishment of new key areas in the second movement is, in this instance, perhaps partially undermined when the arrival of the new key is articulated by the return of the opening theme. In the second movement, the dialectic between harmonic progression and thematic repetition is allied to a dialectic between sonata- and variation-form procedures.

48. The interruption of these static passages fulfills a similar structural function to the famous solo-oboe cadenza that Beethoven inserts into the opening of the recapitulation of the first movement of the Fifth Symphony in C Minor, op. 67 (1808). And since we can also note that the first movement of the Piano Sonata no. 8 in C minor, op. 13 (*Pathétique*) (1799) is likewise punctuated by slow passages, in the form of returns of the opening slow introduction, we might posit that the interaction between anxiously driving fast music and slow reflection is a characteristic of Beethoven's so-called "C-minor mood." For example, see Michael C. Tusa, "Beethoven's 'C-Minor Mood': Some Thoughts on the Structural Implications of Key Choice," *Beethoven Forum* 2, ed. Christopher Reynolds, Lewis Lockwood, and James Webster (Lincoln: University of Nebraska Press, 1993), 1–28.

49. Kerman has related the fugal counterpoint in this movement to two other movements by Beethoven during this period, the last movement of the Piano Sonata, op. 10, no. 2 in F Major (1798) and the Andante of the First Symphony, op. 21 (1800): *The Beethoven Quartets*, 68–69.

50. Kirkendale, *Fugue and Fugato*, 229.

51. Kerman, *The Beethoven Quartets*, 69.

52. During the course of the minuet and trio, the problem created by the sparse ending of the minuet's canon is resolved, in part, by the two hefty passages of homophony with thumping accompaniments that occur in the trio, starting in mm. 44 and 70, respectively. In these two passages, the mild disarray created at the end of the minuet is temporarily resolved by forthright musical gestures. The difficulty of the end of the minuet, though, also continues to have effect in three places in the trio, starting in mm. 38, 52, and 62, respectively. At these points, the music seems to be temporarily disabled by a lack of conviction, as if the uncertainty of the minuet's concluding measures has infected the trio's ability to progress unhindered through its musical processes. In the following chapter, I consider how Haydn exploits irresolution for the purposes of through-composition with regard to the minuet movement of the String Quartet op. 33, no. 5 in G Major.

53. Vladimir Jankélévitch, *Music and the Ineffable,* translated by Carolyn Abbate (Princeton, N.J.: Princeton University Press, 2003), 5.

54. Ibid.

55. Ibid., 4.

56. Ovid, *Metamorphosis*, translated by A. D. Melville (Oxford: Oxford University Press, 1986), 133.

57. Ibid.

58. Ibid.

59. Ibid.

3. EXILE (*HAYDN, STRING QUARTET OP. 33, NO. 5*)

Earlier versions of portions of this chapter come from my article "Waiting for the Viennese Classics," *The Musical Quarterly* 90 (1) (2007): 123–166. Used by permission of Oxford University Press.

1. For an extended elaboration on this idea of the world's nervous system, see Michael Taussig, *The Nervous System* (London: Routledge, 1992).

2. Theodor W. Adorno, *Beethoven: The Philosophy of Music* (Stanford, Calif.: Stanford University Press, 1998), xi.

3. I have elaborated on this political notion of collaboration at greater length and more critically in my "Music and Politics," in *The Routledge Compendium of Philosophy and Music* (London: Routledge, 2011).

4. Lawrence Kramer, *Why Classical Music Still Matters* (Berkeley: University of California Press, 2007), 6, my emphasis.

5. Ibid., 9.

6. Ibid., 33.

7. Ibid., 33.

8. Quoted in Owen Hatherley, "Lash Out and Cover Up: Austerity Nostalgia and Ironic Authoritarianism in Recession Britain," *Radical Philosophy* 157 (September/October 2009), 2.

9. Žižek, *The Sublime Object of Ideology*, 127. For an excellent, optimistic, and remarkably level-headed introduction to the notion of the fundamentally unresolved fact of human social and political life, see Chantal Mouffe, *On the Political* (New York: Routledge, 2005). It should be noted, however, that although Mouffe and Žižek can agree that by definition "Society doesn't exist," the conclusions to which this leads them are pronouncedly different: Mouffe argues for the creation of a kind of radically "agonized" liberal democratic political practice, Žižek for an act of radical refoundation and rejection of the purported authority of liberal democratic terms of debate.

10. Žižek, *The Sublime Object of Ideology*, 127.

11. Ibid.

12. Fredric Jameson, *The Political Unconscious: Narrative as a Socially Symbolic Act* (Ithaca, N.Y.: Cornell University Press, 1981), 79.

13. Claude Lévi-Strauss, *Triste tropiques*, translated by John Russell (New York: Atheneum, 1971), 179.

14. Jameson, *The Political Unconscious*, p. 79.

15. As Jameson writes:

How much more must it be true for the citizen of the modern *Gesellschaft*, faced with the great constitutional options of the revolutionary period, and with the corrosive and tradition-annihilating effects of the spread of money and market economy, with the changing cast of collective characters which oppose the bourgeoisie, now to an embattled aristocracy, now to an urban proletariat, with the great fantasms of the various nationalisms, now themselves virtual "subjects of history" of a rather different kind, with the social and homogenization and psychic constriction of the rise of the industrial city and its "masses," the sudden appearance of the great transnational forces of communism and fascism, followed by the advent of the superstates and the onset of that great ideological rivalry between capitalism and communism, which, no less passionate and obsessive than that which, at the dawn of modern times, seethed through the wars of religion, marks the final tension of our global village?

Ibid., 79–80.

16. Walter Benjamin, "Theses on the Philosophy of History," in *Illuminations*, edited by Hannah Arendt, translated by Harry Zohn (New York: Schocken Books, 1968), 256–57.

17. Theodor W. Adorno, *Minima Moralia: Reflections from Damaged Life*, translated by E. F. N. Jephcott (London: Verso, 1978), 50.

18. Lydia Goehr, *The Quest for Voice: Music, Politics, and the Limits of Philosophy* (Berkeley: University of California Press, 1998), 13.

19. The following discussion of the politics of critique has been adapted from my "Music and Politics."

20. Adorno, *Minima Moralia*, 39.

21. We should note that in *Why Classical Music Still Matters*, Kramer also articulates music in terms of futurity, the new, and the not-as-yet known. So for example: "This music still matters for the same reason that Greek drama or Renaissance painting or modernist fiction matters: because it made discoveries we are far from done with and that are far from done with us. It has imagined forms of experience that became substantial realities in being thus imagined: forms of being, becoming, sensing, witnessing, remembering, desiring, hoping, suffering and more.... The Western world is not only the richer for preserving Sophocles' *Antigone* or Beethoven's Ninth Symphony, but different" (33).

22. Adorno, *Minima Moralia*, 39. I have elaborated further on this kind of point in my "Music after All," *Journal of the American Musicological Society* 62 (Spring 2009), 161.

23. Ibid., 39.

24. For an extended analysis of the paradoxes of subjection – whereby being subordinated to power allows for our possible emergence as subjective agents – see Judith Butler, *The Psychic Life of Power: Theories in Subjection* (Stanford, Calif.: Stanford University Press, 1997).

25. Kramer, *Why Classical Music Still Matters*, 33.

26. The question of the remaining trace of musical autonomy in Kramer's work was the primary focus of Gary Tomlinson's critique in the well-known interchange between himself and Kramer that appeared in *Current Musicology* 53

(1993): Kramer, "Music Criticism and the Postmodern Turn: In Contrary Motion with Gary Tomlinson," 25–35; Tomlinson, "Musical Pasts and Postmodern Musicologies: A Response to Lawrence Kramer," and "Tomlinson Responds," 18–24, and 36–40. At that time, Tomlinson had argued strongly against the status of music as an object that can be distinguished from the context by which it is mediated; by comparison, Kramer had been more prepared to admit a kind of provisional status for the musical object, even though his concern has remained with musical meaning and, therefore, not with musical objects per se. I have discussed their positions in "Music after All," where I also reject such rejections of musical autonomy as both logically contradictory (via an engagement with the work of Giles Hooper and Kevin Korsyn) and politically self-defeating.

27. Kramer, *Why Classical Music Still Matters*, 33.

28. Richard Leppert, "Music 'Pushed to the Edge of Existence' (Adorno, Listening, and the Question of Hope)," *Cultural Critique* 60 (2005): 97–98.

29. Chua, *Absolute Music and the Construction of Meaning*, 3.

30. See Walter E. Rex, "A Propos of the Figure of Music on the Frontispiece of the Encyclopédie: Theories of Musical Imitation in d'Alembert, Rousseau, and Diderot," in *Report of the Twelfth I.M.S. Congress Berkeley 1977*, edited by Anthony Newcomb and Bonnie Wade (Kassel: Bärenreiter, 1981), 214–25.

31. For a discussion of how the idea of art as artifice affected audience behavior, see James J. Johnson, "Musical Experience and the Formation of a French Musical Public," *Journal of Modern History* 64, no. 2 (1992): 191–226.

32. Charles Batteux, *Les Beaux-arts reduits à un même principe*, in Edward Lippman, *Music Aesthetics: A Historical*

Reader I (New York: Pendragon Press, 1986), 264.

33. Ibid., 264.

34. Carl Dahlhaus, *Esthetics of Music,* translated by William Austin (Cambridge: Cambridge University Press, 1983), 20.

35. Ibid., 17.

36. Ibid.

37. We should note here that Kramer's work has been marked by a sustained effort to prove, to the contrary, that words in fact can go an exceedingly long way into articulating the terrain of music's capacity for, as it were, existential meaning.

38. Goehr, *The Quest for Voice,* 32.

39. In a discussion of Schopenhauer's aesthetics of music, Goehr writes that "from the perspective of Will, [music] expresses *abstractly, universally,* and *essentially.* . . . So if it expressed the different emotions at all, it expresses them 'in themselves' abstracted from any ordinary human motives or experiences that might generate their particularized instantiation" (*The Quest for Voice,* 22).

40. Lydia Goehr, *The Imaginary Museum of Musical Works: An Essay in the Philosophy of Music* (Oxford: Clarendon Press, 1992), 154.

41. Ibid.

42. Cited in David Charlton, ed., *E. T. A. Hoffman's Musical Writings:* Kreisleriana, The Poet and the Composer, *Music Criticism,* translated by Martyn Clark (Cambridge: Cambridge University Press, 1989), 96.

43. Friedrich Nietzsche, *The Birth of Tragedy and The Case of Wagner,* translated by Walter Kaufmann (New York: Vintage Books, 1967), 55.

44. Nietzsche, *The Birth of Tragedy and The Case of Wagner,* 180. Usually, "effect" is the "result of an action" (*Chambers English Dictionary,* 452), where the "action" implies the presence of something that could create the effect. However,

"effective," in the sense in which it appears within essentially Romantic discourses of the transcendent, is more akin to the present-day spectacle of cinematic special effects, where the cause seems to remain unknown. An early example of this kind of use of the word is to be found in Jean-Jacques Rousseau's 1768 *Dictionnaire de Musique,* where the "effective" denotes "when the sensation produced seems superior to the means employed in creating it" (191).

45. E. T. A. Hoffman, "Beethoven's Instrumental Music," in *E. T. A. Hoffman's Musical Writings,* 98.

46. "Who, if I cried out, would hear me among the angels' hierarchies? and even if one of them pressed me suddenly against his heart: I would be consumed in that overwhelming existence. For beauty is nothing but the beginning of terror, which we still are just able to endure, and we are so awed because it serenely disdains to annihilate us. Every angel is terrifying" (Rainer Maria Rilke, *Duino Elegies,* the first elegy, in *The Selected Poetry of Rainer Maria Rilke,* edited and translated by Stephen Mitchell [New York: Vintage Books, 1989], 150–51).

47. For a modern reassertion of the structural and formal ground of autonomy and freedom in the human subject, see Slavoj Žižek, *Tarrying with the Negative: Kant, Hegel, and the Critique of Ideology* (Durham, N.C.: Duke University Press, 1993), chap. 1 ("*Cogito:* The Void Called Subject"), 9–44.

48. Even in James Webster's work, where arguments in favor of assigning classical music to a separate period have been most strong, classical music is understood in terms of a mixture of divergent historical influences. And so, for example, Haydn's *Creation*

helped to found music's new-found status as the highest and most romantic art, albeit in a form that simultaneously maintained its traditional function as mimesis. Among the elements that made this triumph possible, the musical sublime was arguably the most important. From this perspective, Haydn's final triumph itself almost seems sublime, not only in elementary human terms, but in historical ones as well. For his triumph was the artistic touchstone of an entire historical period: a period for which we have no name, because it links, rather than divides, the Enlightenment and Romanticism.

Webster, "The *Creation,* Haydn's Late Vocal Music, and the Musical Sublime," in *Haydn and His World,* edited by Elaine Sisman (Princeton, N.J.: Princeton University Press, 1997), 97. See also Webster, "The Eighteenth Century as Music-Historical Period?," *Eighteenth-Century Music* 1 (2004): 47–60, "Between Enlightenment and Romanticism in Music History: 'First Viennese Modernism' and the Delayed Nineteenth Century," *Nineteenth-Century Music* 25 (2002): 108–26; "The Concept of Beethoven's 'Early' Period in the Context of Periodizations in General," *Beethoven Forum* 3 (1994): 3–27; and *Haydn's "Farewell" Symphony,* 335–66.

49. Harold Powers, "Reading Mozart's Music: Text and Topic, Syntax and Sense," *Current Musicology* 57 (1995), 29.

50. Allanbrook, *Rhythmic Gesture in Mozart,* 3.

51. In a similar fashion, George Edwards has noted that the use of a pitch at the top of a chord other than the root is frequently employed at the end of movements in Haydn's late quartets (opp. 74, 76, and 77) as a means of undermining a sense of closure (Edwards, "The Nonsense of an Ending: Closure in Haydn's String Quartets," *Musical Quarterly* 75 [1991]: 240).

52. Donald Francis Tovey, "Haydn's Chamber Music," in *The Main Stream of Music and Other Essays* (New York: Oxford University Press, 1979), 51.

53. A comparison can be made here with Haydn's A Major Sonata, Hob. XVI: 30, part of a set whose composition began in 1774 and that was distributed in 1776. As Sisman has written: "Its Tempo di Menuet finale with six easy variations might easily be dismissed as quotidian and unserious. Yet it concludes a sonata in which not a single previous movement came to a final cadence, the first and only such fully linked cycle in Haydn's *oeuvre;* indeed, the theme provides the first structural final cadence in the sonata. That the theme is then followed by six such final cadences in the variations drives home the point emphatically: the finale acts as a kind of reiterated cadential pattern for the sonata as a whole." *Haydn and the Classical Variation* (Cambridge, Mass.: Harvard University Press, 1993), 43. See also James Webster's interpretation of this sonata: *Haydn's "Farewell" Symphony,* 288–94.

54. Kant, "An Answer to the Question: 'What Is Enlightenment?',", in *Kant: Political Writings,* 2nd ed., edited with an introduction and notes by Hans Reiss, translated by H. B. Nisbet (Cambridge: Cambridge University Press, 1991), 54.

55. Ibid.

56. Ibid., 54–55.

57. Ibid., 55.

58. Ibid., 58.

59. Ibid., 55.

60. Ibid., 56.

61. Cited in O'Neill, "Enlightenment as Autonomy: Kant's Vindication of Reason," 193.

62. Ibid., 194.

63. Žižek, *The Sublime Object of Ideology,* 80.

64. Ibid., 81.

65. Ibid., 80–81.

4. ENCHANTMENT (MOZART, LA CLEMENZA DI TITO)

Earlier versions of portions of this chapter come from my article "Better the Puppet?" *Current Musicology,* 74 (2002): 4–45.

1. Julia Kristeva, *Powers of Horror: An Essay on Abjection,* translated by Leon S. Roudiez (New York: Columbia University Press, 1982), 2–3.

2. See, for example, George Steiner, *Real Presences: Is There Anything in What We Say?* (London: Faber and Faber, 1989).

3. Ibid., 4.

4. I have elaborated in somewhat different terms on the potential ideological violence inherent in the association of the marginalized with dance in "Music after All."

5. Walter Benjamin, "The Work of Art in the Age of Mechanical Reproduction," in *Illuminations,* edited by Hannah Arendt, translated by Harry Zohn (New York: Schocken Books, 1968), 217–51.

6. Ibid., 242.

7. The preservation of myth within the ongoing distortions of modernity is, of course, a key argument in Theodor Adorno's and Max Horkheimer's *Dialectic of Enlightenment,* translated by John Cumming (New York: Continuum, 1991).

8. Benjamin, "The Work of Art," 242.

9. Ibid., 223. For a somewhat damning historical and theoretical critique of Benjamin's claims regarding mechanical reproduction, see Robert Hullot-Kentor, "What Is Mechanical Reproduction?," in *Things Beyond Resemblance: Collected Essays on Theodor W. Adorno* (New York: Columbia University Press, 2006), 136–53.

10. Ibid., 233.

11. Ibid., my emphasis.

12. John Keats, "To Sleep," *A Selection from John Keats,* edited by E. C. Pettet (London: Longman, 1974), 230.

13. Johan Huizinga, *Homo Ludens: A Study of the Play-Element in Culture* (Boston: Beacon Press, 1955), 8.

14. Ibid.

15. Ibid.

16. Ibid.

17. John A. Rice, "Leopold II, Mozart, and the Return to a Golden Age," in *Opera and the Enlightenment,* edited by Thomas Bauman and Maria Petzoldt McClymonds (Cambridge: Cambridge University Press, 1995), 290.

18. Reinhart Koselleck, *Critique and Crisis: Enlightenment and the Pathogenesis of Modern Society* (Cambridge, Mass.: MIT Press, 1988), 19.

19. Ibid., 55.

20. For example, see James Van Horn Melton, *The Rise of the Public in Enlightenment Europe* (Cambridge: Cambridge University Press, 2001), in particular chapter 6 ("Women in Public: Enlightenment Salons"), 197–225.

21. Koselleck, *Critique and Crisis,* 63.

22. This, for example, is James Van Horn Melton's essentially positive reading of the situation, in *The Rise of the Public in Enlightenment Europe,* 197–205.

23. Mary Wollstonecraft, *A Vindication of the Rights of Woman* (London: Penguin, 1992), 87.

24. Thomas Laqueur, *Making Sex: Body and Gender from the Greeks to Freud* (Cambridge, Mass.: Harvard University Press, 1990), 5.

25. Linda Schiebinger, *The Mind Has No Sex? Women in the Origins of Modern Science* (Cambridge, Mass.: Harvard University Press, 1989), 191–200, and "Skeletons in the Closet: The First Illustrations of the Female Skeleton in Eighteenth-Century Anatomy," *Representations* 14 (1986): 42–82.

26. On the relationship between women as mothers and Enlightenment thinking, see Nancy K. Miller's classic *The*

Heroine's Text: Readings in the French and English Novel 1722–1782 (New York: Columbia University Press, 1980).

27. Jean-Jacques Rousseau, *Emile, or On Education,* translated by Allan Bloom (New York: Basic Books, 1979), Book V, 361.

28. In Evelyne Berriot-Salvador, "The Discourse of Medicine and Science," translated by Arthur Goldhammer, in *A History of Women in the West: Renaissance and Enlightenment Paradoxes,* edited by Natalie Zemon Davis and Arlette Farge (Cambridge Mass.: Harvard University Press, 1993), 387.

29. In her introduction to Wollstone-craft's *Vindication,* for example, Miriam Brody writes that although "a small receptive circle of liberal reformers . . . would welcome the *Vindication* with enthusiasm . . . once concern grew over the association of English radicalism with the ideas of the French revolution, Wollstonecraft's assault on established authority . . . was greeted with predictable alarm and outrage." Wollstonecraft, *A Vindication of the Rights of Women,* 41–42.

30. "Protectresses of the community, they rose to defend its rights. Thanks to their mobility, their constant presence in the streets, their familiarity with public spaces, and their role in the neighborhood, they soon learned of any violation of the tacit rules governing the balance between public power and its subjecters. They were quick to rise to protest any situation they judged intolerable, dragging their men along with them." Dominique Godineau, "The Woman," in *Enlightenment Portraits,* edited by Michel Vovelle and translated by Lydia G. Cochrane, 416. See also Arlette Farge, "Protesters Plain to See," translated by Arthur Goldhammer, in *A History of Women in the West,* 489–505, which includes a list of the studies of this phenomenon.

31. See Godineau, "The Woman," 394.

32. Farge, "Protesters Plain to See," 502–505.

33. See Joan Landes, *Women and the Public Sphere in the Age of the French Revolution* (Ithaca, N.Y.: Cornell University Press, 1988).

34. Dorinda Outram, *The Enlightenment* (Cambridge: Cambridge University Press, 1995), 85.

35. Alan Tyson, "*La clemenza di Tito* and Its Chronology," in *Mozart; Studies of the Autograph Scores* (Cambridge, Mass.: Harvard University Press, 1987), 48–60. On the question of paper types, see also H. C. Robbins Landon, *1791, Mozart's Last Year* (New York: Thames and Hudson, 1988), chap. 8 ("A Journey to Prague"), 84–101.

36. Cited in Leo Treitler, ed., *Strunk's Source Readings in Music History, Revised Edition* (New York: Norton, 1998), 967.

37. Emily Anderson, editor and translator, *The Letters of Mozart and His Family* (London: Macmillan, 1938), vol. 2, 1000.

38. John A. Rice, "Mozart and His Singers: The Case of Maria Marchetti Fantozzi, the First Vitellia," *Opera Quarterly* 11 (1995): 31–52.

39. S'altro che lacrime / Per lui non tenti, / Tutto il tuo piangere / Non gioverà / A questa intutile / Pietà che senti, / Oh quanto è simile / La crudeltà. / S'altro che lacrime, ecc. (parte) [If you do nothing for him but shed tears, all your weeping will be of no avail. Oh, how like to cruelty is this useless pity that you feel. If you do nothing for him, etc. (exit)].

40. Che del ciel, che degli Dei / Tu il pensier, l'amour tu sei, / Grand'Eroe, nel giro angusto / Si mostrò di questo dì / Ma, cagion di maraviglia / Non è già, felice Augusto, / Che gli Dei chi lor somiglia, Custodiscano / così [That you are the care, the darling of heaven and of the gods, great hero, has been shown in the brief course if this day. But there is

no cause for wonder, fortunate Augustus, that the gods thus watch over one so like them].

41. Sulzer, "Menuet," in *Allgemeine Theorie der schönen Künste* (1771–74), translated in Allanbrook, *Rhythmic Gesture in Mozart*, 33–34; for an examination of dance types in *Clemenza* in general, see Judith L. Schwartz, "Rhythmic Gesture in 'La clemenza di Tito': Dance Rhythms as Rhetorical Devices," *Mozart Jahrbuch* (1991), 755–65. Since Sulzer, like many others in the late eighteenth century, here invokes Winckelman's famous remarks regarding the "noble simplicity and calm grandeur" of classical art, it would be interesting to consider further whether the neoclassical potential of the minuet was being aligned with *Clemenza's* neoclassical subject matter in Mozart's intention.

42. C. J. von Feldtenstein, *Die Kunst nach der Choreographie zu tanzen und Tänze zu schreiben* (Braunschweig, 1767), 36–37, translated in Allanbrook, *Rhythmic Gesture in Mozart*, 33.

43. Immanuel Kant, *The Critique of Judgment*, translated by James Creed Meredith (Oxford: Oxford University Press, 1952), 167.

44. The association of Handel with sublimity was already in place during Handel's life – Alexander H. Schapiro, "Drama of an Infinitely Superior Nature: Handel's Early English Oratorios and the Religious Sublime," *Music and Letters* 74 (1993): 215–45; Claudia L. Johnson, "'Giant HANDEL' and the Musical Sublime," *Eighteenth-Century Studies* 19 (1985–86): 515–33. It continued on into the late eighteenth century and beyond – Christoph Wolff, "Mozart's *Messiah:* The Spirit of Handel from van Swieten's Hands," in *Music and Civilization: Essays in Honor of Paul Henry Lang*, edited by Edmond Strainchamps and Maria Rika Maniates (New York: Norton, 1984), 1–14; William Weber, "The Intellectual Bases of the Handelian Tradition, 1759–1800," *Proceedings of the Royal Musical Association* 108 (1981–82): 100–114.

45. The start of the chorus's second phrase – beginning in m. 21 with the words "ma, cagion di maraviglia," and set to essentially the same musical gesture as the opening of the first phrase – begins solidly at the beginning of the measure. More accustomed now to their musical environment, the chorus has no longer need of being stunned; to repeat the initial gesture of awe would have merely stylized it and emphasized artifice over spontaneity.

46. Rousseau, *Dictionnaire de musique* (Paris 1768), in David Charlton, *E. T. A. Hoffman's Musical Writings*, 72.

47. Daniel Heartz, "Mozart and His Italian Contemporaries," in *Mozart's Operas* (Berkeley: University of California Press, 1990), 299–317.

48. John A. Rice, "Leopold II, Mozart, and the Return to a Golden Age," in *Opera and the Enlightenment*, edited by Thomas Bauman and Marita Petzoldt McClymonds (Cambridge: Cambridge University Press, 1995), 271–96.

49. This statement is, for example, at the heart of my critique of DJ Spooky, "Spookier than Spooky," review essay of Paul D. Miller's (aka DJ Spooky, That Subliminal Kid), *Rhythm Science*, in *Popular Music* 26, no. 3 (2007): 505–12.

50. Diderot, *Rameau's Nephew and D'Alembert's Dream*, translated by Leonard Tancock (London: Penguin, 1966), 151–52 and 157, respectively. My historical argument in this passage – moving as it does from eighteenth-century mechanistic thinking through Kant – mirrors a certain historical picture painted by Abbate in her remarkable essay on musical automata, "Outside Ravel's Tomb," *Journal of the American Musicological Society* 52 (1999): 465–530, rewritten in "Outside the Tomb," in Abbate, *In Search of Opera* (Princeton, N.J.: Princeton University Press, 2001),

185–246. For particularly fine pieces on mechanistic aspects of music in the eighteenth century specifically, see Yearsley, *Bach and the Meanings of Counterpoint*, chap. 5 ("Bach the Machine"), 173–208, and Annette Richards, "Automatic Genius: Mozart and the Mechanical Sublime," *Music and Letters* 80 (1999): 366–89.

51. Steiner, *Real Presences*, 122.

52. For an extended and deeply sensitive examination of the possibilities and tragedies attendant upon this short-circuit as it manifested itself within the German tradition, see Hoeckner, *Programming the Absolute: Nineteenth-Century German Music and the Hermeneutics of the Moment*.

53. Chua, *Absolute Music and the Construction of Meaning*, 257.

54. Ibid., 262.

55. Ibid., 264.

56. Ibid.

57. McClary, *Conventional Wisdom: The Content of Musical Form*. McClary, of course, has also been a proponent of the values of the deconstituted subject. This is illustrated, for example, in her discussion of a kind of pluralized model of desire in "Constructions of Subjectivity in Schubert's Music," in *Queering the Pitch: The New Gay and Lesbian Musicology*, edited by Philip Brett, Elizabeth Wood, and Gary C. Thomas (New York: Routledge, 1994), 205–34.

58. bell hooks, *Belonging: A Culture of Place* (New York: Routledge, 2009).

59. In this regard, we should note that Lacan's own linguistic reconstitution of the human psyche is a project that is frequently punctuated with analogies to and resonances with Marx's understanding of capitalism. For a decidedly critical examination of this theme, see Joe Valente, "Lacan's Marxism, Marxism's Lacan (from Žižek to Althusser)," in *The Cambridge Companion to Lacan*, edited by Jean-Michel Rabaté (Cambridge: Cambridge University Press, 2003), 153–72.

60. However, ever since Marx's own critique, this kind of possibility has been read in two ways simultaneously. So, for example, as Fredric Jameson puts it, we need "to think the cultural evolution of late capitalism dialectically, as catastrophe and progress all together" (*Postmodernism, or, The Cultural Logic of Late Capitalism* [Durham, N.C.: Duke University Press, 2003], 47). The classic examination of this split is Marshall Berman's *All That Is Solid Melts into Air: The Experience of Modernity* (New York: Penguin Books, 1988).

61. Cornel West, *Democracy Matters: Winning the Fight against Imperialism* (London: Penguin Books, 2005), 26–27.

62. We should note, however, that unlike most disenchanted postmodern thinking, West's and hook's projects are frequently cut across by a transformative utopian politics.

63. For a more extended discussion of the psychoanalytic understanding of the pleasure principle, see the end of the first chapter of this study.

64. My use of the phrase "Post-Communist Condition" is a play on the title of the political geographer and social theorist David Harvey's famous *The Condition of Postmodernity: An Enquiry into the Origins of Cultural Change* (Oxford: Blackwell, 1989). Harvey's book critiques the claims that postmodernism is a form of liberation, arguing, by contrast, that it is actually yet another distortion emerging from capitalism itself. The phrase "Post-Communism" was recently used as the title of a volume of the journal *Radical Philosophy* 159 (January/February 2010). Like Harvey, the contributors to the volume (many Eastern Europeans) argue that 1989 never managed to articulate a new beginning after the world of communism, but simply devolved into a negative globalization of the problems of capitalism itself that the First World/Second World

rifts had similarly helped to keep successfully afloat. For the beginnings of an understanding of the logic of how capitalism
thrived within, for example, the Cold War,
see Eric Hobsbawm, *The Age of Extremes:
A History of the World, 1914–1991* (New
York: Vintage Books, 1996), chap. 8 ("Cold
War"), 225–56. Also of relevance would be
the work of the Cold War and Music Study
Group, affiliated to the American Musicological Society. Here, one might start
with *Journal of Musicology* 26, no. 1 (winter
2009), which was devoted to their work.

65. In Lacan, "forced choice" is the
phrase used to articulate how we get interpolated into the symbolic of language.
To "choose" not to enter into language is
no choice at all, since it leads to psychosis,
where we cannot properly speak about a
subject making choices. So it is only once
we have become, as it were, subject to the
symbolic, that we can understand that by
being forced into the symbolic we were
given the very possibility of choice in
the first place. It is a classic case of what,
in Lacanian discourse, is referred to as
future anteriority. However, this creates
a certain ambivalence with regard to how
the subject perceives its symbolically
ordained freedom to choose; since choice
has come from coercion, the subject is
haunted by a certain guilt regarding what
it has given up: in other words, the *jouissance* created by the ultimate excess of *not*
choosing to be forced to choose choice.

66. Žižek, *The Sublime Object of Ideology*, 165.

67. Paul Griffiths, *New Sounds, New
Personalities: British Composers of the 1980s
in Conversation with Paul Griffiths* (London: Faber and Faber, 1985), 119.

68. Ibid., 118.

69. Ibid., 119.

70. Ibid., 120.

71. Alenka Zupančič, *The Odd One
In: On Comedy* (Cambridge, Mass.: MIT
Press, 2008), 4.

72. Ibid., 5.

73. Ibid.

74. Earlier versions of this following
argument of mine are to be found in "Music after All," particularly 157–61, and "Musicology after Identity – Four Fragments,"
Women and Music 12 (2008): 87–93.

75. Zupančič, *The Odd One In*, 7.

76. Ibid.

77. Ibid., 6.

5. FORGETTING (*EDWARD SAID*)

1. This point is nicely contextualized
by Moustafa Bayoumi in "Reconciliation
without Duress: Said, Adorno, and the
Autonomous Intellectual," *Alif: Journal of
Comparative Poetics* 25 (2005): 46–64.

2. "My Right of Return" (an interview
with Ari Shavit, *Ha-aretz Magazine,* Tel
Aviv, 2000), reprinted in Edward Said,
*Power, Politics, and Culture: Interviews with
Edward W. Said,* edited by Gauri Viswana-
than (New York: Vintage, 2002), 458.

3. Bayoumi, "Reconciliation without
Duress."

4. Said, "My Right of Return,"
447–48.

5. Daniel Barenboim and Edward
W. Said, *Parallels and Paradoxes: Explorations in Music and Society,* edited by
Ara Guzelimian (London: Bloomsbury,
2003), xvii.

6. "Returning to Ourselves" (an
interview with Jacqueline Rose, *Jewish
Quarterly,* Winter 1997/1998), reprinted in
Said, *Power, Politics, and Culture,* 419.

7. Ibid.

8. Ibid.

9. Ibid., 429.

10. For example, this trope makes its
presence felt on 425.

11. Ibid., 426.

12. Ibid., 425.

13. Ibid., 423.

14. Ibid.

15. Ibid., 424.

16. Ibid., 425.

17. The identification of this aspect of Said's work as somehow Enlightenment in orientation is made by Rose early on in the interview (420). She contrasts it with Said's interest in modernism, which "by your own [Said's] account, is skeptical of certain concepts of truth, certainty, and so on" (420).

18. Ibid., 419–20.

19. Ibid., 420–21.

20. Some of this material appears as the third chapter ("*Così fan tutte* at the Limits") of Said's posthumously published *On Late Style: Music and Literature against the Grain* (New York: Vintage Books, 2006), 48–72.

21. Said, "Returning to Ourselves," 430.

22. Ibid., 430.

23. Ibid.

24. Ibid.

25. Ibid.

26. Said, *On Late Style*, vii.

27. Said, "Returning to Ourselves," 430–31.

28. Toward the beginning of *On Late Style,* Said acknowledges: "Each of us can readily supply evidence of how it is that late works crown a lifetime of aesthetic endeavor. Rembrandt and Matisse, Bach and Wagner." However, with an almost self-reflective interrogative he changes direction: "But what of artistic lateness not as harmony and resolution but as intransigence, difficulty, and unresolved contradiction?" Said then turns to Ibsen for illustration, but his conclusion that Ibsen's late plays "leave the audience more perplexed and unsettled than before" is equally as descriptive of the effect of his own late work. *On Late Style*, 7. Likewise, as Stathis Gourgouris points out, "The writing of [Said's] memoir *Out of Place* (1999) – which by his own account, proved difficult to complete – was hardly an attempt to round out the contours of his life or provide a retrospective reference

for some sort of Saidian totality." "The Late Style of Edward Said," *Alif: Journal of Comparative Poetics* 25 (2005): 37.

29. As Michael Wood writes in his introduction: "Said was not attracted by the idea of a late, dissolving self. He doesn't inhabit his last works as 'a lamenting personality,' his own phrase in this book for Adorno's picture of late Beethoven. Said wanted to continue with the self's making, and if we divide a life into early, middle, and late periods, he was still in the middle when he dies at the age of sixty-seven.... Still a little too early, I think he would have said, for real lateness" (*On Late Style*, xviii). Said's most extended statement about the making of the self and the question of the conscious formation of beginnings is to be found in his *Beginnings: Intention and Method* (New York: Basic Books, 1975).

30. Said, "Returning to Ourselves," 431.

31. Goehr, *The Quest for Voice: Music, Politics, and the Limits of Philosophy*.

32. The famous passage from the preface to the *Phenomenology* from which the phrase comes is, in its own way, an argument against forgetting: "But the life of the spirit is not the life that shrinks from death and keeps itself untouched by devastation, but rather the life that endures it and maintains itself in it. It is this power, not as something positive, which closes its eyes to the negative, as when we say of something that it is nothing or is false, and then, having done with it, turn away and pass on to something else; on the contrary, Spirit is this power only by looking the negative in the face, and tarrying with it. This tarrying with the negative is the magical power that converts it into being." G. W. F. Hegel, *Phenomenology of Spirit*, translated A. V. Miller (Oxford: Oxford University Press, 1977), 19.

33. For further elaboration on the interesting interaction between personal

and political import in Said's late relationship to Adorno, see Bayoumi, "Reconciliation without Duress," 46–64.

34. The presence of ethical and political inconsistencies in Said's late work with, and theorizing with regard to, the West-Eastern Divan Orchestra lies at the heart of Rachel Beckles Willson's critique in "Whose Utopia? Perspectives on the West-Eastern Divan Orchestra," *Music and Politics* 3, no. 2 (2009).

35. Paul Smaczny, *The Ramallah Concert – Knowledge Is the Beginning and West-Eastern Divan Orchestra/Barenboim* (EuroArts Music International and Warner Classics, 2005), track 5.

36. Friedrich Nietzsche, "On the Uses and Disadvantages of History for Life," *Untimely Meditations,* edited by Daniel Breazelae, translated by R. J. Hollingdale (Cambridge: Cambridge University Press, 1997), 64.

37. Walter Benjamin, "Theses on the Philosophy of History," in *Illuminations,* edited Hannah Arendt, translated Harry Zohn (New York: Schocken Books, 1968), 257.

38. Alain Badiou, *Ethics: An Essay on the Understanding of Evil,* translated by Peter Hallward (London: Verso, 2001), 109.

39. As an aside, we might also note that one of the characteristic notions of Jean Genet, whom Said discusses at length in his work on lateness, is that our emotions and sensations somehow survive beyond our own death. Take, for example, this characteristic passage from Genet's last novel, *Captif amoureux,* completed just before his death in 1986: "A little while ago I wrote that though I shall die, nothing else will. And I must make my meaning clear. Wonder at the sight of a corn-flower, at a rock, at the touch of a rough hand – all the millions of emotions of which I'm made – they won't disappear even though I shall. Other men will experience them, and they'll still be there because of them. More and more I believe I exist in order to be the terrain and proof which show other men that life consists in the uninterrupted emotions flowing through all creation. The happiness my hand knows in a boy's hair will be known by another hand, is already known. And although I shall die, that happiness will live on. 'I' may die, but what made that 'I' possible, what made possible the joy of being, will make the joy of being live on without me." Genet, *Prisoner of Love,* translated by Barbara Bray (New York: New York Review Books, 2003), 361.

40. Said, *On Late Style,* 51.

41. Ibid., 66.

42. Ibid., 68.

43. Ibid., 79.

44. Ibid., 82.

45. Ibid., 90.

46. Ibid., 82–83.

47. In a similar vein see Milan Kundera's remarkable analysis of ecstasy in "Improvisation in Homage to Stravinsky," in *Testaments Betrayed,* translated by Linda Asher (London: Faber and Faber, 1995), in particular 84–87.

48. Said, *On Late Style,* 131.

49. As Bruce Fink writes, "The hysteric pushes the master – incarnated in a partner, teacher, or whomever – to the point where he or she can find the master's knowledge lacking. Either the master does not have an explanation for everything, or his or her reasoning does not hold water." "The Master Signifier and the Four Discourses," *Key Concepts of Lacanian Psychoanalysis,* edited by Dany Nobus (New York: Other Press, 1998), 36.

50. Said, *On Late Style,* 18.

51. Ibid., 18.

52. Ibid.

53. Ibid., 131–32.

54. For example, see chapter 1, section iii ("Two Visions in *Heart of Darkness*") in

Said, *Culture and Imperialism* (New York, Vintage, 1993), 19–31.

55. I have elaborated on the dialectical volatility of the politics of visibility in "Musicology after Identity – Four Fragments."

56. Of course, one could easily argue that with Gould one is dealing with the ultimate form of hysteric visibility, and that his attempts to disenable us from viewing him were simply instrumental in keeping us fixated on the possibility of a sighting of his idiosyncratic and contradictory Gothic distortions: a tall wraith sitting on a short chair, but hunched over like some vile golem, while simultaneously conducting the piano nobly as if it were an invisible orchestra. Children like to play hide-and-seek because the pleasure of being able to escape the gaze of the Other is protected from transforming into the horror of abandonment by the thrilling terror of being found again.

57. Said, *On Late Style*, 144.

58. Ibid., 24.

59. Ibid., 145.

60. Ibid.

61. Ibid., 41.

62. Ibid., 46.

63. Ibid.

64. Ibid., 45.

65. Willson, "Whose Utopia?"

66. Said's reading appears as chapter 2, section ii ("Jane Austen and Empire") of *Culture and Imperialism*, 80–97.

67. Ibid., 40.

68. Ibid., 44.

69. Ibid., 45.

70. See, for example, Jameson's *The Political Unconscious*.

71. An excellent discussion of the complex interactions between the political pedagogy taking place in the orchestra's workshops and the music making itself is to be found in Willson's "The Parallax Worlds of the West-Eastern Divan Or-

chestra," *Journal of the Royal Musical Association* 134 (2009): 319–47.

72. Willson, "Whose Utopia?," and "The Parallax Worlds of the West-Eastern Divan Orchestra."

73. In taking this line of argumentation, I have been influenced by Giles Hooper's strongly Habermassian argument with regard to the still much-contested notion of the "music itself": that we have to "recognize a 'quasi-transcendental' necessity in the prior presupposition of a 'music in itself' in order that we can *then*, if we choose, proceed to explore *its* multiply mediated condition." *The Discourse of Musicology* (Aldershot: Ashgate, 2006), 95.

74. It is a recurrent theme, for example, in her chapter on musical performance ("Conflicting Ideals of Performance Perfection in an Imperfect Practice") in *The Quest for Voice*, 132–73.

75. Barenboim and Said, *Parallels and Paradoxes*, 9.

76. Ibid.

77. Through recourse to the work of Jacques Attali and Elias Canetti, Willson has elaborated further on the potentially authoritarian and disciplinary qualities of the structures of orchestras ("The Parallax Worlds of the West-Eastern Divan Orchestra"). Anyone who has been an orchestral musician (as indeed for many years I was, both in the National Youth Orchestra of Great Britain, various amateur orchestras, and as a freelance professional) will recognize that these things are never far away from the order of things in orchestral life. However, my feeling is that in Willson's argument, multifaceted as it is, these features sometimes threaten to devolve into Pavlovian bells; intentionally or not, once rung they easily encourage us to salivate instinctively with a somewhat self-righteous postmodern ire that bespeaks of the presence of

orthodoxy rather than critique. What is perhaps more effective – and thankfully profoundly disenabling for any attempt to narcissistically secure the sanctity of an ethical position – is fully to take on board the radical strategic variability of such notions as authority, discipline, hierarchy, and the like. (Perhaps ironically, since Willson draws loosely on his notion of the parallax, this has been fundamental to much of Žižek's political arguments, notably in *In Defense of Lost Causes* [Verso: London, 2008].) At points in her argument, it seems to me less that we are dealing with what's potentially wrong with the West-Eastern Divan and more that we are being asked to reject orchestras per se. My own argument is that without a certain focus, forgetting, authority, and the like, orchestras simply can't exist; this is linked to my argument above regarding the need for an orchestra to be an orchestra. Perhaps then we might see orchestras as potentially places where usually negative terms are momentarily capable of being redeemed. Moreover, I argue that through recourse to this disciplined closing off of certain freedoms – a form of closure that Willson rightly sees as potentially contradictory to some of the orchestra's purported claims – a space might then be made available. In short, my position is that freedom is a discipline that must be practiced.

78. Ibid., 9–10.

79. This pervasive theme surrounding the activities of the West-Eastern Divan became dramatically realized when Barenboim put pressure on the orchestra to make the incredibly difficult decision to go and give a concert in the cultural palace in Ramallah in the West Bank territories. In order to minimize difficulties at the border crossings and to guarantee a certain degree of security to the musicians, the Spanish government provided all members of the orchestra with Spanish diplomatic passports. So in a quite literal sense, all members of the orchestra, with the exception of the Spanish musicians, changed citizenship in order to perform as orchestral musicians. In this regard, we might also mention the fact that after the Ramallah concert (12 January 2008), Barenboim was given and accepted honorary Palestinian citizenship, the first Israeli ever to have been offered it.

80. For the beginnings of a sociological investigation into this phenomenon, see Richard Sennett's *Respect: The Formation of Character in an Age of Inequality* (London: Penguin Books, 2004).

81. Barenboim and Said, *Parallels and Paradoxes,* 146.

82. Ibid., 147.

83. Ibid.

84. Bernard Williams, "Moral Luck," in *Moral Luck: Philosophical Papers 1973–1980* (Cambridge: Cambridge University Press, 1981), 20–39.

85. Hans Ulrich Gumbrecht, *Production of Presence: What Meaning Cannot Convey* (Stanford, Calif.: Stanford University Press, 2004), 104.

86. On which note, Willson states that "players from Egypt, Syria and Lebanon do not undertake the collaboration without concerns, because even if the government allows them to take part, anti-Israel sentiment is sufficiently strong for collaboration to alienate them from friends and colleagues, and to disadvantage them professionally at home. (For this reason many players' names have not, historically, been made available to the public.)" "The Parallax Worlds of the West-Eastern Divan Orchestra," 325.

87. See Cheah's *An Orchestra beyond Borders.*

88. Barenboim and Said, *Parallels and Paradoxes,* 49.

89. Productive here might be some kind of interaction between Barenboim's ideas and those of Vladimir Jankélévitch,

for example, "Music and Silence" from *Music and the Ineffable*, translated by Carolyn Abbate (Princeton, N.J.: Princeton University Press, 2003), 130–55.

90. Ibid., 30–31.

91. Ibid., 31.

92. Ibid., 31.

93. *Parallels and Paradoxes*, 146. Professionalism would seem to script, for example, being an orchestral musician as a sometimes enjoyable job that nevertheless primarily functions to collect a salary so that one can perform what is perhaps perceived as the "real job" of consolidating one's economic securities and allowing thereby for the possibility of participating in life's extramusical pleasures. (In the sections of her argument where she focuses on how the youths' participation in the West-Eastern Divan can be a means, via Barenboim, of them gaining professional advancement elsewhere, Willson gives enormous weight to this modality of orchestral life – somewhat depressingly, and under the guise of a potentially questionable anthropological realism, she gives far more to this than to more musical alternatives. "The Parallax Worlds of the West-Eastern Divan Orchestra.") One is tempted to wonder whether Barenboim's distaste for professionalism – a distaste that is echoed and encouraged in the discussions by Said's own well-known criticisms of specialization – is, in part, the product of his experiences with American orchestras. Barenboim claimed that he stepped down from his long-time position (1991–2006) as music director of the Chicago Symphony Orchestra because of the large amounts of fund-raising activities that such American positions necessitate. Subsequently, when Lorin Maazel put Barenboim's name forward as the next music director of the New York Philharmonic, he said

no, and has stated that he has no interest at present in holding such a position in the United States.

94. Barenboim and Said, *Parallels and Paradoxes*, 60.

95. Elena Cheah, *An Orchestra beyond Borders: Voices of the West-Eastern Divan Orchestra* (London: Verso, 2009), vii.

96. However, for the beginnings of a more critical political contextualization of musicology's own characteristic political contextualizations of music, see my "Music after All."

97. Barenboim's and Said's document originally read as follows: "This year, our project stands in sharp contrast to the cruelty and savagery that denies so many innocent civilians the possibility to continue living, fulfilling their ideals and dreams. Israel's destruction of life-giving infrastructure in Lebanon and Gaza, uprooting a million people and inflicting heavy casualties on civilians, and Hezbollah's indiscriminate shelling of civilians in northern Israel are in total opposition to what we believe in. The refusal to have an immediate ceasefire and the refusal to enter into negotiations for resolving once and for all the conflict in all its aspects goes against the very essence of our project as well." Cheah, *An Orchestra beyond Borders*, 4–5.

98. Barenboim and Said, *Parallels and Paradoxes*, 10.

99. As Barenboim states in his next remark: "What seemed extraordinary to me was how much ignorance there was about the 'other.' The Israeli kids couldn't imagine that there are people in Damascus and Amman and Cairo who can actually play violin and viola. And I think that Arab musicians knew that there is a musical life in Israel, but they didn't know very much about it." Ibid., 10.

100. Ibid., 11.

BIBLIOGRAPHY

Abbate, Carolyn. *In Search of Opera.*
Princeton, N.J.: Princeton University
Press, 2001.
———. "Music – Drastic or Gnostic?" *Crit-
ical Inquiry* 30 (Spring 2004): 505–36.
———. "Outside Ravel's Tomb." *Journal
of the American Musicological Society* 52
(1999): 465–530.
Adorno, Theodor W. *Beethoven: The
Philosophy of Music.* Translated by
Edmund Jephcott. Edited by Rolf Ti-
edemann. Stanford, Calif.: Stanford
University Press, 1998.
———. *Minima Moralia: Reflections from
Damaged Life.* Translated by E. F. N.
Jephcott. London: Verso, 1978.
———. *Prisms.* Translated by Samuel and
Shierry Weber. Cambridge, Mass.: M I T
Press, 1981.
Adorno, Theodor W., and Max Hork-
heimer. *Dialectic of Enlightenment.*
Translated by John Cumming. New
York: Continuum, 1991.
Agawu, Kofi. *Playing with Signs: A Se-
miotic Interpretation of Classic Music.*
Princeton, N.J.: Princeton University
Press, 1991.
Allanbrook, Wye J. "Comic Issues in Mo-
zart's Piano Concertos." In *Mozart Pi-
ano Concertos: Text, Context, Interpre-
tation,* edited by Neal Zaslaw, 75–106.
Ann Arbor: University of Michigan
Press, 1996.

———. "A Millennial Mozart?" *Mozart
Society of America Newsletter* 3 (1999):
2–4.
———. *Rhythmic Gesture in Mozart.* Chi-
cago: University of Chicago Press, 1983.
———. "Theorizing the Comic Surface."
In *Music in the Mirror: Reflections on
the History of Music Theory Literature
for the 21st Century,* edited by Andreas
Giger and Thomas J. Mathiesen, 195–
246. Lincoln: University of Nebraska
Press, 2002.
———. "Two Threads through the Laby-
rinth: Topic and Process in the First
Movements of K. 332 and K. 333." In
*Convention in Eighteenth- and Nine-
teenth-Century Music: Essays in Honor
of Leonard G. Ratner,* edited by Wye J.
Allanbrook, Janet M. Levy, and Wil-
liam P. Mahrt, 125–71. Stuyvesant, N.Y.:
Pendragon Press, 1992.
Anderson, Emily, ed. and trans. *The Let-
ters of Mozart and His Family.* Volume
2. London: Macmillan, 1938.
Badiou, Alain. *Ethics: An Essay on the Un-
derstanding of Evil.* Translated by Peter
Hallward. London: Verso, 2001.
Bakhtin, Mikhail. *Rabelais and His World.*
Translated by Hélène Iswolsky. Bloom-
ington: Indiana University Press,
1984.
Barenboim, Daniel, and Edward W. Said.
Parallels and Paradoxes: Explorations

in Music and Society. London: Blooms-bury, 2003.

Bayoumi, Moustafa. "Reconciliation without Duress: Said, Adorno, and the Autonomous Intellectual." *Alif: Journal of Comparative Poetics* 25 (2005): 46–64.

Benjamin, Walter. *Illuminations*. Edited by Hannah Arendt. Translated by Harry Zohn. New York: Schocken Books, 1968.

Berman, Marshall. *All That Is Solid Melts into Air: The Experience of Modernity*. New York: Penguin Books, 1988.

Berriot-Salvador, Evelyne. "The Discourse of Medicine and Science." Translated by Arthur Goldhammer. In *A History of Women in the West: Renaissance and Enlightenment Paradoxes*, edited by Natalie Zemon Davis and Arlette Farge, 348–88. Cambridge, Mass.: Harvard University Press, 1993.

Bonds, Mark Evan. "Haydn, Laurence Sterne, and the Origins of Musical Irony." *Journal of the American Musicological Society* 44 (1991): 57–91.

———. "Haydn's 'Cours complet de la composition' and the Sturm und Drang." In *Haydn Studies,* edited by W. Dean Sutcliffe, 152–76. Cambridge: Cambridge University Press, 1998.

Bowie, Malcolm. *Lacan*. Cambridge, Mass: Harvard University Press, 1991.

Brown, A. Peter. "The Sublime, the Beautiful, and the Ornamental: English Aesthetic Currents and Haydn's London Symphonies." In *Studies in Music History, Presented to H. C. Robbins Landon on His Seventieth Birthday*, edited by Otto Biba and David Wyn Jones, 44–71. London: Thames and Hudson, 1996.

Butler, Judith. *The Psychic Life of Power: Theories in Subjection*. Stanford, Calif.: Stanford University Press, 1997.

Charlton, David, ed. *E. T. A. Hoffman's Musical Writings:* Kreisleriana, The Poet and the Composer, *Music Criti-cism*. Translated by Martyn Clark. Cambridge: Cambridge University Press, 1989.

Cheah, Elena. *An Orchestra beyond Borders: Voices of the West-Eastern Divan Orchestra*. London: Verso, 2009.

Chua, Daniel, K. L. *Absolute Music and the Construction of Meaning*. Cambridge: Cambridge University Press, 1999.

———. *The "Galitzin" Quartets of Beethoven: Opp. 127, 132, 130*. Princeton, N.J.: Princeton University Press, 1995.

Currie, James. "Garden Disputes: Postmodern Beauty and the Sublime Neighbor (A Response to Judith Lochhead)." *Women and Music* 12 (2008): 75–86.

———. "Music after All." *Journal of the American Musicological Society* 62 (Spring 2009): 145–203.

———. "Music and Politics." In *The Routledge Companion to Philosophy and Music,* edited by Theodore Gracyk and Andrew Kania. London: Routledge, 2011.

———. "Musicology after Identity – Four Fragments." *Women and Music* 12 (2008): 87–93.

———. "Spookier than Spooky." *Popular Music* 26 (2007): 505–12.

d'Alembert, Jean le Rond. *Preliminary Discourse to the Encyclopedia of Diderot*. Translated by Richard N. Schwab. Bloomington: Indiana University Press, 1963.

Dahlhaus, Carl. *Analysis and Value Judgement*. Translated by Siegmund Levarie. New York: Pendragon, 1983.

———. *Esthetics of Music*. Translated by William Austin. Cambridge: Cambridge University Press, 1983.

Deleuze, Gilles, and Félix Guattari. *Anti Oedipus: Capitalism and Schizophrenia*. Translated by Robert Hurley, Helen R. Lane, and Mark Seem. Minneapolis: University of Minnesota Press, 1983.

———. *A Thousand Plateaus: Capitalism and Schizophrenia*. Translated by Brian

Massumi. Minneapolis: University of Minnesota Press, 1987.

Derrida, Jacques. *Specters of Marx: The State of the Debt, the Work of Mourning, and the New International.* Translated by Peggy Kamuf. New York: Routledge, 1994.

Diderot, Denis. *Rameau's Nephew and D'Alembert's Dream.* Translated by Leonard Tancock. London: Penguin, 1966.

Eagleton, Terry. *The Ideology of the Aesthetic.* Oxford: Basil Blackwell, 1990.

Edwards, George. "The Nonsense of an Ending: Closure in Haydn's String Quartets." *Musical Quarterly* 75 (1991): 227–54.

Farge, Arlette. "Protesters Plain to See." In *A History of Women in the West,* edited by Natalie Zemon Davis and Arlette Farge, translated by Arthur Goldhammer, 489–505. Cambridge, Mass.: Harvard University Press, Belknap Press, 1993.

Fink, Bruce. "The Master Signifier and the Four Discourses." In *Key Concepts of Lacanian Psychoanalysis,* edited by Dany Nobus, 29–47. New York: Other Press, 1998.

Fink, Robert. "Going Flat: Post-Hierarchical Music Theory and the Musical Surface." In *Rethinking Music,* edited by Nicholas Cook and Mark Everist, 102–37. Oxford: Oxford University Press, 1999.

Freeman, Michael. "Human Rights and the Corruption of Governments, 1789–1989." In *The Enlightenment and Its Shadows,* edited by Peter Hulme and Mudmilla Jordanova, 163–83. London: Routledge, 1990.

Freud, Sigmund. *The Interpretation of Dreams.* In *Standard Edition of the Complete Psychological Works of Sigmund Freud,* vol. 5, translated and edited by James Strachey in collaboration with Anna Freud. London: Hogarth Press and the Institute of Psycho-Analysis; New York: Norton, 1953–74.

Genet, Jean. *Prisoner of Love.* Translated by Barbara Bray. New York: New York Review Books, 2003.

Girdlestone, Cuthbert. *Mozart and His Piano Concertos.* New York: Schirmer, 1958.

Godineau, Dominique. "The Woman." In *Enlightenment Portraits,* edited by Michel Vovelle and translated by Lydia G. Cochrane, 393–426. Chicago: University of Chicago Press, 1997.

Goehr, Lydia. *Elective Affinities: Musical Essays on the History of Aesthetic Theory.* New York: Columbia University Press, 2008.

———. *The Imaginary Museum of Musical Works: An Essay in the Philosophy of Music.* Oxford: Clarendon Press, 1992.

———. *The Quest for Voice: Music, Politics, and the Limits of Philosophy.* Berkeley: University of California Press, 1998.

Gourgouris, Stathis. "The Late Style of Edward Said." *Alif: Journal of Comparative Poetics* 25 (2005): 37–45.

Grave, Floyd K., and Margaret G. Grave. *In Praise of Harmony: The Teachings of Abbé Georg Joseph Vogler.* Lincoln: University of Nebraska Press, 1987.

Griffiths, Paul. *New Sounds, New Personalities: British Composers of the 1980s in Conversation with Paul Griffiths.* London: Faber and Faber, 1985.

Gumbrecht, Hans Ulrich. *Production of Presence: What Meaning Cannot Convey.* Stanford, Calif.: Stanford University Press, 2004.

Harvey, David. *The Condition of Postmodernity: An Enquiry into the Origins of Cultural Change.* Oxford: Blackwell, 1989.

Hatherley, Owen. "Lash Out and Cover Up: Austerity Nostalgia and Ironic Authoritarianism in Recession Britain." *Radical Philosophy* 157 (2009): 2–5.

Heartz, Daniel. *Mozart's Operas*. Berkeley: University of California Press, 1990.

Hegel, G. W. F. *Phenomenology of Spirit*. Translated by A. V. Miller. Oxford: Oxford University Press, 1977.

Hobsbawm, Eric. *The Age of Extremes: A History of the World, 1914–1991*. New York: Vintage Books, 1996.

Hoeckner, Berthold. *Programming the Absolute: Nineteenth-Century German Music and the Hermeneutics of the Moment*. Princeton, N.J.: Princeton University Press, 2002.

Hoffmann, E. T. A. "Beethoven's Instrumental Music." In *Source Readings in Music History: Volume 6: The Nineteenth Century*, edited by Ruth A. Solie, 151–56. New York: Norton, 1998.

hooks, bell. *Belonging: A Culture of Place*. New York: Routledge, 2009.

Hooper, Giles, *The Discourse of Musicology*. Aldershot: Ashgate, 2006.

Hosler, Bellamy. *Changing Aesthetics of Instrumental Music in 18th Century Germany*. Ann Arbor, Mich.: UMI Research Press, 1981.

Huizinga, Johan. *Homo Ludens: A Study of the Play-Element in Culture*. Boston: Beacon Press, 1955.

Hullot-Kentor, Robert. *Things beyond Resemblance: Collected Essays on Theodor W. Adorno*. New York: Columbia University Press, 2006.

Irving, Howard. "Haydn and Laurence Sterne: Similarities in Eighteenth-Century Literary and Musical Wit." *Current Musicology* 40 (1985): 34–49.

Ivashkin, Alexander, ed. *A Schnittke Reader*. Translated by John Goodliffe. Bloomington: Indiana University Press, 2002.

Jameson, Fredric. *The Political Unconscious: Narrative as a Socially Symbolic Act*. Ithaca, N.Y.: Cornell University Press, 1981.

———. *Postmodernism, or The Cultural Logic of Late Capitalism*. Durham, N.C.: Duke University Press, 1991.

Jankélévitch, Vladimir. *Music and the Ineffable*. Translated by Carolyn Abbate. Princeton, N.J.: Princeton University Press, 2003.

Johnson, Claudia L. "'Giant HANDEL' and the Musical Sublime." *Eighteenth-Century Studies* 19 (1985–86): 515–33.

Johnson, James J. "Musical Experience and the Formation of a French Musical Public." *Journal of Modern History* 64 (1992): 191–226.

Judt, Tony. "The Gnome in the Garden: Tony Blair and Britain's 'Heritage.'" *New York Review of Books* (July 2001). Reprinted in *Reappraisals: Reflections on the Forgotten Twentieth Century*. New York: Penguin Press, 2008. 219–32.

Kant, Immanuel. "An Answer to the Question: 'What is Enlightenment?'" In *Kant: Political Writings*, 2nd ed., edited by Hans Reiss, translated by H. B. Nisbet, 54–60. Cambridge: Cambridge University Press, 1991.

———. *The Critique of Judgment*. Translated by James Creed Meredith. Oxford: Oxford University Press, 1952.

Keats, John. *A Selection from John Keats*. Edited by E. C. Pettet. London: Longman, 1974.

Keefe, Simon P. *Mozart's Piano Concertos: Dramatic Dialogue in the Age of Enlightenment*. Rochester, N.Y.: Boydell, 2001.

Keller, Hans. *The Great Haydn Quartets: Their Interpretation*. London: Dent, 1986.

Kerman, Joseph. *The Beethoven Quartets*. New York: Norton, 1966.

Kirkendale, Warren. *Fugue and Fugato in Rococo and Classical Chamber Music*. Translated by Warren Kirkendale and Margaret Bent. Durham, N.C.: Duke University Press, 1979.

Koselleck, Reinhart. *Critique and Crisis: Enlightenment and the Pathogenesis of Modern Society*. Cambridge, Mass.: MIT Press, 1988.

Kramer, Lawrence. "Music Criticism and the Postmodern Turn: In Contrary Motion with Gary Tomlinson." *Current Musicology* 53 (1993): 25–35.

———. *Why Classical Music Still Matters.* Berkeley: University of California Press, 2007.

Kramer, Richard. "'Der Organische der Fuge': On the Autograph of Beethoven's Quartet in F Major, Opus 59 No. 1." In *The String Quartets of Haydn, Mozart, and Beethoven. Studies of the Autograph Manuscripts. A Conference at Isham Memorial Library. March 15–17, 1979,* edited by Christoph Wolff, 223–65. Cambridge, Mass.: Harvard University Press, 1980.

Kristeva, Julia. *Powers of Horror: An Essay on Abjection.* Translated by Leon S. Roudiez. New York: Columbia University Press, 1982.

Kundera, Milan. *Testaments Betrayed.* Translated by Linda Asher. London: Faber and Faber, 1995.

Kurrik, Maire Jaanus. *Literature and Negation.* New York: Columbia University Press, 1979.

Lacan, Jacques. *The Seminar. Book II. The Ego in Freud's Theory and in the Technique of Psychoanalysis, 1954–55.* Translated by Sylvanna Tomaselli. New York: Norton; Cambridge: Cambridge University Press, 1988.

———. *The Seminar. Book VII. The Ethics of Psychoanalysis, 1959–60.* Translated by Dennis Porter. London: Routledge: 1992.

Laclau, Ernesto and Chantal Mouffe. *Hegemony and Socialist Strategy: Towards a Radical Democratic Politics.* London: Verso, 1985.

Landes, Joan. *Women and the Public Sphere in the Age of the French Revolution.* Ithaca, N.Y.: Cornell University Press, 1988.

Landon, H. C. Robbins. *1791, Mozart's Last Year.* New York: Thames and Hudson, 1988.

Laqueur, Thomas. *Making Sex: Body and Gender from the Greeks to Freud.* Cambridge Mass.: Harvard University Press, 1990.

Leppert, Richard. "Music 'Pushed to the Edge of Existence' (Adorno, Listening, and the Question of Hope)." *Cultural Critique* 60 (2005): 92–133.

Lévi-Strauss, Claude. *Triste tropiques.* Translated by John Russell. New York: Atheneum, 1971.

Levy, Janet M. "'Something Mechanical Encrusted on the Living': A Source of Musical Wit and Humor." In *Convention in Eighteenth- and Nineteenth-Century Music: Essays in Honor of Leonard G. Ratner,* edited by Wye Jamieson Allanbrook, Janet Levy, and William P. Mahrt, 225–56. Stuyvesant, N.Y.: Pendragon Press, 1992.

Lippman, Edward. *Music Aesthetics: A Historical Reader.* New York: Pendragon Press, 1986.

Lyotard, Jean-François. *The Postmodern Condition: A Report on Knowledge.* Translated by Geoff Bennington and Brian Massumi. Minneapolis: University of Minnesota Press, 1984.

McClary, Susan. "Constructions of Subjectivity in Schubert's Music." In *Queering the Pitch: The New Gay and Lesbian Musicology,* edited by Philip Brett, Elizabeth Wood, and Gary C. Thomas, 205–34. New York: Routledge, 1994.

———. *Conventional Wisdom: The Content of Musical Form.* Berkeley: University of California Press, 2000.

Melton, James Van Horn. *The Rise of the Public in Enlightenment Europe.* Cambridge: Cambridge University Press, 2001.

Miller, Nancy K. *The Heroine's Text: Readings in the French and English Novel 1722–1782.* New York: Columbia University Press, 1980.

Mouffe, Chantal. *On the Political.* London: Routledge, 2005.

Nietzsche, Friedrich. *The Birth of Tragedy and The Case of Wagner.* Translated by Walter Kaufmann. New York: Vintage Books, 1967.

———. *Untimely Meditations.* Translated by R. J. Hollingdale. Cambridge: Cambridge University Press, 1997.

O'Neill, Onara. "Enlightenment as Autonomy: Kant's Vindication of Reason." In *The Enlightenment and Its Shadows,* edited by Peter Hulme and Mudmilla Jordanova, 184–99. London: Routledge, 1990.

Outram, Dorinda. *The Enlightenment.* Cambridge: Cambridge University Press, 1995.

Powers, Harold. "Reading Mozart's Music: Text and Topic, Syntax and Sense." *Current Musicology* 57 (1995): 5–44.

Ratner, Leonard. *Classic Music: Expression, Form and Style.* New York: Schirmer, 1980.

Rex, Walter E. "A Propos of the Figure of Music on the Frontispiece of the Encyclopédie: Theories of Musical Imitation in d'Alembert, Rousseau, and Diderot." In *Report of the Twelfth I.M.S. Congress Berkeley 1977,* edited by Anthony Newcomb and Bonnie Wade, 214–25. Kassel: Bärenreiter, 1981.

Rice, John A. "Leopold II, Mozart, and the Return to a Golden Age." In *Opera and the Enlightenment,* edited by Thomas Bauman and Marita Petzold McClymonds, 271–96. Cambridge: Cambridge University Press, 1995.

———. "Mozart and His Singers: The Case of Maria Marchetti Fantozzi, the First Vitellia." *Opera Quarterly* 11 (1995): 31–52.

Richards, Annette. "Automatic Genius: Mozart and the Mechanical Sublime." *Music and Letters* 80 (1999): 366–89.

Rilke, Rainer Maria. *The Selected Poetry of Rainer Maria Rilke.* Edited and translated by Stephen Mitchell. New York: Vintage Books, 1989.

Rosen, Charles. *The Classical Style: Haydn, Mozart, Beethoven.* New York: Schirmer, 1972.

Rousseau, Jean-Jacques. *Dictionnaire de Musique.* Paris, 1768.

———. *Emile, or On Education.* Translated by Allan Bloom. New York: Basic Books, 1979.

Said, Edward. *Beginnings: Intention and Method.* New York: Basic Books, 1975.

———. *On Late Style: Music and Literature against the Grain.* New York: Vintage Books, 2006.

———. *Power, Politics, and Culture: Interviews with Edward W. Said.* Edited by Gauri Viswanathan. New York: Vintage, 2002.

———. *The World, the Text, and the Critic.* Cambridge, Mass.: Harvard University Press, 1983.

Sandberger, Adolf. "Zur Geschichte des Haydnschen Streichquartetts." *Altbayerische Monatsschrift* 2 (1900): 41–64, rev., reprinted in Sandberger, *Ausgewählte Aufsätze zur Musikgeschichte,* vol. 1, 224–65. Munich: Drei Masken, 1921.

Schapiro, Alexander H. "Drama of an Infinitely Superior Nature: Handel's Early English Oratorios and the Religious Sublime." *Music and Letters* 74 (1993): 215–45.

Scherzinger, Martin. "Negotiating the Music-Theory/African-Music Nexus: A Political Critique of Ethnomusicological Anti-formalism and a Strategic Analysis of the Harmonic Patterning of the Shona Mbira Song 'Nyamaopa.'" *Perspectives of New Music* 39 (2001): 5–117.

———. "Feminine/Feminist? In Quest of Names with No Experiences (Yet)." In *Postmodern Music/Postmodern Thought,* edited by Judith Lochhead and Joseph Auner, 141–73. New York: Routledge, 2002.

Schiebinger, Linda. *The Mind Has No Sex? Women in the Origins of Modern Science.*

Cambridge, Mass.: Harvard University Press, 1989.

———. "Skeletons in the Closet: The First Illustrations of the Female Skeleton in Eighteenth-Century Anatomy." *Representations* 14 (1986): 42–82.

Schnittke, Alfred. "Polystylistic Tendencies in Modern Music." In *A Schnittke Reader,* edited by Alexander Ivashkin, translated by John Goodliffe. Bloomington: Indiana University Press, 2002.

Schwartz, Judith L. "Rhythmic Gesture in 'La clemenza di Tito': Dance Rhythms as Rhetorical Devices." *Mozart Jahrbuch* (1991): 755–65.

Sennett, Richard. *Respect: The Formation of Character in an Age of Inequality.* London: Penguin Books, 2004.

Sisman, Elaine. "Genre, Gesture, and Meaning in Mozart's 'Prague' Symphony.'" In *Mozart Studies,* edited by Cliff Eisen, 27–84. Oxford: Oxford University Press, 1997.

———. *Haydn and the Classical Variation.* Cambridge, Mass.: Harvard University Press, 1993.

———. *Mozart's 'Jupiter' Symphony.* Cambridge: Cambridge University Press, 1993.

Solie, Ruth. *Source Readings in Music History: Volume 6: The Nineteenth Century.* New York: Norton, 1998.

Sontag, Susan. *A Susan Sontag Reader.* London: Penguin, 1983.

Spitzer, Michael. *Music as Philosophy: Adorno and Beethoven's Late Style.* Bloomington: Indiana University Press, 2006.

Steiner, George. *Real Presences: Is There Anything in What We Say?* London: Faber and Faber, 1989.

Taussig, Michael. *The Nervous System.* London: Routledge, 1992.

Tomlinson, Gary. "Musical Pasts and Postmodern Musicologies: A Response to Lawrence Kramer" and "Tomlin-

son Responds." *Current Musicology* 53 (1993): 18–24, 36–40.

Tovey, Donald Francis. *The Main Stream of Music and Other Essays.* New York: Oxford University Press, 1979.

Treitler, Leo, ed. *Strunk's Source Readings in Music History.* Rev. ed. New York: Norton, 1998.

Tusa, Michael C. "Beethoven's 'C-Minor Mood': Some Thoughts on the Structural Implications of Key Choice." *Beethoven Forum* 2, edited by Christopher Reynolds, Lewis Lockwood, and James Webster, 1–28. Lincoln: University of Nebraska Press, 1993.

Tyson, Alan. *Mozart; Studies of the Autograph Scores.* Cambridge, Mass.: Harvard University Press, 1987.

Valente, Joe. "Lacan's Marxism, Marxism's Lacan (from Žižek to Althusser)." In *The Cambridge Companion to Lacan,* edited by Jean-Michel Rabaté, 153–72. Cambridge: Cambridge University Press, 2003.

Waeber, Jacqueline. "Jean-Jacques Rousseau's 'unité de mélodie.'" *Journal of the American Musicological Society* 62 (Spring 2009): 79–143.

Watkins, Holly. "From the Mine to the Shrine: The Critical Origins of Musical Depth." *Nineteenth-Century Music* 27 (2004): 179–207.

Weber, William. "The Intellectual Bases of the Handelian Tradition, 1759–1800." *Proceedings of the Royal Musical Association* 108 (1981–82): 100–114.

Webster, James. "Between Enlightenment and Romanticism in Music History: 'First Viennese Modernism' and the Delayed Nineteenth Century." *Nineteenth-Century Music* 25 (2002): 108–26.

———. "The Concept of Beethoven's 'Early' Period in the Context of Periodizations in General." *Beethoven Forum* 3 (1994): 3–27.

———. "The *Creation,* Haydn's Late Vocal Music, and the Musical Sublime." In

Haydn and His World, edited by Elaine Sisman, 57–102. Princeton, N.J.: Princeton University Press, 1997.

———. "The Eighteenth Century as Music-Historical Period?" *Eighteenth-Century Music* 1 (2004): 47–60.

———. *Haydn's "Farewell" Symphony and the Idea of Classical Style: Through-Composition and Cyclic Integration in His Instrumental Music.* Cambridge: Cambridge University Press, 1991.

West, Cornel. *Democracy Matters: Winning the Fight against Imperialism.* London: Penguin Books, 2005.

White, Hayden. *Tropics of Discourse: Essays in Cultural Criticism.* Baltimore: Johns Hopkins University Press, 1978.

Williams, Alastair. *New Music and the Claims of Modernity.* Aldershot: Ashgate, 1997.

Williams, Bernard. *Moral Luck: Philosophical Papers 1973–1980.* Cambridge: Cambridge University Press, 1981.

Willson, Rachel Beckles. "The Parallax Worlds of the West-Eastern Divan Orchestra." *Journal of the Royal Musical Association* 134 (2009): 319–47.

———. "Whose Utopia? Perspectives on the West-Eastern Divan Orchestra." *Music and Politics* 3, no. 2 (2009). Accessed 6 June 2010 at www.music.ucsb.edu/projects/musicandpolitcs/archive/2009-2/beckles_willson.html.

Wolff, Christoph. "Mozart's *Messiah:* The Spirit of Handel from van Swieten's Hands." In *Music and Civilization: Essays in Honor of Paul Henry Lang,* edited by Edmond Strainchamps and Maria Rika Maniates, 1–14. New York: Norton, 1984.

Wolff, Christoph, ed. *The String Quartets of Haydn, Mozart, and Beethoven: Studies of the Autograph Manuscripts. A Conference at Isham Memorial Library, March 15–17, 1979.* Cambridge, Mass.: Harvard University Press, 1980.

Wollstonecraft, Mary. *A Vindication of the Rights of Woman.* London: Penguin, 1992.

Yearsley, David. *Bach and the Meanings of Counterpoint.* Cambridge: Cambridge University Press, 2002.

Zaslaw, Neal. *Mozart's Symphonies: Context, Performance Practice, Reception.* Oxford: Clarendon Press, 1989.

Žižek, Slavoj. *In Defense of Lost Causes.* Verso: London, 2008.

———. *The Sublime Object of Ideology.* London: Verso, 1989.

———. *Tarrying with the Negative: Kant, Hegel, and the Critique of Ideology.* Durham, N.C.: Duke University Press, 1993.

Zupančič, Alenka. *The Odd One In: On Comedy.* Cambridge, Mass.: MIT Press, 2008.

INDEX

Note: Page numbers in *italics* indicate musical examples.

Abbate, Carolyn, 37, 38, 194n50
abjection, 100–105
absolute music, xv, 76–77, 127–29, 169
Absolute Music and the Construction of Meaning (Chua), 127–28
absolute relativism, 40
absolutism, 107, 108, 131. *See also* authoritarianism
Adorno, Theodor: on Baroque fugues, 44; on Beethoven's "Heroic mode," 94; on home of music and belonging, 72–73; on late capitalism, 140–41; and negative dialects, 141, 150; on otherness, 71–72; on our relationship to music, 66; and Said's late style, 150–51, 153, 155–56, 161, 197n29; on Strauss, 159; and transcendence and ambiguity, 78; and Utopia, 128
aesthetic autonomy in musicology, ix–xi
aesthetic experience, 100–102
Agawu, V. Kofi, 8
agency, 75, 133–35. *See also* autonomy
Albrechstberger, Johann Georg, 10, 47, 50–51
Alexenburg, Menahem, 166, 172
alienation, 3
Allanbrook, Wye Jamison: on finale of Mozart's K. 459, 15, 28; and linguistics, 181n23; on musical surfaces, 4, 26–27; on musical topoi, 82; on *opera buffa* style, 14; and postmodern view of Mozart, 8–9

allegorical verisimilitude, 106–12
ancien régime, 95, 107
André, Johann Anton, 12, 182n34
anti-Semitism, 70
Apollo, 62, 62–64
architecture, 27–28
artifice, 112–14, 116–17, 120–21. *See also* surface
Attali, Jacques, 199n77
authoritarianism, 10–11, 27, 97, 199n77
autonomy: aesthetic autonomy in musicology, ix–xi; and the contextual sublime, 121–25; and the disenchanted subject, 125–27, 129; and exile, 67; "forced choice," 133; and gender politics, 109; and Haydn's op. 33, no. 5, 93–94; human agency, 75; and Kantian philosophy, 123; Kramer/Tomlinson exchange on, 189n26; and mimesis, 77, 80–81; of music, 73; and musical conventions, 83–85; and outsideness, 156–57; and post-ideological happiness, 131–32, 134, 135, 138; Said on, 154; and social role of music, 76–77; and transcendence, 80–81; and Viennese classics, 94, 123; and Vitellia, 112–13
avoidance: and discussing the universal, 2; and the disenchanted subject, 128–29; and disengagement, 168; forgetting contrasted with, 149; and the material unconscious, 35; and nature of friendship, 66; and political reflections,

3; and postmodernism's celebration of
surface, 6

Bach, Johann Sebastian, 13, 44
Bach and the Meanings of Counterpoint
    (Yearsley), 181n26
Badiou, Alain, 153
Bakhtin, Mikhail, 37
Barenboim, Daniel: and Beethoven's
    Moonlight Sonata, 173; and forgetting,
    152; and the Israeli-Palestinian conflict,
    165–67, 172–73, 200n79, 201n97; and
    musical professionalism, 200n93; on
    otherness, 201n99; and "phenomenol-
    ogy of sound," 169–70; and political
    role of music, 169–71, 171–74, 176; Said's
    work with, 140, 141, 161; on successful
    musical performance, 163
Baroque style: and church sonatas, 50;
    and the contextual sublime, 124; and
    counterpoint, 13; and fugal finales,
    57, 60; and fugues, 44–46; and Kant's
    paradox of freedom, 97; and polysty-
    listic method, 9; and stylistic interplay,
    10–11
Barthes, Roland, 5
basset horns, 121
Bastille, 107
Batteux, Charles, 77–78, 83
Bayoumi, Moustafa, 140
Beethoven, Ludwig van
    and absolute music, xv
    C-minor mood, 187n48
    and fugal counterpoint, 42, 43, 60–62,
        185n34, 187n49
    and fugal texture, 50, 55
    and fugatos, 186n34
    and "Heroic mode," 94, 173
    Hoffmann on, 79–80
    and homophonic textures, 54
    and late style, 185n34, 197n29
    and Reicha, 51
    and solo-oboe cadenza in Symphony
        no. 5, 187n48
    works: Cello Sonata op. 102, no. 2, 50;
        Eroica Symphony, 55, 186n34; *Moonlight*
        Sonata, 173; Piano Concerto op. 37, no.

3 in C Minor, 54; Piano Sonata op. 10,
    no. 2 in F Major, 187n49; Piano Sonata
    op. 13, no. 8 in C Minor, 187n48; Piano
    Sonata op. 106 (*Hammerklavier*), 50;
    Piano Sonata op. 111 in C Minor, 60–61;
    Seventh Symphony, 176; String Quartet
    op. 18 in C Minor, no. 4, 61–62; String
    Quartet op. 59, no. 1 in F Major, 57;
    String Quartet op. 133 (*Grosse Fuge*),
    50; Symphony no. 1 op. 21, 187n49;
    Symphony no. 5 op. 67 in C Minor,
    187n48
"Beethoven's Instrumental Music"
    (Hoffmann), 79–80
belief systems, 44, 74, 101–102, 104
belonging: human belongings, 67, 72, 73;
    and music in exile, 67–69; and musical
    autonomy, 80; and nationalism, 147;
    and the postmodern human, 130–31,
    133; and potential for becoming, 72–73;
    and transformation from *epistēmē* to
    technē, 165
Benjamin, Walter, 102–103, 152
Berio, Luciano, 6
Berlin Staatskapelle, 167
Biedermeier era, 129
"bio-morality," 136
The Birth of Tragedy (Nietzsche), 62
birthday celebrations, 1–2
Blair, Tony, xii
Bloch, Ernst, 74
Brody, Miriam, 192n29
buffa style. See *opera buffa* style
Burney, Charles, 10

cadenzas, 35–39, 41, 187n48
Cage, John, 126
camouflage, 35
Canetti, Elias, 199n77
capitalism: Adorno on, 140–41; and
    cultural evolution, 195n60; and the
    disenchanted subject, 130–31; and
    Fukuyama's end-of-history thesis,
    132–33; and gender politics, 109; and
    musicology, xi–xiii; and political
    rivalry, 188n15; and postcommunism,
    195n64; and post-ideological happiness,

137–38; and postmodernism, 195n64; and racism, 70; and road-rage metaphor, 154–55

Capriccio (Strauss), 158–59

Captif amoureaux (Genet), 198n39

caricature, 21

categorical imperative, 96, 98

Catherine II (Catherine the Great), 111

Cavafy, Constantine P., 157–58

"Che del ciel" chorus (Mozart), 114, 116–17, 121, 193n40

Chicago Symphony Orchestra, 201n93

Christo, 32

Chua, Daniel, xv, 77, 127–29

church music, 44, 45–46, 50

cinema, 103

class divisions, 8–9, 111

Close, Glenn, 4

codettas, 19, 23, 25

collaboration, 67, 72

collectivism, 130

colonialism, 30, 164, 176

comedy, 28, 61

"coming out" phenomena, 134–35

commerce, 109

communism, xi, 103, 130–32, 188n15, 195n64

compromise, 170. *See also* Barenboim, Daniel; Said, Edward

concerto style, 15

Condorcet, Marquis de (Nicolas de Caritat), 10

Congress of Vienna, 129

Conrad, Joseph, 156

context of music: Adorno on, 66; autonomy and the contextual sublime, 121–25; and Beethoven's "Heroic" mode, 94; and the disenchanted subject, 125, 129; and enchantment, 105; and Middle-Eastern politics, 173, 176; and Mozart's stylistic discourse, 8–9; and music in exile, 67–77; and music/politics trope, 171; Powers on, 82; and Said's work, 145, 148, 156–58, 173, 176; and textural dissonance, 41

contextual sublime, 121–25

contrapuntal texture. *See* counterpoint; fugal counterpoint

convention: conventional wisdom, 130; and finale of Mozart's K. 459, 28–29; and musical topoi, 82; and repetition, 88; and Said's late style, 156; and Viennese classics, 94

Conversation between Diderot and D'Alembert (Diderot), 122

Così fan tutte (Mozart), 154

counterpoint: and finale of Mozart's K. 459, 16, 18, 21–22, 24–26; and fugal counterpoint, 45; and signification, 39; and stylistic interplay, 10–13. *See also* fugal counterpoint

Coupland, Douglas, 69

Course in General Linguistics (Saussure), 181n23

Creation (Haydn), 190n48

critical historiography, 10

critical music, 72

cryptographic sublime, 37

culture, xviii, 39–41, 195n60

Dadaism, 6

Dahlhaus, Carl, 48, 78

Dasein, 146–47

Daube, Johann Friedrich, 12, 21

death rituals, 33

Declaration of the Rights of Women (Gouges), 111

deconstruction, 105

Del Tredici, David, 135

Deleuze, Gilles, 5, 40

Democratic Party (US), xvi

depth analysis, 26–33, 37, 38, 180n3

Der angehende praktische Organist (Kittel), 11

Der musikalische Dilettant (Daube), 12

Der Rosenkavalier (Strauss), 158–59

Derrida, Jacques, 1–2, 27, 40, 105, 126

Descartes, René, 109

dialectical method: and autonomy, 67; in comparison with forgetting, 150; dialectical mediation, 140; dialectical paradox, xvi, 145; dialectical suspension, 161; and "doubling," 149–50; and finale of Mozart's K. 459, 28; between harmonic progression and thematic

repetition, 186n47; and the Israeli-Palestinian conflict, 152; and politics of the mirror, 160; and Said's late style, 140–41, 145, 149–50; and social role of music, 72–73; between sonata form and variation form, 186n47; and structure of this work, xv–xvii
Diderot, Denis, 122
Die Zauberflöte (Mozart), 14
Dionysus, 62–63
disenchantment. *See* enchantment/disenchantment
disengagement, 168
distance, 79, 102–105, 110–11, 112
distribution of wealth, 138
divertimento style, 92
dogmatism, 95–96, 135
Don Giovanni (Mozart), 117, 154
"doubling," 149–50
dreams and dream theory, 35, 37–38, 41, 63, 157. *See also* material unconscious; unconscious
Dürer, Albrecht, 66

Eagleton, Terry, 5
Eastern European communism, xi
economic bubbles, xiii
economic equity, 6–7
Edwards, George, 191n51
emergence, 34–35
Émile, ou le l'éducation (Rousseau), 110
empiricism, 97
enchantment/disenchantment: and abjection, 104–105; and artifice, 112–14, 121; and the contextual sublime, 121–25; and the disenchanted subject, 125–31; and *La clemenza di Tito*, 112; and post-ideological happiness, 132, 138. *See also* belief systems; faith
The End of History and the Last Man (Fukuyama), 132–33
"end of history" thesis, xi, 2, 132
engagement: and abstraction, 162–63; and *buffa* style, 22; and ethical sacrifices, 168–69, 177; Kramer on, 75; and recent musicology, 125; and veiling, 32
Engels, Frederick, 130

enjoyment (*jouissance*), 31–32, 36, 63, 70, 196n65. *See also* Lacan, Jacques
Enlightenment: and abjection, 103; and the contextual sublime, 123–24; critique of authority, 5; and culturally formed objects, 40; and fidelity to truth, 144; and fugal practices, 47, 57; and gender politics, 109; and learned style, 37; and mechanistic thinking, 124; and paradox of freedom, 94–98; and Said's work, 196n17; and salon culture, 108–11; and scientific discourse, 109–10; and sexual politics, 107; and stylistic pluralism, 10–13, 22–23
epistêmê, 162, 164–65, 168, 175
Eroica Symphony (Beethoven), 55, 186n34
erotics of art, 4
escapism, 35
eschatology, 128
essentialism, 30
ethics: and autonomy, 123, 134; and cultural positions, 39; and the disenchanted subject, 125; and engagement/avoidance, 168–69; and friendship, 66; and gender politics, 107–108, 116; and happiness, 137; and musical autonomy, 76; and musical freedom, 166–67, 170, 172; and political reflections, 5, 8; and Said's work, 142–45, 148, 159, 162, 176–77, 197n134; and tragedy, 68; and West-Eastern Divan Orchestra's discourse, 175–76
Eucharist, 100–101
exile, 67–77, 93
existential meaning of music, 189n37
expectancy, 43
"extimacy," 31

faith, 95. *See also* belief systems
Fantozzi, Maria Marchetti, 113–14
Fascism, 102–103, 152, 188n15
Fatal Attraction (1987), 4
feminism, 109–11, 123
film music, 76
financial crisis, xi
Fink, Bruce, 198n49
Fink, Robert, 6

Fontenelle, Bernard le Bovier de, 77–78, 80
"forced choice," 133–34, 195n65
forgetting, 148–52, 157, 172–75, 197n32, 199n77
Forkel, Johann Nikolaus, 44, 47, 184n14
form of music: Barenboim and Said's positions contrasted, 169; and belonging, 72; and culturally formed objects, 40–41; and dream metaphor, 39–42; and excessive *jouissance*, 63–64; and moral law, 98; and musical autonomy, 81; negative postmodern critique of, 62; as political critique, 72–77; and social antagonisms, 71; as surface, 38; and textural dissonance, 41, 46–47, 56; and thematic development, 54–56
Foucault, Michel, 140
Frederick the Great, 95–96
freedom, 94–98
French overture style, 116
French Revolution: and Fukuyama's "end-of-history" thesis, 132; and gender politics, 111, 192n29; and Kantian idea of freedom, 96; and *La clemenza di Tito*, 107, 111, 123–24; and Utopia, 128
Freud, Sigmund, xv, 30–31, 38
friendship, 65–67
fugal counterpoint: and Beethoven, 44, 60–62, 185n34, 186n43, 187n49; and cadenza of Mozart's K. 459, 41; dynamic quality of, 41, 184n14; and finale of Mozart's K. 459, 14–15, 19–21, 21–25, 42, 55, 56–62, 184n22; in finales, 56–57; and first-movement sonata-allegros, 47, 57–58, 186n45; and homophonic texture, 55; and Marsyas, 62–64; and the material unconscious, 34–42; and outsideness, 157; in religious music, 46; Rousseau's view of, 42–56; and sonata-style syntax, 45–51, 54, 56–58; and strategic placements, 56–62; and stretti, 25–26, 43, 53; and stylistic interplay, 10–13; and the sublime, 54; variety of meanings, 181n26
fugal subjects: and authority, 14; Baroque, 60; and *buffa* style, 23–25; cadenza of

Mozart's K. 459, 35–36; and Haydn's op. 20, no. 2, 185n25; and learned style, 16, 19–21; and melodic material, 43, 45, 51–52; and motet style, 14, 21; and sonata-style syntax, 48
fugato, 14, 18–21, 23–24, 51–52, 55, 186n42
Fugue and Fugato (Kirkendale), 182n34
Fukuyama, Francis, xi, 132–33

galant style, 3, 10–11, 26, 47, 185n25
gender politics, 105, 108, 108–11, 192n29, 193n30. *See also* sexual politics
A General History of Music from the Earliest Age to the Present Period (Burney), 10
Genet, Jean, 155, 198n39
Gerber, Ernst Ludwig, 11
Gibbon, Edward, 10
Girdlestone, Cuthbert, 13
Godineau, Dominique, 111, 193n30
Goehr, Lydia, xv, 71–72, 78, 149, 149–50, 163, 189n39
Gothic style, 124
Gouges, Olympe des, 111
Gould, Glenn, 155–57, 198n56
Gourgouris, Stathis, 196n28
Gramsci, Antonio, 146
Grosse Fuge, op. 133 (Beethoven), 50
Guattari, Félix, 5
Gulf War, 147
Gumbrecht, Hans Ulrich, 168–69
Guzelimian, Ara, 167

Ha-aretz, 140
Habermas, Jürgen, 199n73
Hammerklavier Sonata (Piano Sonata op. 106) (Beethoven), 50
Handel, 116, 121, 126, 184n17, 194n44
happiness, post-ideological, 131–38
"Happy Birthday!," 1–2
Harvey, David, 195n64
Hawkins, Laetitia, 112
Haydn, Joseph
   and church music, 46
   and dialectical suspension, 150
   and end of movements, 191n51
   and fugal counterpoint, 56, 57–58, 59, 60–62, 186n45

and fugal finales, 184n22, 185n25
and fugal texture, 46–48, 49, 50–51,
    54–55
Gerber on, 11
and homophony, 187n52
and motivic connection, 90–91, 91
and musical topoi, 82
and Reicha, 51
and Siciliana theme, 92, 93
Sisman on, 191n53
and sonata-style syntax, 47, 47–48,
    186n45
"Sturm und Drang" works, 56
Webster on, 190n48
works: Creation, 190n48; Lark, 54;
    Lord Nelson mass, 46; St. Cecilia mass,
    46; String Quartet K. 168 in F Major,
    46; String Quartet K. 173 in D Minor,
    46; String Quartet op. 20, no. 2 in C
    Major, 46, 47, 49; String Quartet op.
    20, no. 5 in F Minor, 46; String Quartet
    op. 20, no. 6 in A Major, 46; String
    Quartet op. 33, no. 1 in B Minor, 55;
    String Quartet op. 55, no. 2 in F Minor
    (Razor), 57–61, 59, 60; String Quartet
    op. 76, no. 2 in D Minor (Quinten),
    62; Symphony no. 40 in F Major, 46;
    Symphony no. 95 in C Minor, 55–56.
    See also String Quartet op. 33, no. 5 in
    G Major (Haydn)
Heartz, Daniel, 120
Hegel, Georg Wilhelm Friedrich, xv, 40,
    96, 150, 173, 197n32
hegemonic power: and learned style, 24,
    29; and "mirrorization," 8; and outside-
    ness, 73, 156, 174; and politicization
    of music, 174; and post-ideological
    happiness, 136
Heidegger, Martin, 126, 146–47
hermeneutics, 4, 4–5, 35, 37, 38
hermeticism, 162–63
"Heroic mode" of Beethoven, 94, 173
Hezbollah, 172
hierarchy of the arts, 77
historical relativism, 2–3, 8–9
Historisch-biographisches Lexicon der
    Tonkünstler (Gerber), 11

History of the Decline and Fall of the Roman
    Empire (Gibbon), 10
Hobbes, Thomas, 108
Hoeckner, Berthold, xv
Hoffmann, E. T. A., 4, 79–80, 124, 180n3
Holloway, Robin, 135
"home" of music, 67–77, 93. See also
    belonging; human belongings
Homeland Security, 68
homophony: and accompaniment, 42; and
    Baroque church sonatas, 50–51; and
    Beethoven's Op. 18 no. 4, 61; and finale
    of Mozart's K. 459, 18, 21–22, 25–26,
    53; and fugal counterpoint, 45, 54–55,
    55–56; and fugatos, 51–52; and minuet
    of Haydn's Quinten Quartet, 187n52;
    and Rousseau, 42
homosexuality, 134–37. See also sexual
    politics
hooks, bell, 130, 131, 195n62
Hooper, Giles, 199n73
Huizinga, Johan, 104
human agency, 75
human belongings, 67, 72, 73
human rights, 6–7. See also gender politics
humanism, 161
Humanism and Democratic Criticism
    (Said), 153
humility, 8

Ibsen, Henrik, 196n28
"Idea for a Universal History with a
    Cosmopolitan Purpose" (Kant), 10
identity: and global economic relations,
    xi–xiii; and political role of music, 161,
    164–65, 175–77; and Said's late style, 155
ideology: and Beethoven's "Heroic" mode,
    94; and enjoyment, 31; and Kant's
    paradox of freedom, 98; key features
    of, x; and political rivalry, 188n15; post-
    ideological happiness, 131–38; relation-
    ship of aesthetics to, 71; and stylistic
    interplay, 11; sublime object of, 70
Idomeneo (Mozart), 113
Iliad (Homer), 169
immaturity, 95. See also Kant, Immanuel
improvisation, 37

indifference, xi, xv, xvii, 63, 109, 134, 139, 146, 151, 153, 155, 161, 167, 176
indoctrination, 134–35
instinctual choice, 134–38
interdisciplinarity, 163
Israel-Hezbollah War, 172
Israeli-Palestinian conflict: and the Oslo Accords, 140–41, 144, 147; and outsideness, 154, 157; Said's perception of, 140–41, 142–48, 150, 152; and the West-Eastern Divan Orchestra, 161–66, 169, 170–71, 171–77, 200n79, 201n97; Willson on, 200n86

Jackson, Michael, 74
Jameson, Fredric, 27–28, 71, 160, 188n15
Jankélévitch, Vladimir, 63
Jeanne-Claude, 32
Jewish Quarterly, 142
Joseph II, 107
jouissance (enjoyment), 31–33, 36, 63, 70. See also Lacan, Jacques
Jupiter Symphony (Mozart), 42, 56

Kant, Immanuel, 10, 94–98, 103, 115, 123, 194n50
Keats, John, 4, 104
Keefe, Simon, 13, 28
Keller, Hans, 50
Kerman, Joseph, 57, 61, 187n49
Kierkegaard, Soren, 74
Kirkendale, Warren, 12, 46, 47, 61, 182n34, 184n22
Kittel, J. C., 11
Knowledge Is the Beginning (2005), 165–66, 173, 175–76
Koch, Heinrich Christoph, 12, 43–45, 47
Koons, Jeff, 2, 32, 180n2
Kosselleck, Reinhart, 108
Kramer, Lawrence, 67–68, 72, 75, 188n21, 189n26
Kristeva, Julia, 100–101
Kurrik, Maire Jaanus, xv
"Kyrie" (Mozart), 46

La clemenza di Tito (Mozart): and artifice, 112–21; "Che del ciel" chorus, 114,

116–17, 121, 193n40; and the contextual sublime, 121–25; and the disenchanted subject, 125–31; and gender politics, 108, 112; ideological context of Vitellia character, 105; librettos, 106; and mechanistic thinking, 113, 122–24, 194n50; "Non più di fiori" rondò, 113–14, 118–19, 120–22; and "Or sai chi l'onore" from Don Giovanni, 117; and post-ideological happiness, 131–38; as realistic political allegory, 106–12; "S'altro che lacrime" aria, 114, 116–17, 116, 193n36; Servilia character, 106, 108, 114–15, 117, 121, 126; Sextus character, 106, 114; as stylistically progressive or retrospective, 120–21; Titus character, 106–107, 112, 114. See also Vitellia (La clemenza di Tito character)
Lacan, Jacques: and autonomous force within language, 126; and dream metaphors, 38–40; and enjoyment (jouissance), 31–32, 36, 63, 70, 196n65; and "extimacy," 31; and forced choice, 133, 195n65; on listening ~versus understanding, 48; and Marx and linguistics, 195n59; and musical aspects of psychoanalysis, 183n6; and otherness, 70–71; and the pleasure principle, 31–32; and post-ideological happiness, 133, 135; and Said's late style, 155
Laclau, Ernesto, xvi, 69
Lacombe, Claire, 111
language. See linguistics
Laquer, Thomas, 110
Lark (Haydn), 54
lateness/late style: Beethoven's late style, 185n34, 197n29; and forgetting, 147, 172; Genet's late style, 151, 198n39; Ibsen's late style, 196n28; Said's late style, 140–41, 146–50, 153–61, 172, 176, 197n34; Strauss's late style, 158–60, 165, 171; and temporal displacement, 157–58; Wood on, 197n29
law, 96, 97
Le nozze di Figaro (Mozart), 9
learned style: and authoritarian Other, 27; and cadenza of Mozart's K. 459, 35–37, 39, 41; and finale of Mozart's K.

459, 14–26, 29; and fugal counterpoint, 35–36, 43–44; Sisman on, 181n25; and stylistic interplay, 10–12

Legislated Nostalgia, 69

Leon, Pauline, 111

Leopold II, 106–107, 120

Leppert, Richard, xv, 76

Les Beaux arts reduits à une même principe (Batteux), 77

Les paravents (Genet), 155

Letters on the Female Mind (Hawkins), 112

Lévi-Strauss, Claude, 71, 94

linguistics: and the disenchanted subject, 125–31; Lacan and Marx, 195n59; limits of language, 80; and mimetic theory, 77, 79; and phonic units, 9; and postmodern theory, 181n23

Locke, John, 108

Lord Nelson mass (Haydn), 46

Lord of the Flies (Golding), 74

Lyotard, Jean-François, 26, 31

Maazel, Lorin, 201n93

Mallarmé, Stéphane, 126, 127

Manhattan, New York, 68

Manichaeanism, 143

Mansfield Park (Austen), 160

Mardi Gras, 167

marginalization, 101–102, 136–38

Maria Theresa of Austria, 111, 112

Marie Antoinette, 107

market economics, xi–xii

Marsyas, 62–64

Marx, Karl, 6, 103, 130, 195n60

material unconscious, 34–42. See also dreams and dream theory

materialism, 73, 85

Mazzolà, Caterino, 106

McClary, Susan, ix–x, 7, 130, 179n1, 194n50

mechanical reproduction, 102–104. See also Benjamin, Walter

mechanistic thinking, 113, 122–24, 194n50

melancholy, 65–67, 79, 125–26

melody and melodic writing: and accompaniment, 42; and artifice, 120–21; and finales, 92; and fugal counterpoint, 42–43, 45, 51–52, 54–55; and galant

style, 11; Keats on, 4; and La clemenza di Tito, 114–15, 117, 120–21; melodic variations, 92; and mimesis, 78; and mimetic theory, 78; and resolution of movements, 89

metaphysics, 5, 30, 39–40, 129

Metastasio (Pietro Trapassi), 106

Middle-Eastern politics, 173. See also Israeli-Palestinian conflict

mimesis, 7, 77–81, 85, 93–94, 123

minimalism, 6–7, 163

minuets, 9, 115, 121, 187n52

"mirrorization" of the world, 3–8

modernity, 102–103, 127–28, 154–56

monarchism, 107–108

Moonlight Sonata (Beethoven), 173

Morales, Pablo, 168–69

morality: and home of music, 72–73; and Kant's paradox of freedom, 97–98; and politics, 108; and post-ideological happiness, 136

Mouffe, Chantal, xvi, 69, 188n9

Mozart, Wolfgang Amadeus
    and aesthetic artifice, 113, 117
    birthday observance, 1–2
    creation of La clemenza di Tito, 106
    and death themes, 145
    and finales, 56
    and fugal counterpoint, 14–15, 19–21, 21–25, 42, 55, 56–62, 184n22
    and historical relativism, 2–3
    and homophonic textures, 54
    and postmodernism, 8–9, 62
    and stylistic interplay, 13
    and textural modulation, 51–52
    works: Così fan tutte, 154; Die Zauberflöte, 14; Don Giovanni, 117, 154; Idomeneo, 113; Jupiter Symphony, 42, 56; Le nozze di Figaro, 9; mass in C Major, K. 66, 46; mass in C Major, K. 167, 46; mass in C Major, K. 262, 46; mass in C Minor, K. 139, 46; Piano Sonata in F Major, K. 332, 9; Requiem, K. 626, 46; String Quartet in G Major, K. 387, 55; String Quintet in E-flat Major, K. 614, 54. See also La clemenza di Tito; Piano Concerto in F Major, K. 459

musical topoi, 9, 81–82
mysticism, 37

nationalism, 143, 147, 188n15
negation: and dialectical mediation, 140; and forgetting, 148–52; and irreconcilability, 141; and Kant's paradox of freedom, 95–96, 98; and Said's late style, 156; and "tarrying with the negative," 150, 197n32; and the Viennese classics, 94
New Labour Party (UK), xii
New Orleans, Louisiana, 167
New York City, 68
Nietzsche, Friedrich: and ambiguity of music, 78; and *The Birth of Tragedy*, 62–63; and forgetting, 149, 151; on limits of language, 80; and Said's late style, 146–47
"no music," xiv
"Non più di fiori" rondò (Mozart), 113, 114, *118–19, 120–22*
normative meaning of music, 79

Obama administration, 69
obedience, 95, 98
objectivity, 6, 35
"Ode on a Grecian Urn" (Keats), 4
On Late Style (Said), 146, 159, 161, 196n28
O'Neill, Onara, 96
opera buffa style, 14–26, 36
opera seria style, 89–90, 113
"Or sai chi l'onore" (Mozart), 117
Orientalism (Said), 156
Orpheus, 63
Oslo Accords, 140–41, 144, 147
otherness: and abjection, 104; and anti-Semitism, 70; Barenboim on, 201n99; and fugal counterpoint, 41–42; and the Israeli-Palestinian conflict, 175; and Stein, 163
Out of Place (Said), 196n28
outsideness, 152–61
Ovid, 63, 63–64

Palestine. *See* Israeli-Palestinian conflict
Palestinian Liberation Organization (PLO), 147

Palestinian National Council, 147
paradoxes, 41, 112–21
Parallels and Paradoxes (Said), 141, 200n93
parents, 73–77
petition rights, 111
phenomenology of sound, 169–70
Phenomenology of Spirit (Hegel), 197n32
Piano Concerto in F Major, K. 459 (Mozart): cadenza extract, *18*; and caricature, 21; finale of, 3, 14–26, 26–33, 53, 71; and fugal counterpoint, 14–15, 19–21, 21–25, 42, 55, 56–62, 184n22; and fugal texture, 20; length of instrumental continuation, 16, 17; rhythmic motives, 19, 19, 20; stretto, 25–26, 53; and stylistic interplay, 13; and textural modulation, 51–52
pleasure principle, 30–32, 70, 132
pluralism, 7
Poe, Edgar Allen, 124
politics: and autonomy, 67; and class divisions, 111; and the contextual sublime, 122; and difference, 9; and ethics, 108; and finale of Mozart's K. 459, 26–27; and instinctual choice, 136; in musicology, x–xi; and negation, xvi; political crises, xi; political role of music, 161, 164–65, 169–71, 171–74, 175–77; and postmodern reflection, 3–8, 29–30; of relationship formation, 67–68; and Said's late style, 140, 153; women's political rights, 111–12. *See also* Israeli-Palestinian conflict
politics of the mirror, 26, 29, 150, 160–61
polyphony, 51, 54
polystylistic method, 6, 7, 9
pop art, 180n2
Portman, John, 27–28
possessions, 73
postcolonialism, 164
postcommunism, 195n64
post-ideological happiness, 131–38
postmodernism: and depth analysis, 5–8, 26–33; and the disenchanted subject, 127, 129–30, 131–32; and finale of Mozart's K. 459, 28–29; Harvey on, 195n64; and linguistics, 125; and

"mirrorization" of the world, 3–8; and
Mozart's music, 8–9; and musical
conventions, 28–29; and politics of the
mirror, 26, 29, 150, 160–61; and pop art,
180n2; and post-ideological happiness,
131–34, 138; postmodern musicology,
ix–xi, xiv, xvii, 2–3; postmodern writing, 4–5; and reflective surface, 26–28;
and "reveling in the rubble," 179n1; and
Said's analysis of Strauss, 160–61; and
stylistic pluralism, 22
post-structuralism, 126
Powers, Harold, 82
professionalism, 200n93
psychoanalysis, xviii, 39–40
psychosis, 41

Queer Eye for the Straight Guy (television
    series), 137
queer politics, 134–37
The Quest for Voice (Goehr), 149–50
Quinten String Quartet (String Quartet
    op. 76, no. 2 in D Minor) (Haydn), 62
Quintilian, 22

Rabelais, François, 37
racism, 137–38
rational autonomy, 110
Ratner, Leonard, 8, 45
Razor Quartet (String Quartet op. 55, no.
    2 in F Minor) (Haydn), 57–61, 59, 60
reason, 95, 95–97, 110
Reformation, 107–108
Reicha, Anton, 12, 51
relativism, 40
religion, 6, 95
Republican Party (US), xvi
Requiem, K. 626 (Mozart), 46
research practices, 171
"Returning to Ourselves" (Rose), 142
"reveling in the rubble," 179n1
revisionism, 163
revolution, 95
Rice, John, 106–107, 113, 120
Rilke, Rainer Maria, 80, 190n46
Rimbaud, Arthur, 126
road-rage metaphor, 154–55

rococo style, 61
Romanticism: and depth theory, 7; and
    the disenchanted subject, 128; and
    "effect," 190n48; and music, 79–80; and
    poetry, 158; and political reflections,
    3–4, 7; Romantic hermeneutics, 4; and
    transcendence, 190n44; and Utopia, 128
rondò, 113, 117, 121, 122
Rose, Jacqueline, 142–48, 196n17
Rosen, Charles, 13
Rousseau, Jean-Jacques, 10–11, 42–56,
    110–11, 117, 190n44
Roussel, Pierre, 110
Rozema, Patricia, 160
Russell, Bertrand, 176

Sacred Enemy (Stein), 163
sadness/sad music, 34, 66–69, 72
Said, Edward: and contemporary musicol-
    ogy, 152; death of, 141, 146, 153, 161,
    176; and death themes, 145–47; and
    Enlightenment orientation, 196n17; and
    Genet's work, 155, 198n39; and late style,
    139–41, 153, 196n28; on Mansfield Park,
    160; and Mozart's work, 145, 154; and
    musical professionalism, 201n93; and
    outsideness, 152–61; and Strauss's late
    style, 158–60, 165, 171
Said, Mariam C., 146, 172
salon culture, 108–11
"S'altro che lacrime" aria (Mozart), 114,
    116–17, 116, 193n36
satire, 90
Saussure, Ferdinand de, 181n23
Scenes from Schumann (Holloway), 135
Scheibe, Johann Adolf, 10–11
Schenker, Heinrich, 6, 169
Scherzinger, Martin, xv, 40
Schlegel, August Wilhelm, 41, 78
Schnittke, Alfred, 6, 7
Schopenhauer, Arthur, 78, 146
scientific discourse, 109–10
selfishness, 168–69
September 11 terrorist attacks, 68–69
Servilia (La clemenza di Tito character),
    106, 108, 114–15, 117, 121, 126
Seventh Symphony (Beethoven), 176

Sextus (*La clemenza di Tito* character), 106, 114
sexual politics, 107, 134–37
Siciliana theme/topic, 92, 93
signification, 38–39, 77, 82
Sinfonia (Berio), 6
Sisman, Elaine, 12, 22, 191n53
Sketch for an Historical Picture of the Progress of the Human Mind (Condorcet), 10
slow movements, 91–92
Smaczny, Paul, 165
social bonding, 138
social contract, 108
social custom, 97–98
Société de Citoyennes Républicaines Révolutionnaires, 111
sociological idealism, 76
Somfai, László, 186n43
sonata-style syntax, 13, 15, 45–51, 54, 56–58, 186n45
Sontag, Susan, 4
Spazier, Karl, 12, 182n34
Spitzer, Michael, xv
St. Cecilia mass (Haydn), 46
Stadler, Anton, 121
Stein, Gertrude, 162–63
Steiner, George, 126–27
strategic placements, 56–62
Strauss, Richard, 158–60, 165, 171, 173
stretti, 25–26, 43, 53
String Quartet op. 33, no. 5 in G Major (Haydn), 187n52; and autonomy, 67; cadential figure opening, 82–85, *83, 86, 87, 88*; coda to finale, 83–85, 92–93; and dialectical doubling, 150; finale of, *84*, 93–94, 98–99; and freedom of autonomy, 98; and motivic material, 86–87, *87*, 90–91, *90, 91*; and post-ideological happiness, 138; and postmodern disenchantment, 129–31; relationship to Mozart's D minor "Haydn" quartet, 92; Siciliana theme/topic, 92, 93
"Sturm und Drang" works of Haydn, 56
stylistic pluralism, 10–13, 14, 20, 22–23
sublimity: contextual sublime, 121–25; cryptographic sublime, 37; and

enjoyment, 31; and fugal counterpoint, 54; and Handel, 194n44; and otherness, 70–71; and "sublime object of ideology," 70
Sulzer, J. G., 115
superego, 137
surface, 27–33, 38–39, 125
Surrealism, 6, 126
symbolism, 31, 80
syntax of music: and cadential figures, 82–83, 85, 86, 89–93; and finales, 83, 93; fugal-style syntax, 47–51, 54, 56–58; and *galant* instrumental style, 11, 185n25; sonata-style syntax, 13, 15, 45–51, 54, 56–58, 186n45; and tonal closure, 60
Système physique et moral de la femme (Roussel), 110

Te Deum hymn, 46
technê, 162, 165, 168, 170, 175
Tel quel, 130
the Terror, 96
textural dissonance, 41, 43, 46–47, 51–52, 56, 59–60
textural modulation, 51, 53
Thatcher, Margaret, xii, 69
therapeutic role of music, 68
"Theses on the Philosophy of History" (Benjamin), 152
Titus (*La clemenza di Tito* character), 106–107, 112, 114
Tomlinson, Gary, 37, 189n26
tonal closure, 58
totalitarianism, 128, 133. *See also* authoritarianism
Tovey, Donald, 92, 94
tragedy and tragic style: and Haydn, 91; and human interaction, 68; and Mozart, 28, 117, 120; Nietzsche on, 62–63; and outsideness, 156
Traité de haute composition musicale (Reicha), 12
transcendence: and Haydn's op. 33, no. 5, 93; and mimetic theories, 77–81; and musical topoi, 85; Romantic discourses on, 190n44; transcendental subject, 123; and Viennese classics, 94

transubstantiation, 101
Tyson, Alan, 113

Über das neue Fugensystem (Reicha), 51
unconscious, 34–42, 53. *See also* dreams
    and dream theory
Unité de Mélodie, 42
United Kingdom, xii
United States, 143
Utopianism: and forgetting, 148–52; and
    Fukuyama's "end of history" thesis,
    132–33; and Israeli-Palestinian conflict,
    143; and redemptive power of music,
    128; and Said's late style, 148; West and
    hooks on, 195n62; and the West-Eastern
    Divan Orchestra, 162

veiling, 32–33, 34–35, 38–39
Viennese classical repertoire, xiv, 81–82,
    85, 94, 96, 123
A Vindication of the Rights of Woman
    (Wollstonecraft), 112, 192n29
virtuoso figuration, 24–25, 29
Vitellia (*La clemenza di Tito* character):
    and artifice, 112–14, 116–17, 120–21; and
    autonomy, 112–13; and the contextual
    sublime, 121–25; and disenchantment,
    105–107, 126–27, 129, 131; and gender
    roles, 110–12; and post-ideological hap-
    piness, 132, 138
vocal styles, 113–14. *See also* "Non più di
    fiori" rondò (Mozart)
Vogler, Georg Joseph, 44, 47

Waeber, Jacqueline, 54
wealth inequality, 138

Webster, James, 46, 50, 190n48
welfare state, xii
West, Cornel, 130–31, 195n62
West-Eastern Divan Orchestra: and for-
    getting, 152; and the Israeli-Palestinian
    conflict, 161–66, 169, 170–71, 171–77,
    200n79, 201n97; and musical profes-
    sionalism, 200n93; and Said's late
    style, 139–40; and structure of or-
    chestras, 199n77; and totalitarianism,
    167
Why Classical Music Still Matters
    (Kramer), 188n21
Williams, Alastair, xv
Williams, Bernard, 168
Willson, Rachel Beckles, 93, 159, 162,
    199n77, 200n86
Wolf Foundation Prize, 165–66, 173
Wollstonecraft, Mary, 109, 111–12, 192n29
Wood, Michael, 197n29
"The Work of Art in the Age of
    Mechanical Reproduction"
    (Benjamin), 102–103
worldliness, 145

Yearsley, David, 44, 181n26

Zionism, 141
Žižek, Slavoj: and absolute relativism, 40;
    and "forced choice," 133; and Freudian
    dream theory, 38; and Kantian philoso-
    phy, 97–98; and negation of society,
    69–70, 188n9; and parallax concept,
    199n77; and "sublime object of ideol-
    ogy," 70
Zupančič, Alenka, 135, 137–38

MUSICAL MEANING & INTERPRETATION

Robert S. Hatten, editor

A Theory of Musical Narrative
BYRON ALMÉN

Approaches to Meaning in Music
BYRON ALMÉN &
EDWARD PEARSALL

*Voicing Gender: Castrati, Travesti,
and the Second Woman in Early
Nineteenth-Century Italian Opera*
NAOMI ANDRÉ

The Italian Traditions and Puccini
NICHOLAS BARAGWANATH

*Debussy Redux: The Impact of His
Music on Popular Culture*
MATTHEW BROWN

Music and the Politics of Negation
JAMES R. CURRIE

Il Trittico, Turandot, *and
Puccini's Late Style*
ANDREW DAVIS

Neil Young and the Poetics of Energy
WILLIAM ECHARD

*Interpreting Musical Gestures, Topics, and
Tropes: Mozart, Beethoven, Schubert*
ROBERT S. HATTEN

*Musical Meaning in Beethoven: Markedness,
Correlation, and Interpretation*
ROBERT S. HATTEN

Intertextuality in Western Art Music
MICHAEL L. KLEIN

*Musical Forces: Motion, Metaphor,
and Meaning in Music*
STEVE LARSON

*Is Language a Music? Writings on
Musical Form and Signification*
DAVID LIDOV

*Pleasure and Meaning in the
Classical Symphony*
MELANIE LOWE

*Decorum of the Minuet, Delirium of
the Waltz: A Study of Dance-Music
Relations in ¾ Time*
ERIC MCKEE

The Musical Topic: Hunt, Military, Pastoral
RAYMOND MONELLE

*Musical Representations, Subjects,
and Objects: The Construction
of Musical Thought in Zarlino,
Descartes, Rameau, and Weber*
JAIRO MORENO

*Deepening Musical Performance
through Movement: The Theory and
Practice of Embodied Interpretation*
ALEXANDRA PIERCE

*Expressive Forms in Brahms's
Instrumental Music: Structure and
Meaning in His* Werther *Quartet*
PETER H. SMITH

*Expressive Intersections in Brahms:
Essays in Analysis and Meaning*
HEATHER PLATT &
PETER H. SMITH

*Music as Philosophy: Adorno
and Beethoven's Late Style*
MICHAEL SPITZER

*Music and Wonder at the Medici Court:
The 1589 Interludes for* La pellegrina
NINA TREADWELL

*Reflections on Musical Meaning
and Its Representations*
LEO TREITLER

Debussy's Late Style
MARIANNE WHEELDON

JAMES R. CURRIE is Associate Professor of Music at the University at Buffalo (State University of New York), where he teaches courses on music history and music and philosophy. In addition to his work as a scholar, which has remained consistently political in orientation, he is also active as a performance artist and poet.